Innocent III

Innocent III

Vicar of Christ or Lord of the World?

edited with an introduction by

JAMES M. POWELL

Second, expanded edition

The Catholic University of America Press
Washington, D.C.

The paper used in this publication meets the minimum require-
ments of American National Standards for Information Science—
Permanence of Paper for Printed Library materials, ANSI Z39.48-
1984.

∞

LIBRARY OF CONGRESS CATALOGING-IN-
PUBLICATION DATA

Innocent III : vicar of Christ or lord of the world? / edited with an
     introduction by James M. Powell.—2d, expanded ed.
          p.   cm.
     Includes bibliographical references and index.
          1. Innocent III, Pope, 1160 or 61-1216.   I. Powell, James M.
BX1236.166   1994
282'.092—dc20
[B]
93-12609
ISBN 0-8132-0783-5

CONTENTS

THE CONFLICT OF OPINION

". . . for many centuries before and after Innocent, no one more learned, more pure in his way of life, more rich in merit to the Church and illustrious for great works sat on the throne of St. Peter."

—FRIEDRICH HURTER

"Now is the Pope [Innocent] no more primarily priest, but before all a secular lord." —ALBERT HAUCK

". . . it seems clear that the jurisdiction claimed by Innocent III was almost illimitable and his exercise of it without parallel either in extent or effectiveness. Yet it was a jurisdiction in its nature primarily spiritual, and temporal only incidentally (*casualiter*), a power grounded on the Pope's duty as Vicar of God to judge of the sins (*de peccato*) of all Christians, not on his right as a temporal ruler to administer law for his subjects."

—CHARLES H. MCILWAIN

"That Innocent wished to submit rulers to the control of the Holy See without otherwise mixing in their administration proper . . . , there is no doubt; but, if he desired the political unity of Christendom under the hegemony of the papacy, it was before all to ensure, in religious unity, the defense and the glory of the Catholic faith and Christian morality."

—AUGUSTIN FLICHE

"Innocent did take it for granted that, under the pope, secular rulers had a permanent and necessary role to play in the governance of Christian society, and that this role was a part of the divinely-ordered scheme of things. He assumed that two hierarchies were necessary for the government of the Christian world but, in his view, both hierarchies culminated in the pope."

—BRIAN TIERNEY

"[Innocent] took advantage of all possible legal arguments that were granted him for leading the Christian world. He took it seriously if a ruler resisted his claim, and sought in cases of conflict a solution just to both sides. To this elasticity we must credit his deep insight into the limits of his spiritual political—claims to lead, with the result that—in spite of many setbacks—he reached a position of political power that exceeded that of his predecessors and that his successors would not surpass, because they lost sight of political realities and made the mistake of pursuing a rigid hierocratism."   —FRIEDRICH KEMPF

Innocent III

Introduction

THIRTY YEARS AGO, the title of this volume meant something different from what it means today. Although historical scholarship in the early 1960s had already moved away from the narrow political interpretation of Innocent's pontificate that had dominated much of the writing on the medieval papacy in the pre–World War II era, the dichotomy represented in the terms "Vicar of Christ" and "Lord of the World" still implied a sharp distinction between those historians who viewed the papacy chiefly from the perspective of its spiritual mission and those who focused on its political impact. True enough, extreme statements on either side of the issue already found little support. The apologetic tone taken by Friedrich Hurter was widely criticized and dismissed. Even the views of Albert Hauck, distinguished though his contributions to German church history were, lost force in the next generation. While apologetical defenses and efforts to cast papal motives in purely political terms continued to find expression among other writers even in the post-war period, the trend was away from the polemical positions that had defined earlier discussions. The new directions in research on Innocent III in the fifties and early sixties provided the rationale for the first edition. The preparation of the present edition made it clear that a substantial body of new literature has advanced our understanding of the pontificate of Innocent III well beyond the positions outlined in the introduction to the first edition.

Recent historical writing continues to accord Innocent III a special place in the history of the medieval papacy. Without granting him the title "the Great" withheld by his contemporaries, it has recognized in him one of the most significant of medieval popes, during whose reign the papacy reached its medieval apogee. But this characterization still harbors more than a little of the idea that the papacy operated mostly as a political force in the later Middle Ages. The stress on Innocent's importance in political affairs continues to overshadow his strong commitment to the reform agenda of the twelfth-century papacy in the writings of some historians, although the primacy of the spiritual aspects of the papal office as the motivating power behind his political involvement is generally acknowledged. The term "reform," moreover, contains numerous pitfalls. Not merely does its meaning change during the century and a half after the reform papacy gained ascendancy in the eleventh century, but developments in papal government, the growth of a system of ecclesiastical law, and papal involvement in the crusade movement did much to redefine its content. Political issues certainly occupied a considerable place in papal affairs, but historians have come increasingly to recognize substantial changes in the causes of conflict between the spiritual and temporal powers in the eleventh and twelfth centuries and those of the later Middle Ages and early modern period. In essence, the earlier period was marked by the attempt of the reform papacy to use temporal means to define its spiritual role in a rapidly changing world marked by the growing influence of royal governments; the later period witnessed a papacy on the defensive in the face of temporal powers that viewed it as a political competitor. The thirteenth century was pivotal to this change. Some have even argued that the reign of Innocent III was the beginning of an intrusion of the papacy into the secular sphere leading directly to a decline of its power under Pope Innocent IV (1243–54). Others have pointed, however, to the limited nature of Innocent's claims and his hesitancy on more than one occasion about a particular course of action as evidence of his reluctance to intervene in secular matters. The selections that follow enable us to pursue this discussion further and to explore other issues that add to the still-developing picture of this major figure in the history of the papacy.

In the view of many scholars, Innocent III represented a marked break from the elderly pontiffs who had ruled the church in the late twelfth century. If he had a model, it was perhaps Pope Alexander III, whose political involvement, administrative activities, and commitment to reform often seemed to parallel his own efforts. Like Alexander, he was enmeshed in controversy with the Empire and other temporal rulers. Like him, he summoned a council of the Church to meet in Rome. He was more outspoken in his rhetoric than Alexander, but hardly less diplomatic in his relations with contemporary rulers. On the other hand, his efforts to promote the Crusade, coming in the aftermath of the failure of the Third Crusade to recapture Jerusalem in the early 1190s, may well have been influenced by the program set forth by Pope Gregory VIII (1187) and Clement III (1187–91), whose plans had led to the involvement of the emperor as well as the French and English kings in that Crusade. At that time, Innocent was scarcely two years beyond the canonical age for ordination. He was very much a product of the vigorous intellectual life of the twelfth century. He studied in Paris and may well have associated there with men who were destined to be leaders in the theological schools at the turn of the century. He spent at least some time in Bologna, then the major center of legal studies in Western Europe. Scion of the noble Roman family of Scotti, as well as of the Conti di Segni from the Roman Campagna, he rose quickly to prominence at the court of his relative Pope Clement III. It was a challenging period in the history of the papacy. The prestige of the papal office had achieved wide recognition in the twelfth century. During the pontificate of Celestine III (1191–98), Innocent witnessed the efforts of that pope to maintain the alliance of the papacy with the Normans of southern Italy despite the changes that had occurred after the death of King William II in 1189 and the successful attempt of Emperor Henry VI to secure the throne for himself and his wife, Constance of Sicily, the daughter of King Roger II, in 1194. We can only speculate whether these events had any influence on Innocent's election as pope following the death of Celestine in 1198.

Innocent III's pontificate was clearly in line with those of the major reform popes of the previous century and a half. He was not, however, merely a continuator of an existing program of reform. In fact, no such program can be said to have existed, though certain concerns and ideals did influence the major directions of papal policy. In the first place, the eleventh-century reform had drawn on diverse elements from the religious experiences of the period. Its roots in monasticism ensured that its aims would at least partially reflect those of the monastic reformers. Thus, concern for monastic liberty produced strong efforts to protect monasteries from lay control and also heightened the desire of some to seek isolation from the world, which found expression in the revival of the eremetical movement. Monastic influence on the reform papacy from the pontificate of Pope Leo IX (1049–54) onward was critical to the development of its emphasis on clerical celibacy, its opposition to simony, and its concern with ecclesiastical liberty. By the last quarter of the eleventh century, the issue of lay investiture moved to a central position in the reform program. Lay investiture touched the root of the relationships between the churches and the dominant political forces in a period of increasingly intense competition among central authorities in church and secular society. The papacy took the lead under Pope Alexander II (1061–73) and Gregory VII (1073–85) in defending episcopal liberty and opposing lay investiture (the conferring of the spiritual symbols of ecclesiastical office on bishops by secular rulers). In practical terms, lay investiture was analogous to the forms of patronage over monasteries that monastic reformers had worked to eliminate or, at least, to limit throughout this period, and from which they continued to seek protection, often with papal support. The debate over lay investiture, however, inevitably provoked confrontations on a much broader scale than local conflicts over monastic immunity from lay jurisdictions or episcopal supervision. It affected the interests of the German emperors and the kings of western Europe. They stood to lose the most if the reform popes succeeded in making good their claims for freedom to ecclesiastical appointments, especially of bishops. The situation was particularly critical for northern Italy, where the tenuous control established by the Saxon emperors depended heavily on the loyalties of pro-imperial bishops supported by leading members of the upper lay aristocracy. Italy was the flash point of this struggle that resulted in protracted conflict between Gregory VII and Henry IV and continued until a compromise was reached under Calixtus II and Henry V in 1122.

Understandably, nineteenth-century historians focused on the political aspects of this controversy. For them, lay investiture stood for a conflict between two very different conceptions of European Christian society. In the first, the emperor or king stood at the apex. The act of lay investiture confirmed the legitimate role of monarchy in Christian society, affirming the sacral role of kingship. Within the Empire, from the Carolingian period on, and most especially after the Ottonian revival in the tenth century, bishops were important linchpins in the government of the realm. Their loyalty was essential to good government. In the opposing view, advanced in various forms by papal reformers in the eleventh century, lay investiture was an intrusion of the laity into the sphere of the sacred. The reformers rejected all notions of hierocratic kingship, but were divided over attempts to define the nature of the relationship between the papacy and secular rulers. Their opposition to lay investiture, however, enabled them to subordinate their differences on the nature of papal authority in the church and in secular society in the interest of defending ecclesiastical liberty from temporal rulers.

The compromise that brought the investiture controversy to an end in the early twelfth century did not entirely resolve the issues that had created a rift between the papacy and the Empire. The brutal military campaigns waged by Henry IV and Henry V against the papacy and its supporters had gained little for the Empire. The political conflicts exploited by the reformers involved the church in local animosities that often continued for long periods. The political settlement achieved at Worms in 1122 was also ambiguous. Only by seeing the way in which the papacy was able to exploit the advantages it had gained during the remainder of the twelfth century can we begin to appreciate the critical importance of the controversy and its settlement for the development of the papacy during the next three centuries. Its immediate effect was evident in the decrees of the First Lateran Council in 1123. That council witnessed the first stages in the consolidation of the position of the papacy at the head of the ecclesiastical hierarchy, building on the work begun almost seventy-five years earlier. But the papacy did not anticipate fully the direction that the reform movement would take. The degree of separation between the church and temporal powers that resulted from this settlement may not appear very significant to some modern historians, but it represented a major alteration of established relationships within the twelfth-century world. The potential for reform within the church took on new meaning as a result of the freedom that had been gained. The structure of the hierarchical society, which had found its support in the imperial and royal churches of the early Middle Ages, was badly shaken. The deep conflicts unleashed in the investiture controversy encouraged those who had found little room for the expression of their religiosity under the old system to identify with the cause of reform. The papal reformers had early supported such groups as the "Pataria" of Milan, who opposed their pro-imperial bishop but espoused a still-vague goal of reform for the church. Indeed, most of the leading voices of monastic reform, who were calling for a return to the "apostolic life" enshrined in the gospels, supported the papacy against the emperor. But it was not possible to contain all of these aspirations and desires within a reform program that had been largely aimed at protecting churches and monasteries from spoliation and from the subversion of their spiritual functions. As a consequence, the twelfth century witnessed increasing diversity and even confusion with the reform movement. The development of new religious orders, such as the Cistercians, the Praemonstratensians, the Gilbertines, and the Order of Grandmont, was accompanied and followed by the foundations of the *Humiliati,* the Beguines, and the Waldensians. Among the latter, the potential for heresy, especially notable among those who virulently attacked the shortcomings of a clergy that often still reflected traditional forms of religious practice, was considerable and has tended to obscure the orthodox links of these groups. Confronted by such unstable conditions, the reform papacy was slow to react. Pope Lucius III's condemnation of the Waldensians has generally been regarded as indicative of a papal policy toward movements of this kind, but should more likely be regarded as evidence of the lack of any policy. The pontificate of Innocent III is, therefore, all the more notable, not merely for its commitment to the work of reform carried forward by Alexander III and the Third Lateran Council, but also for his effort to formulate solutions to those problems that had emerged in the years after 1179. The meaning of Innocent's reign lay in the establishment of a sharper papal agenda and his effort to set down ways for meeting it.

The historical writing of the last thirty years has revealed a marked departure from the themes that had dominated the history of the medieval papacy and temporal powers early in this century. The brief excerpts from Friedrich Hurter and Albert Hauck included here serve to illustrate positions current at that time among apologists for and critics of papal power. Hurter's complaint that his contemporaries engaged in invective against Innocent has a certain merit. Hauck's critique reflects the developing scholarship of the early twentieth century but remains imbedded in a Protestant and nationalist view of Innocent and the papacy. The French historian Achille Luchaire, who has presented a somewhat more sympathetic view of Innocent, shares the political emphasis characteristic of most of the writings of this period. Luchaire's biography of Innocent, from which the account of his accession to the papacy has been taken, devoted an entire volume to the Fourth Lateran Council and another to the Crusade. His attention to the movement of reform, evident in his treatment of such figures as St. Francis of Assisi and St. Dominic, reflected the growing interest in these topics among historians at this time. Although Luchaire's Innocent was still deeply enmeshed in political affairs, he caught the spirit of the pope's own desire to order his priorities according to spiritual rather than temporal concerns. For Luchaire, Innocent was a realistic man of affairs, committed to principle, but far from intransigent.

The major break with the older tradition of historiography, however, came in the post–World War I era, in the work of such scholars as A. J. and R. W. Carlyle and C. H. McIlwain. The Carlyles' massive *Medieval Political Theory in the West* commanded serious attention from scholars in the English-speaking world for the then-neglected field of medieval European political and legal theory. Where earlier scholarship had emphasized English legal and constitutional history, they looked to the continent. What was especially important in their view of Innocent III was his reliance on the inherent powers of the priesthood and the papal office as the basis for his actions in both the spiritual and temporal spheres. Relying on a better understanding of canon law than most earlier English writers (with the exception of S. R. Maitland), they presented a more coherent picture of his pontificate than that found in Luchaire. Innocent had based his power to appoint and depose kings on "his office as Christ's vicar." On this same foundation, he promoted peace and worked to resolve issues involving the powerless of society, widows and orphans. The trend toward an ecclesiological interpretation of Innocent's activity was also evident in the work of Charles H. McIlwain, whose influence on the writing of medieval legal and constitutional history remained important in the United States into the 1960s. In his view, Innocent claimed almost illimitable power, but conceived his jurisdiction as "primarily spiritual and only incidentally temporal." It was already quite evident, therefore, by the late 1930s that the narrow political interpretation of the medieval papacy no longer commanded the assent of many leading scholars in the field.

The decline of this view opened the way for various other interpretations, represented here by the selections from Michele Maccarrone and Augustin Fliche, though some scholars continued to maintain the older position—for example, the German historian of the papacy Johannes Haller. The persistence of national "schools" of historiography continued to influence the writings of these scholars, as did their various religious commitments. But there was a notable lessening in the impact of these ties as the study of church history entered the mainstream of the maturing academic discipline of history. These developments are evident in the ambitious research program carried out by Augustin Fliche, represented by a selection from his contribution to the *Histoire de l'église,* which he edited together with Victor Martin. Fliche, who had focused his research interest on the era of the Gregorian Reform, viewed Innocent as the leader in a struggle to reform Church and society, building on the work of Gregory VII. This approach also influenced Helene Tillmann's biography of Innocent and, perhaps most of all, the writings of Michele Maccarrone, who emphasized the "uniquely spiritual character" of Innocent's conception of the mission of the pope. He stressed that the notion of the pope as a possessor of royal power belongs to Innocent IV, "who carried it to its ultimate systemization," rather than to Innocent III.

The major contributor to a new interpretation of Innocent III's relations to secular powers in the last thirty years has been Brian Tierney, whose studies have provided the basis for a reappraisal of medieval ecclesiology and political theory. Building on the insights of scholars such as McIlwain and the Carlyles, as well as his mentor, Walter Ullmann, Tierney has insisted that the issue of Innocent's claim to the exercise of temporal power must be confronted directly within the context of medieval political and legal thought. In so doing, he has charted a course that avoids too exclusive an emphasis on the spiritual aspects of papal authority while placing Innocent's political ideas into the context of the legal and political culture of his period. More than earlier scholars, Tierney has made it possible to explore both the spiritual and temporal aspects of papal authority. At the same time, his work has opened the way to a better understanding of the influences pressing on the papacy from other directions, particularly the reform ideas that had captured the hearts of important segments of the laity in the late twelfth and early thirteenth centuries.

The political aspects of Innocent III's pontificate have continued to interest scholars, but recent approaches reveal a sharp break with the views fashionable down to the World War II era. The selections by Elizabeth Kennan, John C. Moore, and the late Christopher Cheney demonstrate not merely the breadth of Innocent's political concerns, but the way in which the issues involved were enmeshed in his religious goals as well as in his effort to defend the rights of the papacy as he saw them. In her very suggestive piece, Elizabeth Kennan has put Innocent's involvement in political crusades in Europe into a context with the activities of his successors, Honorius III and Gregory IX. Not only does her account demonstrate the concerns that led to papal summonses of crusades within Europe, it also stresses the ambiguities and reluctance that often accompanied these decisions. Her presentation of such controversial papal involvements as the Albigensian Crusade and the Stedinger revolt provides insight into the actual role of the papacy in local affairs. John Moore shows how Innocent's view of the papal patrimony in Italy affected his relations with Sardinia. Christopher Cheney, whose important contributions to the study of Innocent III and England are represented by a brief excerpt, provides a nuanced picture of the role of politics in Innocent's program. Recently, Friedrich Kempf, known for his numerous works on Innocent, has given us a very helpful summary of Innocent's claims to political authority. Drawing on Innocent's use of images from Scripture and his grasp of canon law, Kempf reveals the profound unresolved tensions between the spiritual and the political claims of the papacy. The terms "Vicar of Christ" and "Lord of the World" remain pregnant with meaning, but are now largely deprived of their former polar significance. Instead, they express an interrelationship whose true nature requires continued investigation.

Scholarship in the seventies focused more attention on the sources of Innocent's views and his implementation of the pastoral and spiritual concerns of his office. In a valuable essay, Kenneth Pennington raised questions about Innocent's legal education that have stimulated discussion of the mainsprings of his thought. While Innocent's contributions to canon law remain central to an understanding of his thought, historians have begun to pay more attention to his sermons and treatises. Wilhelm Imkamp has drawn on these sources to provide a theologically informed view of the development of Innocent III's views of the church. In yet another direction, Brenda Bolton's study of Innocent's handling of the *Humiliati* has opened the door to further research on relations between the papacy and groups of clerical and lay Christians, whose role in the church and in society at large has increasingly become the focus of studies on such topics as confraternities and the work of the mendicants. Innocent's traditionally assigned role in the encouragement of these groups has come in for considerable attention. The relations of the papacy to these groups were difficult and complex, as the study of Cardinal Robert Courçon's legation in France on the eve of the Fourth Lateran Council demonstrates. The tendency of some historians to read sources solely in terms of pro- or anti-reform messages is clearly inadequate when subjected to an examination that shows how efforts to insure the reform of a religious community could fall victim to conflicting notions about what constituted reform.

The preoccupation with political conflicts between the papacy and temporal powers that characterized most of the writing on Innocent III earlier in this century has given way to research that places the political role of the papacy in a context that cannot be separated from its spiritual concerns. The recognition that such involvement threatened to divert the efforts of even the most spiritual-minded popes—and Innocent was certainly among their number—away from the spiritual role of the papacy has forced scholars to reject the overly-simple judgments of that period. The growing awareness of the importance of the Middle Ages in the formation of both modern institutions and the ideas that encapsulate them has given a new meaning to the way in which Innocent III agonized over these issues. But we also recognize that the conflict over church and state is ultimately merely one aspect of a discussion of the reform of the church. For this reason, the agenda Innocent laid down for the Fourth Lateran Council in 1215 may well be the best key to understanding his view of the papacy. Far from being overwhelmed by the political problems that threatened to consume the major energies of the council, he succeeded in keeping to his agenda of reform of the church and promotion of the Crusade.

PART I

Two Views

FRIEDRICH HURTER

Innocent III: Victim of Partisan Historians

THE JUDGMENTS of historians and writers, ancient and modern, who knew how to evaluate [Innocent] honestly on the basis of his accomplishments, the problems he solved, and his position as the central animator of his age, agree entirely in saying that for many centuries before and after [him] no one more learned, more pure in his way of life, more rich in merit to the Church, and illustrious for great works sat on the throne of Peter. No one after him possessed these qualities to such an extent, so that, save for Gregory VII, he was not only the most powerful, but also the wisest of popes—on a par with St. Bernard and Peter the Venerable, who knew how to surpass their age. He was praised by writers who witnessed his work and his influence on social life, because he spread Christianity in the north, restrained heresy in the south, subjected Constantinople to the Holy See (though the means may have been contrary to his intention), overcame the arrogance of the Moslems, and surpassed all in learning and devotion. In his writings he expressed joy at having lived in an age during which Christ granted victory to Christendom—while under the guidance of His faithful servant—over three enemies: schismatics, heretics, and infidels. Likewise, when he recalled the vain attempts of his predecessors, he was forced to render humble thanks to the Lord. He had, he said, by His command, cast nets for the fish and, with the aid of the friars in Livonia, won the pagans, converted the schismatics of Wallachia and Bulgaria, reunited Armenia— too long separated—and, finally, re-attached Greece to the Church. This

From Friedrich Hurter, *Storia di Papa Innocenzo III*, IV (Milan: Battezzati, 1858), 346–49. Translated by the editor.

is not to pretend that some were not made happy rather than sad by his death, because of the way he had pushed his influence, the intensity of his involvement in his work, and the severity with which he governed. Recent authors take up the invectives of a few contemporaries and attach great importance to them without having a complete knowledge of his work and with less understanding of the feelings he revealed so many times in so many ways. But there is nothing strange about this fact; it is the result of the preconceived opinions and the sinister designs of these writers.

Other scholars have judged Innocent differently; if their representation of his position was valid, they knew how to rise above the prejudices of the age. The alterations or, at least, exaggerations, fruit of partisan spite, have not come from that group and ought not to be taken as historical truth. If, indeed, Innocent is accused of ambition for power, the solution depends on whether the authority he exercised, the way he mixed in secular affairs, the confidence with which he made the highest decisions in all cases, whether all this was for himself, for his own benefit, or for that single goal: his concept of duty and the importance of the papal office.

ALBERT HAUCK

Innocent III Desired to Rule the World

NOT KNOWLEDGE, but the feeling for order and rule, the prospects for reconciling and incompatibles, and the cleverness to overcome all things in pursuit of a goal, make the ruler. To a high degree, Innocent possessed these gifts. The young cardinal was so little blinded by the splendor of the curia that he did not delude himself about the numerous abuses in its rule. Hardly was he pope than he ruthlessly reduced its size. Also, in these first days, he dismissed the swarm of servants that had collected under Celestine. To expedite the progress of business, he urged officials to work harder; he forbade them to demand presents for their services. The workshops in which false bulls were produced were forced to discontinue their profitable services. He paid special attention to the reorganization of the treasury. Nor did he overlook little things: under him, for the first time, the chancery collected fees for drawing up bulls; but he also knew how to manage important matters: one did not hear that the curia was overburdened by debts during his rule. As he ruled in Rome, so in the Church and the world: subjectively and objectively, locally and universally, nothing escaped his notice. He knew how to win influence in all things. But in this thousandfold splintered occupation he never lost sight of the goal: the enforcement of papal rule in the Church and in the world.

He had not established the goal, but found it when he entered office. The ideology of the curia had known a long development. He had taken it over and restated it in the old formulas; even the proofs he used, the com-

From Albert Hauck, *Kirchengeschichte Deutschlands,* IV (Leipzig: Hinrichs'sche Buchhandlung), 684–91. Translated by the editor.

parisons with which he illustrated it, were borrowed. But the borrowings sounded different, as the emphasis was put on this or that point. Here is a case in point. With Nicholas I, the statement of the supreme hegemony of the papacy arose out of the necessity to safeguard moral and religious interests; with Gregory VII, conviction of duty to accomplish Church reform provided the starting point. With Innocent, these points of reference were put aside; his goal was papal world dominion. Now was the pope no more primarily priest, but before all a secular lord. The language is concerned with his rule over Church and world, so before "Church" a "not only" should be introduced: not only the Church but also the world has been given to him to rule; so the latter appears in opposition to the former as the greater concern. Therefore, to Innocent, the essence of papal power was in the union of the priestly and the imperial dignity. In conformity with its origins and purpose, the imperial power belonged to the pope. Italy stood at the pinnacle of the world because Rome, as a result of its primacy, was the seat of priesthood and of kingship. It was logical for Innocent to take up the theory of the translation of the emperorship from the Greeks to the Romans by the popes. Now it won a more sure acceptance for the first time. It is still more remarkable that he stated the relationship of the two powers from the viewpoint of feudal law: the pope invested the candidate with the imperial power. It followed therefore that the pope had the right to examine the imperial election and to decide whether or not the candidate was fit for imperial office; and, again, the assertion that the pope should be empowered to raise an illegal candidate to the throne if he recognized him as the more suitable person was only one result. He treated princes in general as he did the emperors. That he allowed both to remain was a concession to actuality, not to any conviction that the secular power was necessary. His ideal was much more the immediate hegemony of the papacy in the world. Only if the secular and spiritual power were united in the hand of the pope could a situation completely satisfactory to the Church be established. Especially was this the natural situation for Italy.

We cannot deny that the assertion of an all-powerful papacy was at this point revolutionary. What was natural was exalted over historical right. Innocent had the courage to draw the conclusions of his viewpoint. Especially did his theory of the binding force of oaths prove this point. It was not enough that he conferred on the pope the right to repeal every oath according to his free judgment; he asserted that oaths sworn by princes generally were opposed to God and his precepts, *i.e.*, the papal commands, and were not binding. For it would not be permitted to him to hold the truth who would not hold God as the Truth. Therewith the permanence of all constitutional provisions of the secular power was left to the will and judgment of one man. The highest bishop of the Church was the absolute ruler in secular affairs. But, at the same time, the transformation of the papacy to a primarily secular power was accomplished.

Innocent was deeply conscious of the fact that he held this position. He identified himself consciously with hierarchical ideas. I, so he preached to the Roman people on the day of his consecration, I have been put over the house of God so that my honor like my office towers over all. Of me it has been said by the prophets: I will put you over peoples and kingdoms; I will give you the keys of the kingdom of heaven. The servant, who has been put in charge of the whole house, is the representative of Christ, the successor of Peter, the anointed of the Lord, the God of the Pharaohs; he is the mediator placed between God and men, lesser than God but greater than man. Innocent thought he was on such a lonely pinnacle that what was said of Christ in the Bible seemed to him to refer to himself as pope: his utterances were God's, his business was God's business. Already, a doubt about his intentions was a sin. Sinners did not have to answer secular judges on judgment day, but him, the pope.

One thinks of Innocent himself as a man who, from the ideas in his writings, lived in contempt of the world. Therefore, one must look for a tragic conflict between his intentions and his practices. But nowhere do we find a trace of it. For Innocent was no kindred soul of the poor man of Assisi; he was a man of this world, a man of great gifts, of sharp intelligence and unbending will, but also of strong individuality. Also, his friends have not denied that he could not endure opposition: he was violent and quick to anger. He thought himself above the pleasures of the world, so much did he deceive himself; unwillingly he confessed that he was fortunate because the papacy gave him the highest earthly rank; glory among men meant scarcely less to him than service before God. He thought and asserted that he had the unchangeable will to permit him to pursue the road of right; thus he also deceived himself in this. For, in general, he conducted business under the influence of preference and dislike. He liked France even as he hated Germany. In the former land the memories of a happy youth captivated him; in the latter he saw nothing but crudity and power. Likewise, devotion to his family blinded his moral judgment: he had no misgivings about enriching relatives from the wealth of the Church and he was prepared to sacrifice the claims of the Church in order to obtain the daughter of an emperor as wife for a nephew. He shielded his cousins in Rome by his authority, when they assassinated an enemy; there was no judge to bring them to account. Can one wonder that his political morality was all too open to criticism? He knew only one rule for politics, that of opportunity and what was opportune; he formed his opinions like a man who saw through men and esteemed them little. He was not afraid to appeal to their base impulses to get them to serve him. He knew that unworthy men held church offices, but he put up with them, for their depravity would enslave them. Hypocrisy and deception were not offensive if they were in his service. On the other hand, he did not recognize the need for truthfulness in his political negotiations. As he undermined the purposes of enemies who could not protect themselves, so he gave assurances he knew he could not give; he managed events just as he needed them and, finally, was not afraid of open alliances. With moral scepticism, he believed that men of his kind tended to be the same: that he who seizes pitch besmirches himself seemed to him excuse enough.

Certainly Innocent was one of the most powerful of the Roman bishops. But he was not the ideal bishop that he has been judged by some; he belonged, however, in the procession of political popes. As the ecclesiastical idea of the papacy was, as it were, defeated in him by the idea of political hegemony, so also was his personality: he tended to speak in traditional religious formulae, but for his negotiations the rules of religion and morality were never unconditional law. We are informed that almost none of his contemporaries trusted him; his own Italians cast up to him his false deeds and his deceitfulness. They did not believe in his Italian patriotism, trotted out for show so ostentatiously. In Germany, they were convinced that he entertained the idea of destroying the empire. His death did nothing to alter this judgment.

ACHILLE LUCHAIRE

A Realist Ascends the Papal Throne

A ROUND AND YOUTHFUL visage with large eyes and high-arched eyebrows, a straight nose, and a small mouth. On the head, a cloth tiara, a simple pointed headdress which ends in a tassel at the top and in a circle of metal at the bottom. On the breast, the insignia of the high priest, the pallium, a band of white wool sewn with red crosses. It is thus that the fragment of mosaic preserved in the villa of Duke Torlonia at Poì, and the painting from the underground church at Sacro Speco represent Innocent III. History adds that he was of small stature, agreeable appearance, had a facile tongue and a voice so sonorous and well-modulated that everyone listened and understood him even when he spoke in a low voice.

When we take the old Roman road from Rome to Naples, we enter the valley of the River Sacco about ten miles from Rome. Above, on the foremost summits that surround the valley, the old Hernician towns, Segni, Anagni, Firentino, Palestrina, appear perched on the eternal seat of their cyclopean walls. Their churches have been built on the foundations of pagan temples. San Pietro of Segni, Santa Maria of Anagni, massive as fortresses, dominate still the stone houses and ramparts of their cities.

Here was the patrimony of Innocent III. The owners of the castle of Segni, of Lombard origin, had held the "county" of Roman Campagna since the tenth century. But it was only after Innocent III that, possessed of important properties in Rome and its environs, they came to use the surname "count," in Italian *conti*. This was the origin of the powerful Roman house of Conti, rival of the Orsini, the Colonna, and the Savelli. It is

From Achille Luchaire, *Innocent III* (Paris: Librairie Hachette, 1905), 1–34. Translated by the editor.

not surprising that it should have furnished several popes to the Christian world in the thirteenth century.

Lothario, or Lothar, of Segni was born in 1160 or 1161 at Anagni or Gavignano. Latin through his father, Trasimondo of Segni, and Roman through his mother, a member of the Scotti family, the future Innocent III was of a race of nobles and men of steel. Indeed, something of this remained in him: the greed of ambition, the warlike energy, the anger, the toughness. But an ecclesiastical education tempered, in this feudal man, the hereditary combativeness. Vowed to the clergy, he demonstrated a rare aptitude for learning. "He studied at Rome, Paris, and Bologna," according to his biographer or, rather, his panegyrist, the author of the *Gesta Innocentii Tertii* [The Deeds of Innocent III], "and he surpassed all his contemporaries by his success in philosophy, theology, and law."

We know little about his youth. At Rome his first master was Peter Ismaël, whom he named, in recognition of this fact, bishop of Sutri. He had better memory for the years he passed in the great international school of Paris. He took constant pleasure in France and Frenchmen. "It is to the University that I owe, by the grace of God, all the knowledge I have," he wrote to Philip Augustus. He asked Richard the Lion-Hearted for an archdeaconry for his former professor at Paris, the theologian Peter of Corbeil: "Master Peter, man of letters and savant of world renown, would be nothing to me were it not for his merits and his virtues. But how can I forget that I have followed his lessons and that he has taught me theology? I am not ashamed to say that I even pride myself in this." In 1198, he procured for him the bishopric of Cambrai. In 1200, he conferred on him the archbishopric of Sens in spite of the king of France and the Canons, partisans of another candidate. Peter of Corbeil was treated as an intruder by his clergy. But Innocent was obstinate: he preserved for his former teachers an affection that surpassed everything.

He did not, however, go so far as to tolerate their opposition. In 1203, while Peter of Corbeil was delaying the execution of the rigorous measures that the court of Rome had taken against a relative of Philip Augustus, Peter of Courtenai, Count of Auxerre, he received a thundering letter from the Lateran: "When we named you archbishop we thought we were doing something useful to the church of Sens and all France. In placing on the candlestick the light which was under a bushel, we thought we had given the service of God a pastor, not a mercenary. But behold, your lamp is out; it is no more than a smoking wick. You have hardly seen the wolf than you have let go your flock and fled; you have become like a mute dog that cannot bark." The archbishop took this remark so much to heart that Innocent felt obliged to console him: "It is only because everyone knows that I love you more than the other bishops of France that I have chosen you to give an example to the whole episcopate." Master Peter had the desire: but the pope was far, the king was near, and when Philip Augustus became the uncontested master of the country after Bouvines [1214], it was expedient to be a royalist before all else. In 1216, with all his colleagues, the archbishop of Sens refused to accept the excommunication launched by Innocent against the king of France, who was blamed for encouraging his son to invade England. The Roman authority ordered an investigation into the disobedience of Peter of Corbeil. Unfortunate vicissitudes of policy! Death alone, perhaps, prevented the former scholar of Paris from excommunicating also his professor.

Nonetheless, Innocent remained the protector of the nascent University and its real head. It owed to him more than to the king the first privileges that gave it its independence. Interested in the good organization of the school where he had studied, he imposed on it regulations of intellectual and moral discipline. He defended it against abuses of power by the bishop and the chancellor of Notre Dame: "From my time," he wrote in 1212, "I have never seen that the scholars were treated in this fashion." And the suspension of 1213, ordered by the delegates whom he charged to bring peace between the University and the bishop, was a victory for the masters and the students. Beyond doubt, his policy acted to remove the great associations of scholars from the bishops and to make them instruments of the Roman power. But in his relations with the school of Paris, he was inspired by memories of his youth and by feelings of gratitude that he always proclaimed loudly. A great admirer of this University which he wished to be free and to flourish, he had the idea, after the founding of the Latin Empire of Constantinople [1204], of sending Paris professors to the Bosphorus to reform education there.

Bologna taught the young Lothar of Segni civil and canon law, the two sciences in which he excelled. After he became pope, he never forgot the canonists who were his masters or his companions in study. Huguccio of Pisa, bishop of Ferrara, one of his habitual correspondents, Peter Collivacino, his notary, Bernard of Pavia, and Sicard of Cremona received benefices, bishoprics, cardinalates, and missions of trust. The court of Innocent III was filled with lawyers and Bolognese men of law. A doctor of canon law, Gregory, was the principal executor of his wishes at Bologna. And it was in this city of jurisprudence, to the body of professors and students that he addressed in 1210 the collection of his decretals edited by Collivacino.

On his return to Rome, Lothar had all that a cleric needed in order to advance rapidly: acquired knowledge, family contacts, and even relationship with certain cardinals. Early he received a prebend in the chapter of St. Peter's in Rome. In 1187, Pope Gregory VIII ordained him subdeacon; in 1190, Clement III made him deacon and cardinal at the age of twenty-nine. The seat of his deaconry was the small church of Saints Sergius and Bacchus in the Roman forum between the arch of Septimius Severus and the Capitol. From there, until the end of the pontificate of Celestine III, Lothar of Segni led the busy life of all the cardinals, occupied with the reconstruction and embellishing of his diaconal church, preserving, amid the intrigues of the curia, an attitude of moderation and habits of disinterest whereby his ambition was well served.

But the brilliant student of Paris proceeded to give the world proof of his success in school. He composed his three most important treatises before his accession to the papacy.

We lack the courage to read them entirely; the feeling of deception is strong. The ordinary method of the scholastic, the accumulation of texts of Holy Scripture or the Fathers, surpasses all limits here: an ocean of citations, where at long intervals some phrases that express the thought or personal judgment of the author float on the surface. In the writings of Innocent III, treatises or sermons, one finds almost nothing of Innocent III.

Christian pessimism views the world as ugly and belittles it in order to abase man's pride. It has inspired the most celebrated of these opuscula, the *De contemptu mundi* [On the contempt of the world] or *De miseria conditionis humanae* [On the misery of the human condition], a work which had an extraordinary vogue, for we find numerous copies in all the European libraries. The cardinal said modestly in his dedication that if one recognized some merit in it, he must attribute it to the grace of God. The merit consists in carvings out of the Old and New Testaments joined together by some common ties.

This treatise opens with a description of physical illness at various ages of life. All the deformities, unhappiness, and sufferings of mankind are here accumulated and exaggerated in a truly curious way. The infant, for example, conceived in filth and blood, made of the vilest matter; what does one think of this little nude being, whimpering, weak, without defense, with an intelligence little different from that of an animal? He is inferior even to the animals, "for, after all," writes the cardinal, "when beasts are born, they walk immediately, while we, made to have rights, we are not able even to go on four feet." And the sorrows of infancy, and the cries of the miserable newly-born! Lothar informs us in passing that the boy cries A, the girl E, and that the word Eve is only a double exclamation, *Heu Ha*. What is the first covering of our nakedness? A bloody film of skin! How is man, born under such conditions, above other created beings? "The vegetables produce flowers and fruits; but you, O man, what do you bring forth? Some worms, some spit, some dung."

He has spoken in the same way of the discomforts of old age, the vanity of knowledge and human occupations, the shortness of life, the misery of poor and rich, of serf and master, of celibacy and marriage. As an exception, Lothar has depicted the married woman with a rather lively touch, her eccentricities, her caprices, her love of dress, and her contrariness. "What a misfortune," he concludes, "that one never knows to what one binds himself when he marries! A horse, an ass, a cow, a dog, a cloak, a bed, a glass, a pot, all these objects we try before we buy, save for a young woman! If one shows her to her suitor, it is difficult to determine whether she displeases him; and whatever she becomes later, once the marriage is over, it is for life." In short, man is ever tormented; when he is young, by nightmares, when old, by cares, reverses of fortune, and illness. A list of the more serious illnesses leads the author to remark that men are no longer healthy and that their nature has deteriorated. Finally, to leave us in a yet more somber mood, he enumerates the diverse punishments human cruelty has invented and ends with the lugubrious history, borrowed from Josephus, of a mother who devoured her baby.

In the second book, moral evil appears as the result of three principal vices in men: cupidity, sensuality, ambition. Beside some barely-outlined portraits, of the drunkard, the *parvenu,* the proud man, that of the intriguer or pusher stands out: the cardinal must have seen this type frequently. In the chapter on luxury the clergy are taken to task with the crudity of expression proper to moralists of this period. A final book, very short, of a strict theology with little originality, demonstrates the eternity of the pains of hell and the irrevocable condemnation of the damned.

Exercise of a scholar, this is the work of a theoretician newly sharpened by scholasticism. It is not the work of a man who knew from experience the realities of life. And the historians who have vaunted it as the last word on the asceticism of the Middle Ages have been duped by an illusion. In his preface Lothar declares he is ready, on request, to develop the contrary thesis. "I will show, by the grace of God, the grandeur of the human condition so that if, by the present work, the proud man is beaten down, by its successor the humble will be exalted." Has he written this counterpart? In any case, we possess no more than the pessimistic thesis, pressed so far to the black side that, if it were necessary to take the quibbles of this Roman prelate seriously, nothing would be left of the justice and bounty of the divine being.

The two other treatises, *The Sacred Mystery of the Altar* and *The Four Kinds of Marriage,* are only applications of mystical symbolism dear to the theologians of this period. In these Lothar compares the unions represented in Christ and his Church, in God and the love of the just, in the Word and human nature, in carnal marriage and a legitimate wife. He poses and resolves some strange problems, among others "whether Christ ought to be called a bigamist." Here he interprets by symbols all the elements of the sacrifice of the mass: words, deeds, and movements of the priest, priestly vestments and the accessories of the cult. Allegory is everywhere, even in the miter of the bishop. The two horns are the two testaments; the two little bands at the fringe, the spirit and the letter. The crosier, sign of the power of correction possessed by the bishop, has a pointed tip to goad the lazy; its stem is straight because the bishop has the duty to reprimand the weak; it is curved at the top because he is charged with gathering in errant souls.

These works of the young Innocent III in no way announce the political genius and the firmness of spirit of one of the greatest popes of the Middle Ages. But contemporaries did not judge them as we do. They were pleased with this rhetoric and enraptured before these subtle puerilities. We must indeed believe, since they said it, that the prestige of Lothar of Segni as theologian, moralist, and writer had a bearing on his accession.

About Christmas, 1197, Pope Celestine III, a nonagenarian, fell ill, and the approach of the end redoubled the agitation of the cardinals. The youngest of them, Lothar, was the foremost; for a long time a devoted party had supported him. This is perhaps the reason why Celestine decided to seek another successor. The old do not like to be replaced by one too young, and besides, he was a member of the Orsini family, an enemy of Lothar's family. He immediately began to prepare the way for the cardinal of St. Prisca, a Colonna. He made him a coadjutor, insinuating that he would abdicate voluntarily if someone promised to name his candidate.

In all periods there have been popes who, for family interests or to avoid a schism, have tried to choose their own successor. All established power looks to its perpetuation either by heredity proper or by prior designation. But the cardinals unanimously repulsed a combination that would annul their electoral right. The opinion of the church, little favorable to practices of this kind, refused to abase the character of the highest religious office. The recommendations that Celestine III made at his death to his entourage met with no success.

The candidates were numerous. "The Lord Cardinal Bishop of Ostia," said a contemporary, the chronicler Richard of Hovedon, "worked to become pope himself, as well as the Cardinal Bishop of Porto and Lord Jordan of Fossanova and Master Gratian. And all the other cardinals attempted, each on his own account, to reach the same goal." The Englishman could indeed make fun of the court of Rome. Celestine III died on January 8, 1198, and on the same day, in spite of the abundance of candidates, he was replaced.

The election was held in a Roman ruin that the Middle Ages had transformed into a fortress, the Septizonium, the debris of a magnificent three-storied monument built by Septimius Severus on the southeast of the Palatine between the Circus Maximus and the Colosseum. It belonged to the monks of St. Andrew, possessors of the Coelian hill, and its name occurred often in the annals of medieval Rome. It was there that the nephew of Gregory VII had defended himself against Henry IV, that Pascal II had escaped the pursuit of the Germans, and that Victor III had been elected. One could deliberate there without fear. When Lothar and part of his colleagues had concluded the funeral at the Lateran, they hastened to rejoin the rest of the conclave enclosed in the Septizonium, and the decisive operation began.

After the mass of the Holy Spirit, the cardinals prostrated themselves and then gave each other the kiss of peace. They named the tellers who would collect the written ballots and read the tally. Lothar obtained the greatest number of votes; Cardinal John of Salerno had ten; two other cardinals divided the rest. They then discussed the outcome. The problem was Lothar's age: to elect the youngest member of the curia! to choose a thirty-seven year-old pope! But this candidate was learned, of irreproachable morals, and finally, the impelling reason was that the situation of the Church demanded an active, vigorous, and militant head. The electors therefore agreed on the name of Lothar of Segni. John of Salerno himself rallied to the choice of the majority and the final vote was unanimous.

Following a tradition of ecclesiastical humility which emphasized the distressing side of the task to be fulfilled, the elect refused at first the honor they wished to bestow on him: "he wept and sobbed," then he gave in. The eldest of the cardinal-deacons put the purple mantle on his shoulders and gave him the name Innocent III. Two cardinal-bishops led him to the altar where he prayed face down, while the cantors and the whole college intoned the *Te Deum*. He then sat down behind the altar, and the cardinals came there in rotation to kiss his foot and his lips. The first phase of the accession, the election, was ended.

Could such an important event in the history of the Middle Ages as the exaltation of Innocent III occur without a sign from the divine will? Three doves flew into the hall of the conclave: one of these birds, of immaculate whiteness, settled at his right and did not stir. In addition, the elect had a vision. He had been told that he would marry his mother, i.e., the Roman Church. Other revelations on this subject were made to pious personages, but we shall pass over them in silence, for Innocent himself did not want them talked about.

For more than a century, the lower clergy and people of Rome had not taken part in the election, which was the responsibility of the cardinals alone. But they were far from being uninterested. A crowd of clerics and laymen awaited the result of the voting outside the Septizonium. When it was announced, they escorted the elect, in acclamation, to the basilica of St. John Lateran where he would be enthroned.

The palace of the Lateran, contiguous to the sanctuary, was the seat of papal government, the center of the Christian world. It occupied the largest part of the square of St. John, from which, as seen today, the view embraces the red line of the ancient walls, the ruined aqueducts, and, in the background, the violet slopes of the Alban hills prominent against the snow of the Sabines. Two groups of buildings contained, on the west, the great council hall supported on its demi-turrets; on the east, the private apartments of the popes, the dining room of Leo III, where public banquets were given, the oratories of St. Sylvester and St. Lawrence, the chapel, and the chancery. The palace disappeared in the time of Sixtus V [1585–90], but the basilica of St. John still remains, though renovated, with its ancient baptistry and its cloister; it was before the portico that was then in front of the church that the new pope was immediately presented to the Roman people.

The cardinals installed Innocent III on a sculpted marble seat, the *sedes stercoraria,* the throne of dung, used because of the verse in Scripture: "He has caused the poor man to arise from dirt and dung so that he sits with princes on the throne of glory." The chamberlain who remained at the pope's side gave him three handfuls of pennies, and he threw them to the crowd massed in the square, saying: "Gold and silver are not for my pleasure; what I have, I give you." When that was done, he was greeted by a new acclamation: "St. Peter has chosen the Lord Innocent." Followed by the prior and canons of St. John Lateran, he entered the church and went to sit on the papal throne behind the altar. Then he mounted the great interior stairway which led from the basilica to the chapel of St. Sylvester, where other ceremonies awaited him.

Two red marble curule thrones were there. Innocent first sat in the one on the right. The prior of St. Lawrence, head of the chapel clergy, put a scepter in his hand, as well as the keys of the church and the palace, signs of his authority over the personnel and of possession of even the property itself. The new master then sat on the throne on the left and the prior passed a cincture of red silk, from which a scarlet purse hung, around his body. It contained twelve seals of precious material and a bag of musk. By this Innocent was given the papal treasure and some objects of value it contained. Then the officials of the palace were presented and permitted to kiss him. Again he threw pieces of money to those assisting with these words: "He has thrown away his treasures, he has distributed them to the poor, and his justice will endure forever." Finally they led the pope from the chapel of St. Sylvester to the oratory of St. Lawrence or the Sancta Sanctorum [Holy of Holies], the only part of the ancient palace preserved today. Innocent prayed there before a special altar; then he entered his private apartments.

The essentials were over. After the ceremonies at the Septizonium and the Lateran, the pope, elected and installed, held power legally. The consecration remained, but it was not necessary for this third act of the accession to follow the other two immediately. Since Innocent was only a deacon, it was necessary to ordain him to the priesthood before consecrating him bishop. The ordination took place on February 21, 1198, six weeks after the election, and on the following Sunday, the feast of St. Peter's Chair, he was consecrated in the basilica of the Vatican.

Protected by the fortified walls of the Leonine city for which the Castello di Sant'Angelo served as an advance bastion, the famous Church of St. Peter offered as a first view its campanile and the triple entrance of its portico. Here, as at the Lateran, the sanctuary lay beyond an atrium, a vast interior court where pilgrims stopped before the tomb of the Emperor Otto II and drank at the huge fir cone in gilded bronze, the *pigna,* from which water poured profusely between eight columns of porphyry. Next the façade of the basilica came into view, with its windows, its five doors, and the immense mosaic which showed Christ seated between St. Peter and the Virgin, the Evangelists and their symbolic animals. Inside, five aisles ended, as in most Roman churches, in a straight transept and a semicircular apse. At the back of the apse was the throne of St. Peter; in the middle of the transept, the *Confession,* an inestimable treasure. The whole world knew its mosaics of gold, its altar of silver, its gilded canopy with four twisted columns of oriental alabaster. Just below the *Confession* a shaft communicated with the funerary chamber where a constant tradition placed the bones of the Apostle. It was there especially that the crowd pressed, but they also besieged the numerous chapels open at the sides. The main aisle, finally, as the curious miniature of the French painter, John Fouquet, shows it, had an imposing character, with its double range of antique columns and the elegant balustrade on its circumference. A small square chapel occupied the extreme left.

It was into this chapel, on February 22, 1198, that Innocent III was led by the canons of the basilica to put on ceremonial sandals and to vest in the papal robes. Then, passing behind the main altar, he sat at the foot of the steps that led to the throne of St. Peter. The bishops and cardinals, according to ritual, formed a circle around him. The consecrator, the Bishop of Ostia, put the gospels on his head and all, without saying a word, extended their right hands to him. After the ceremony of anointing, they gave him the ring and the pallium; they put the gospels into his hands. Then he arose and was put on the throne of the Apostle. At this moment, at the chant of *Gloria in excelsis,* began the procession of assistants, who rendered the customary homage to him.

Remaining seated, Innocent watched the deacons, secretaries, and papal judges, vested in red mantles, divide into two groups. The one sang: "Hear, O Christ!" The other responded: "Long life to our Lord Innocent, Sovereign Pontiff and Universal Pope." And the dialogue continued: "Savior of the world!"—"Come to his aid." And the one side invoked the series of great Roman saints: Gabriel, Raphael, John the Baptist, Peter, Paul, Andrew, Stephen, Leo, Gregory, Benedict, Basil, Saba, Agnes, Cecilia, Lucy. To each name the one choir pronounced, the other responded: "Come to his aid." A *Kyrie eleison,* chanted in unison, closed the solemnities.

When the pope had said mass, preached, gone to communion, and blessed the faithful, he went out to the entrance of the basilica surrounded by a crowd of clergy. There, in view of the Romans singing the *Kyrie eleison,* the first of the cardinal-deacons raised over him the episcopal miter and tiara, the royal power. From that time he was vested with political dominion over the churches and their peoples.

Then the great procession was organized and began to move. The pope and his clergy had to go by way of the "Triumphal Road" from St. Peter's of Rome to St. John Lateran. At the head of the cortege was the magnificently adorned ceremonial horse of the pontiff. A subdeacon carried the cross. Twelve officers of the militia with red banners and two others with lances surmounted by gilded cherubim [followed]. Then [came] the maritime prefects, the notaries, lawyers, judges, choir, abbots from outside Rome, bishops, archbishops, the Roman abbots, the cardinal-priests, the cardinal-deacons. Finally, the pope himself appeared, mounted on a horse with a scarlet saddlecloth. A valet carried an umbrella over his head. At his sides rode the two most notable personages of Rome, the senator and the prefect of the city, followed by the nobility and representatives of the Italian cities, friends or subjects of the papacy.

The cavalcade crossed the Tiber at the bridge of Nero. It stopped at the palace of Maximus in the Campo dei Fiori, then dominated by a fortress, and at the church of St. Mark. Passing the ruins of the imperial fora, it stopped again at the church of St. Adrian, then entered the Roman forum, which it crossed lengthwise in the direction of the Via Sacra. It passed to the north of the Colosseum, skirted the church of St. Lawrence and finally arrived at the pontifical palace by the Via San Giovanni in Laterano. On the whole route, the corporations (the *scholae*) or rich individuals had erected arches of greenery. At each street corner, the clergy of the Roman parishes had gathered, incense-burners in their hands. An enormous crowd, bearing palms and flowers, singing and shooting arrows, acclaimed the sovereign as he passed.

But he had to pay for his welcome. Money played a large part in this triumph. At certain places on the way, the papal servants threw small sums of money to the people. For each of the arches under which the procession passed, for each of the groups of clergy who flowed into the crossroads, a duty was paid and the amount inscribed in the book of Cardinal Cencio, a ritual repeated by a financial secretary. Even the Jews of Rome, come down to the foot of the Campo dei Fiori, offered the pope the book of the law and received a present of money. Each of the major and minor officials of the curia had the right to a meal, to a small sum, to a provision of bread and meat. Even the lay authorities of Rome, Senator, prefect, judges, claimed their part of the food and money.

When he had returned to the palace, Innocent sat once more in the oratory of St. Sylvester and all the prelates came, one after another, to genuflect before him. A surpliced chamberlain, assisted by a clerk of the chamber and two bankers of the city, stood before a large table covered with piles of money and handed the pope, in a cup of silver, the amount due each personage. That night, there was a ceremonial banquet in the great dining room of Leo III, decorated with mosaics, paved with marble, cooled by the stream of water from an enormous porphyry fountain. The table of the pope, higher than the others, sparkling with gold and silver vases, was served by the eldest and noblest of the lay assistants. At the table to the right, the cardinal-bishops and priests were seated; at that on the left, the cardinal-deacons. Farther away, the bishops and nobles of the city sat.

We would like to know the attitude of Innocent III to these ceremonies and feasts. History furnishes only a detail. At the moment of his anointing, "he had such a contrite heart that he shed abundant tears." Perhaps this too was a tradition.

It was an established custom for the new pontiff himself to announce his accession to the churches and princes of Christendom. Innocent had the greater reason to follow the custom because he had to explain his accession to the papal throne at the age of thirty-seven. An encyclical, dated the very day after his election, announced to Europe, therefore, what had happened the day before at the Septizonium. The pope did not speak of the first ballot, which had brought only a majority of votes to his name; he devoted himself to the rallying ballot, which was unanimous for him.

"All have turned their eyes on us, insufficient as we are, mindful, perhaps, that it was Benjamin who found the cup of money at the bottom of the sack. Several, however, were by age, by position, and by merit more worthy than we of such an honor. Convinced of our lack of ability, we at first refused this office, so heavy for our weak shoulders; but we had to surrender to the insistence of our brethren. In prolonging resistance we could have opened the door to a dangerous schism or appeared to oppose the decrees of the divine will." But why the preference shown for the youngest? He himself did not explain it well: "The ways of God are mysterious and his judgments incomprehensible. And it is not without surprise that we sometimes see the young man come before the old in the exercise of the highest authority." In this letter to the Patriarch of Jerusalem, he insists once more, with good nature, on the unanimity of the vote and remarks that the cardinals, contrary to rule, held the election on the same day as the funeral of his predecessor.

Despite the formulae of official modesty, Lothar of Segni, after having reached the highest goal the ambition of man could then seek believed that he was ready to bear the enormous burden. He wanted to take charge with full knowledge of his duties and his rights. Scarcely was he enthroned than he seized the opportunity to tell the Roman people and the whole Church what he thought of his office and the authority it conferred on him.

The sermon he preached on the day of his consecration permitted him to justify the pre-eminence of papal power. In this view, it was based on the superiority of the Apostle Peter attested by the *Tu es Petrus* ["Thou art Peter, and upon this rock I will build my church. . . ." Matthew 18] and the gospel account of the barque of the Apostle. Without doubt, to remain faithful to the duty of humility the Church prescribed for its members, Innocent called himself the servant of the servants of God and dwelt on the obligations rather than on the advantages of his office. But in the same phrase where he spoke of his personal unworthiness, he defined, with a kind of transport of pride, the immense extent of the papal power: "Who am I myself or what was the house of my father that I am permitted to sit above kings, to possess the throne of glory? For it is to me that the words of the prophet apply: 'I have placed you above peoples and kingdoms that you may uproot and destroy as well as build and plant.' It is to me that he has said: 'I will give you the keys of the kingdom of heaven and what you will loose on earth will be loosed in heaven.' See therefore what kind of servant he is who commands the whole family. He is the Vicar of Jesus Christ, the Successor of Peter . . . he is the mediator between God and man, less than God but greater than man."

When he celebrated the anniversary of his accession the next year, he treated the same subject again in a different way. He was spouse of the Roman Church and the Bishop of Rome has no superior but God himself. But what is the explanation (here the spirit of scholasticism reappears) for the fact that the spouse of the Roman Church is in charge of the other churches? Is it not contrary to the laws of marriage, which prohibit more than one wife? To this objection, he answered that, in fact, certain bishops have two churches, *e.g.*, the Bishop of Ostia, who is at the same time Bishop of Velletri. And besides, the Roman Church has the right to do with the pope what Sarah in the Bible did, who led Agar to the bed of her husband Abraham. Rome brought to the pope all of the other churches, its servants. Innocent perceived, however, that he was spending a little too much time on this scholastic argument. "You who are interested in these problems look for the reasons to justify this apparent violation of the laws of marriage; for myself, my other cares do not leave me the time." But the love of symbolism drove him further: "The Roman Church, which I have espoused, did not have empty hands; she brought me a dowry: the fullness of spiritual power and vast temporal possessions. For the Apostle Peter alone is the one who has been called to enjoy the dual authority. I have received from Rome the miter, sign of my religious office, and the tiara, which confers terrestrial dominion on me."

This idea is often expressed in the sermons of Innocent III. For him, Rome has always occupied and will occupy forever the first rank in the universe. It rules over bodies as over souls. At other times, it possessed only the temporal power; it joined to that the spiritual authority. "It held both the keys of heaven and the government of earth."

Make no mistake about the Pope's thought: he believed that Rome, with its dual power, with its double character of "Apostolic" and imperial town, was his. And when he spoke of empire, he did not think of the German sovereign. He was at the same time pope and emperor. He stated this in positive terms in the sermon he delivered on the Feast of Pope Sylvester. Then, the question was no longer merely one of the superiority of the Apostle Peter; the papal power was based on an actual event which had taken place several centuries before. Like all his predecessors Innocent adapted to his use the famous legend of the Donation of Constantine. "This excellent emperor learned by a heavenly revelation that Pope Sylvester had, at his baptism, delivered him from leprosy. When he was established at Byzantium, he took for himself the Eastern Empire and gave the pope at Rome the senate and the whole Western Empire. He even wanted to put his own crown on the pope's head, but Sylvester refused, contented to wear as a diadem the royal headdress circled with gold. In virtue of his religious authority, the pope named patriarchs, primates, metropolitans, and bishops; in virtue of his kingly power, the senators, prefects, judges, and notaries. As king he wore the tiara, as chief bishop, the miter. He used the miter on all occasions; he used the tiara less because the spiritual authority was more ancient, higher, and more extensive than the royal authority. Among the people of God, the priesthood surpassed the empire."

From this very clear teaching proceeded the whole history of Innocent's pontificate. One finds there the essential thread of his doctrine and his deeds. The power he held was at the same time evangelical and historical, by nature spiritual and temporal. Without doubt, like all great clerics of the Middle Ages, he believed that the religious power was very superior to the other; but he would use both, and as both seemed to him legitimate, he would devote his life to strengthening both.

Enunciated from the lofty throne at the Vatican and the Lateran, these principles were proclaimed with tremendous force in the correspondence Innocent carried on with the clergy and sovereigns of Europe. It is enough to peruse the letters of the first year of his rule to be struck by the number of passages where there is a question of the nature and extent of papal power. On each page we find statements like this one: "We are placed by God above peoples and kingdoms. . . . We hold the place of Christ on earth, and, by his example, we have the duty and the desire to bring peace to men. . . . Seated on the throne of dignity, we judge in justice even the kings themselves. . . . Nothing that happens in the universe ought to escape the attention and control of the sovereign pontiff." Writing to the clergy of France to announce the arrival of their legate, he excused himself for not being able to be everywhere. But human nature had its limits and forced him to have recourse to his brethren. He seemed to regret it: "If the interest of the Church would permit it, I would like best to do everything for myself." This depicts the man and the enormous need for activity he desired to satisfy during the eighteen years of his pontificate.

Two of the letters from the year 1198 attract special attention. In a letter to the Archbishop of Monreale, Innocent demonstrated once again the thesis of the pre-eminence of the Apostle Peter, i.e., of the supremacy of the Roman Church and he stated the view, historically false, that Peter and his successors had established archbishops and bishops throughout the whole world and divided the Christian world into provinces and dioceses. The letter to the Rectors of Tuscany began with a comparison still famous: "God, creator of the world, has put two great stars in the firmament to enlighten it: the sun which presides over the day, the moon which commands the night. Likewise, he has instituted two high dignitaries in the firmament of the universal Church: the papacy, which reigns over souls, and the royalty, which rules bodies. As the moon receives its light from the sun, which is so much more important because of the amount and quality of its light, so the royal power draws all its luster and prestige from the papal power. But the two supremacies, the two powers, have their seat in Italy. Italy, by a decree of Providence, possesses, therefore, superiority over all the lands of the earth. The font of the Christian religion is in Italy and, in the primacy of the Apostolic See, the authority of the empire and the priesthood are intertwined." Here again, Innocent seems to ignore the Germanic Empire and its pretensions to dominion over the world.

That this man took pride in his title and wished to push to the extreme limit the exercise of his rights, of his religious and terrestrial authority, there can be no doubt, and he himself did not conceal it. Elsewhere, he moderated the very real expression of his intoxication with power by the formulae demanded by priestly humility. His pen was not sparing of the words "unworthiness" and "insufficiency." In ending his sermon on the apostolic primacy, he said to the faithful gathered at St. Peter's in Rome: "Lift up your pure hands to heaven and ask God in your prayer to make me fulfill worthily this office of pontifical servitude under which my shoulders bow; that He permit me to act for the glory of His name, for the salvation of my soul, for the profit of the church, and the good of all Christian people."

His office of judge and statesman absorbed him, crushed him. He did not cease to complain in his correspondence as in each of the prefaces to his theological treatises: "I am devoured utterly in the abyss of my many occupations and of the cares the government of the world causes me. It is above human resources. . . . Caught up in the infinite network of affairs," he wrote elsewhere, "I am so divided that I find myself inevitably inferior to each of my tasks. They do not leave me time to meditate, scarcely to breathe. A servant to the interests of others, I belong no more to myself. Nevertheless, so as not to neglect the care of God's affairs, so that no one can say that I permit myself to be monopolized by earthly matters with which the misfortunes of the times crush me, I have drawn up these sermons."

A significant admission. Innocent III recognized that he was obliged to neglect the spiritual for the temporal, and he laid the fault on the wickedness of men. He reproached himself, evidently, for being embroiled thus in the whirlwind of the age. Addressing himself to the Abbot and religious of Citeaux, he implored the monks to intercede for him before God. "Your holy prayers will give me the strength that I lack. He who aided the Apostle Peter at the moment of his shipwreck will restore me, too, to the road of salvation; He will prevent me from being plunged, more than necessary, into the vanities of life."

This was not a banal formula, but the sincere expression of a justified scruple. Elsewhere, the new pope lost no time in debating with his conscience. From the day following his election, we see him acting everywhere at once with a decision and vigor of which the papacy had seemed incapable.

PART II

The Vicar of Christ

ALEXANDER J. AND ROBERT W. CARLYLE

Judged by God Alone

THE COMPILER of the Decretals did not hesitate to include very strong statements regarding the powers and pre-eminence of the popes; these do not, however, give a complete idea of Innocent's claims. So far as they go we have shown, in discussing the relevant passages, that while Innocent held that the spiritual power was greatly superior in dignity to the temporal, yet he also held that both alike were of divine appointment. In the case of the empire Innocent admitted the right of the German princes to elect their king to be promoted to the empire, after his coronation by the pope, but he claimed the right and authority to examine the person elected and to decide whether he was fit for empire. He also claimed the right to decide in the case of disputed elections. In the case of disputes between rulers, Innocent claimed the right to arbitrate where a question of sin was involved.

In the Vercelli case he laid down the rule that suitors would not be heard by the Holy See in matters within the jurisdiction of the secular courts, unless justice were refused by the civil authorities concerned. Should justice be refused, recourse might be had to the bishop or to the pope; especially at a time when the empire was vacant and there was no superior to whom they might appeal for justice. Finally, it seems that he maintained that it was for the pope to decide in cases where it was uncertain whether the matter was one for ecclesiastical or for secular authorities to deal with. The passages cited in the Decretals, from Innocent, do not include any reference to Constantine's donation, but there is an important statement on this subject in one of his sermons to which we shall refer later on.

From A. J. and R. W. Carlyle, *Mediaeval Political Theory in the West,* V (Edinburgh: Wm. Blackwood & Sons, 1903), 151–86. By permission of the publisher.

Every reader of Innocent's letters must be struck by his tremendous assertion of the pope's exalted position. Gregory VII was content to be the vicar of St. Peter. For Innocent, the pope is the vicar of Christ (or sometimes of God); less than God but greater than man; the successor of Peter and vested with the same powers. Thus in a sermon on the consecration of the pope (possibly the sermon preached by him on the day of his own consecration) he speaks of himself as placed above all peoples and kingdoms, endowed with the fullness of power, less than God but greater than man, judging all, but judged by God alone. In another sermon on the anniversary of his consecration he speaks of his marriage to the Church (of Rome) and of the dowry he has received—a priceless dowry, the fullness of spiritual and the "latitudo" of temporal powers. As a sign thereof he has received the mitre to indicate his spiritual and the crown to indicate his temporal power. His authority is divine rather than human. He has received of God such fullness of spiritual power that no increase thereof is possible. Innocent complained in March 1211 to the archbishop of Ravenna of the behaviour of Otto IV. From his letter it appears that many held that he had brought his sufferings on his own head by raising Otto to the throne. His reply was that God Himself said He repented having created man. As there is no acceptance of persons with God, so there can be none with him. He has been exalted to a throne where he judges even princes, and should the king of France, trusting in his might, oppose the pope's commands, he will be unable to stand before the face of God, of whom the pope is viceregent. Innocent compares the dispatch of his envoys to the faithful, to the missions entrusted by Christ to his disciples. He cannot tolerate contempt shown to himself, nay, rather to God whose place he holds on earth. Philip (of France) should recognize what honour and glory he had received from all Christians for his obedience to the pope's orders. Kings so revere him that they hold devoted service to him to be a condition of good government. Injured persons may have recourse to the pope, the highest authority, and bound to do justice as "debtor both to the wise and to the unwise." The archbishop of Tours is commended for consulting the pope about matters regarding which he was in doubt, as the Apostolic See has by divine ordinance been placed over the whole world, and should be referred to by all in doubt on any matter. The king of Armenia is praised because he sought the help of the Roman Church, not only in spiritual but also in temporal matters, and because he appealed to it to help him in defending his just claims (*in justitiis suis*). The name of the Apostolic See is revered even among nations which do not know God. God who "wrought effectually in Peter to the apostleship," also "wrought effectually" through Innocent, persuading Philip by means of the papal legate to make a truce with Richard. He writes to Richard of

England that he has taken action after consulting with the cardinals, and in accordance with divine revelation (*divinitus revelatum*). The pre-eminence of the Apostolic See is due, not to the decree of any synod but to divine ordinance. There proceeds from the Apostolic See a sword, very sharp and swift, and it binds those whom it strikes, not on earth alone but also in heaven.

It is as the successors of Peter that Innocent claims for the popes their exalted position. In virtue of this succession they are vicars of Christ, and as his vicars they have received from him authority (*principatum et magisterium*) over all churches, over all clerics, nay more, over all the faithful. Others have limited rule, the pope alone has the fullness of power. While the popes are inferior to Peter in sanctity and in the power of working miracles, they are in every respect his equals so far as their jurisdiction is concerned. It is from St. Peter that the Apostolic See (or as Innocent also calls it the Roman Church, or the Universal Church) has received the primacy over all other churches. James, the brother of our Lord, content with Jerusalem, left to Peter the government not only of the Church Universal, but also of the whole world (*sæculum*).

We must now examine what authority Innocent did claim as pope in temporal matters. In a previous volume we have seen that in one of his letters he compared the pontifical and the royal authority to the sun and moon. In another letter he developed this. As the moon receives its light from the sun, so the splendour of the royal power and authority is derived from the pontifical authority. The logical conclusion would appear to be that the royal authority is derived from the pontifical. Innocent, however, did not draw the conclusion, though here as in other cases he appears, consciously or unconsciously, to be laying a foundation for future explicit claims. It is clear from other letters that Innocent did not as pope claim supreme temporal power. Thus, in a letter to the consul and people of Jesi, he speaks of his unlimited spiritual jurisdiction over peoples and kingdoms, while by the grace of God he has also much power in temporal matters. Again, in a letter to the archbishop of Ravenna, he writes, that ecclesiastical liberty is nowhere better secured than where the Roman Church has authority both in temporal and in spiritual matters. In the Government of the Ecclesia two swords are required, the spiritual and the material. Both are given by God direct; the one to spiritual and the other to temporal rulers. We shall deal later on with Innocent's reference to Constantine's donation; we need only mention here that he treats the donation by the emperor as of grace, and there is no suggestion, as in Innocent IV's letters, that the pope only received from Constantine that to which he was already entitled.

We have still, however, to explain Innocent's explicit assertion of Peter's supremacy, not only over the whole Church, but also over the whole *"sæc-ulum"* or *mundum."* It was in virtue of his office as Christ's vicar, in succession to Peter, that he appointed and deposed kings, that he gave them protection, that he ordered contending parties to make peace, that he took the orphans and widows of crusaders under his protection, and that he confirmed treaties of peace, agreements, grants, and statutes. We shall give some examples of the action taken by him in various cases, and the grounds given by him for taking it.

Towards the end of 1199 or the beginning of 1200 Innocent had written Kaloyan of Bulgaria (whom he addressed simply as "nobilis") asking him to receive his legate. Kaloyan did not reply till 1202. In his letter Kaloyan, who styled himself emperor, asked the Church of Rome to grant him a crown and the honours given to his ancestors. Innocent replied on 27 November 1202, addressing Kaloyan this time as *"dominus"* of the Bulgarians and Wallachians, informing him that he found in the papal registers that many kings, of the lands now subject to him, had been crowned, and that his chaplain whom he was sending to Bulgaria would, among other matters, inquire into the facts regarding the crown conferred by the Church of Rome on his ancestors.

As Bulgaria had only regained its independence from the Greek Empire a few years before, and the fourth crusade had just commenced, caution was obviously necessary in formally recognizing the Bulgarian kingdom. In the following year, after the capture of Constantinople in July and the restoration of the emperor Isaac Angelus to the throne, the situation had altered. Some time before September, 1203, Kaloyan wrote Innocent telling him that the Greeks had sent him their patriarch, promising to crown him as emperor, and to make his archbishop a patriarch (Innocent had not done so), but he refused their advances and again asked the pope to have him crowned as emperor and to promote his archbishop. Innocent replied holding out to the "dominus Bulgarorum" hopes that his requests would be granted. A few months later the pope wrote Kaloyan, "the King of the Bulgarians and Wallachians," that he was sending him by a cardinal, a sceptre and a diadem. In virtue of his power as vicar of Christ, and bound to feed his sheep, he appointed him king over his flock, trusting in the authority of him by whom Samuel anointed David as king, and seeking to provide for the welfare of the people both spiritually and temporally. Before his legate crowned him, Kaloyan was to swear that he and his successors, and all the lands and peoples subject to him, would remain devoted and obedient to the Roman Church. As requested by Kaloyan's envoy, he gave the king authority to mint money with his image on it (*tuo charactere insignitum*). There is no reference in this letter to the previous history of Bulgaria, nor to the inquiries previously ordered by Innocent, the action is based solely on Innocent's authority as vicar of Christ. In a separate letter, probably written at the same time, he sent the king a standard (*vexillum*) to "use against those who honour the crucified one with their lips, but whose heart is far from him."

Sverre, the king of Norway, had for some time been engaged in a serious conflict with the Church in Norway, and Innocent directed that his followers should be excommunicated and their lands placed under interdict. He also ordered the king of Denmark (*per apostolica scripta mandamus*) to take up arms against him. He also directed the archbishop of Norway to excommunicate a bishop supporting him. This was in 1198. In 1211, long after Sverre's death, the disputed succession again came before Innocent, the supporters of his descendants still refusing to accept the pope as arbiter.

Besides appointing and deposing kings, we find Innocent actively supporting them. Thus in March 1202, before John's final breach with Philip, Innocent wrote the archbishop of Rouen, directing him to take action against John's rebellious barons in Normandy, or in his other lands in France. He was, on the pope's authority, to warn them, and if this failed he was to inflict ecclesiastical punishments.

We may take other instances of Innocent's action in protecting kings from his dealings with Hungary. It is noticeable that, though the Roman Church had longstanding claims on Hungary as a feudal State, the pope does not issue any of his orders as feudal lord of the kingdom. Bela, king of Hungary, was succeeded by his son Emerich, who had been crowned during his father's lifetime. Coelestine III forbade the Hungarians to assist Andrew, Emerich's brother, on pain of excommunication, and in support of this policy one of the first letters written by Innocent after his accession was to the abbot of St. Martin's, summoning him to Rome to answer for the support he had given to Andrew. Before his consecration he also wrote Andrew, directing him to carry out the promise he had given his father to go on crusade. In case of failure he would be anathematised, and should his brother die childless he would be passed over in the succession by his younger brother. In June the same year, at Emerich's request, Innocent allowed the king, so long as Hungary was in a disturbed state, to retain in the kingdom any twenty crusaders he chose. He wrote at the same time to Andrew, ordering him (*per apostolica scripta tibi mandamus*) to be faithful to his brother, and forbidding him to make an armed attack on the king or to stir up sedition against him. Disobedience was to be punished by excommunication, and his lands and those of his supporters were to be placed under interdict. In February 1203 he directed the archbishops and bishops in Hungary to give an oath of fidelity to Ladislaus before his father, Emerich, started on crusade. He gave his order that the pontifical authority should so guard and defend the kingdom that it could not be transferred to another. A year later, at the king's request, he ordered the archbishop of Gran to crown his son, though a minor; the father giving, on behalf of his son, the customary oath of obedience to the Roman Church, and an undertaking to maintain the liberty of the Hungarian Church. In April 1205, after the death of Emerich, the pope wrote, as vicar of Christ and bound by his apostolic office to protect minors, directing Andrew not to allow the regalia to be dispersed during the minority of his nephew, Ladislaus. At the same time he directed the Hungarian clergy to defend the king against attack. In June 1206 he again addressed the Hungarian prelates and nobles on behalf of Ladislaus, directing them on pain of ecclesiastical penalties to take the oath of fidelity.

We must turn to another important aspect of Innocent's relations to the temporal power. We find him frequently intervening in conflicts between rulers, endeavouring to persuade or compel them to peace with each other. We shall in later chapters have to consider the similar action specially of Boniface VIII, and in our next volume we shall have to deal with some works which seem to indicate that the conception of some international system or method of setting forward peace was, for some time at least, of importance.

In a previous volume we have dealt with Innocent's letter to the French archbishops and bishops regarding his claim to arbitrate between Philip, king of France, and John, king of England, and requiring the cessation of hostilities.

There were many previous and subsequent cases in which Innocent directed the contending parties to make peace or a long truce, but this case is remarkable from the stress laid by Innocent on the fact that he was taking action on a complaint by John that Philip had sinned against him, and that he was therefore bound as pope to deal with the complaint and to inquire into the charge. This was the letter finally selected for the Decretals, no doubt because it appeared to give the pope all the power he required, while avoiding the appearance of direct intervention in political controversies. It would be difficult to conceive of a case in which one or both of the contending parties could not be accused of sin.

According to Wendover, a papal legate had endeavoured, in 1189, to compel Philip of France and Richard to come to terms with Richard's father, Henry II, and had threatened to put all Philip's lands under interdict. Philip refused to submit to the legate's orders, and denied that the Roman Church had any right to sentence a king of France for punishing a rebellious vassal, the very point taken by Philip in 1203. In 1198, the first year of Innocent's pontificate, Richard appears to have complained to the pope of injuries he had received during his absence on crusade. One of the persons he accused was Philip. The pope replied that Philip had brought counter charges, and that he hoped to be able to come himself and inquire into the matter. Should he be unable to come, he would have the matter settled by a legate. He concluded his letter by a peremptory order to Richard to make peace and to keep it; otherwise, trusting in the power of the Almighty, whose vicar he was, he would by ecclesiastical pressure (*districtione*) compel him and the king of France to keep the peace. He also wrote a similar letter to Philip, dwelling on the obligation that lay on himself as pope to restore peace among those at variance with one another.

While Philip and John were at war in 1203 the Pope issued peremptory orders to Philip to make peace, or a truce with a view to a lasting peace.

He threatened Philip in case of disobedience with ecclesiastical penalties, and wrote a similar letter to John. In his letter to Philip he based his action on the duty laid on him to seek peace and ensure it. He dwelt on the horrors of war, and on the encouragement given to the Saracens by this conflict between Christians. He was bound to interfere lest the blood of the multitudes slain be required at his hand, and he therefore sent his envoys to secure peace, or a truce leading to peace, between the two kings. Philip, before answering, called a meeting of his magnates, ecclesiastical and lay. After he was assured of their support, he replied, according to a papal letter, that he was not bound to submit to the papal decision in feudal matters (*de jure feodi et hominii*), and that the Pope had no say in controversies between kings (*nihil ad nos* [i.e., the pope] *pertinet de negotio quod vertitur inter reges*). Innocent, in his reply, expressed his astonishment that the king should appear to wish to limit the Pope's jurisdiction in matters. He expressly disclaimed any intention of dealing with a feudal matter, but with the question of sin, raised by John's complaints against Philip. This is the first letter in which the pope refers to these complaints. He still dwells in this letter on the evils and wickedness of war. This was on 31 October 1203. A few months later, probably in April 1204, Innocent wrote the French ecclesiastics a letter, portions of which were incorporated in the Decretals, and to which we have previously referred. In this letter the pope lays much more stress than in his letter to Philip, on the fact he does not desire to diminish or to interfere with Philip's powers, and he emphasizes the fact that he is dealing with a question of sin in which the pope's jurisdiction could not be questioned. He makes a very brief reference to the horrors of war (*religiosorum locorum excidium, et stragem . . . populi christiani*), but the special feature of the letter, included in the Decretals, is the stress laid on John's complaint that he had been sinned against.

Innocent asserted his right to intervene in quarrels between secular rulers before and after his contest with Philip, but he did not endeavour to justify his action as based on a complaint by one of the parties. We shall cite a few cases.

In 1199 there was a dispute regarding Borgo San Donino between Piacenza and Parma. Innocent wrote that "inasmuch as according to the apostle, love is the fullness of law, dissension makes men transgressors of the divine law," and he directed his representative to require Piacenza and Parma to come to terms, and if they failed to do so of their own accord, to compel them, if necessary by excommunication, to submit to the pope's judgments. Here it will be observed that the mere fact of dissension is treated as a sin, and as giving the pope ground for compelling submission to his judgment. In 1207 Innocent wrote the Florentines requiring them to make peace on reasonable terms with the Siennese, as the quarrel was the cause of "grave *rerum dispendium*," grave injury to men's bodies, and "immane" danger to their souls, while it belonged specially to the pope, as vicar of Christ, to restore peace. He had accordingly instructed one of his cardinals to take the necessary action, and should either party prove contumacious, he was to deal with it be ecclesiastical censure.

In 1209, in a letter to the consuls and citizens of Genoa, Innocent dwells on the danger to souls, the injury to property, and the *"personarum dispendium"* caused by the quarrel between Genoa and Pisa, and on his duty to deal with those disregarding his orders. He refers also in his letter to the way in which the quarrel hindered relief being given to the Holy Land.

The last letter we shall refer to, in this connection, is one addressed by Innocent to John in April, 1214, a few months before the battle of Bouvines. In it Innocent directed John, on pain of ecclesiastical censure, to make a truce with Philip to last at least till after the General Council, summoned for 1215, was over, and it appears from that letter that he also wrote to Philip in similar terms. He gave these orders as the war between John and Philip prevented help being sent to the Holy Land and was causing other dangers, and he was therefore bound in virtue of his office to intervene. Besides ordering an immediate truce, Innocent directed that two arbitrators (*mediatores pacis*) be appointed to treat for a permanent peace. Should they fail, the two kings were to submit to Innocent's decision, and give guarantees that they would obey. There is no reference to any complaint by either party, and it is singular Innocent should have ventured to give peremptory orders after his previous rebuff by Philip. Possibly he counted on the political situation to compel the parties to yield.

The cases we have cited appear to show that Innocent held that as vicar of Christ he could require the rulers of States or cities at war with one another to cease hostilities and to submit to his judgment, even though neither party had appealed to him.

There was another class of cases in which Innocent frequently intervened—namely, where the interests of widows and minors were concerned. He describes himself as "debtor to widows and orphans"; and one of those whose wrongs he endeavoured to right was Berengaria, the widow of Richard I. In this capacity in 1204 he wrote John that he had given orders that unless he voluntarily did justice to Berengaria, he would be compelled to do so by ecclesiastical pressure. Next year he wrote again on the same subject, as the representative of Christ, who is no acceptor of persons and who does justice to all, and accordingly directed John to carry out his agreement regarding Berengaria's dowry. Should John fail to do so, an inquiry was to be made and the proceedings referred to the pope for orders. In 1208 the dowry had still not been paid, and Innocent wrote to John that if he did not admit any obligation to her, he should refer to the pope, who as the vicar of Christ was inspired by God in his judgments. John had failed to appear before the pope, though Berengaria had been represented, and Innocent could no longer postpone action. Should he not appear within a month all lands included in Berengaria's dowry would be placed under interdict.

Shortly after his accession there was a remarkable case of papal intervention. Innocent gave as the ground of his action that by virtue of his office he was bound to give comfort to the afflicted, and he therefore ordered the release of Sibilla, widow of Tancred, and of others all imprisoned by the orders of Henry VI in Germany. It seems very unlikely that Innocent would have ventured to issue such orders except in the state of confusion in Germany due to the death of Henry VI and the dispute as to the succession. Innocent not only ordered the release of Sibilla and other prisoners, but directed the recipients of his letter to excommunicate those holding the prisoners in custody, and to place the whole diocese in which they were imprisoned under interdict. There is no suggestion in the letter that the pope had acted as feudal overlord of Sicily. He based his action entirely on his duty as pope to comfort those in trouble.

Crusaders were under the special protection of the Church. We need only refer to a few letters issued in the first year of Innocent's reign as pope. In one letter to the archbishop of Magdeburg and his suffragans, he directs that the property of all crusaders, from the time they take the cross, be taken under the protection of St. Peter and of himself, as well as of all archbishops and bishops. He also gave instructions regarding the action to be taken in the case of wrongs done to crusaders placed under the protection of the Church during their *"peregrinatio."* In the same year he gave orders to Philip of Swabia and to the duke of Austria to return the ransom paid by Richard for his release while he was on his way back to England from Palestine.

An important function of the pope at this time was to confirm agreements between secular rulers. For obvious reasons it was often of great advantage to both parties to have an agreement solemnly confirmed by the head of the Church and recorded in his registers. A case in point is his confirmation at the request of the king of France of an agreement between him and Count Baldwin of Flanders. It was, Innocent wrote, his duty in virtue of his apostolic office to provide for the peace and quiet of all, but it was specially incumbent on him in this case owing to his affection for the king and owing to the advantage (*commodum*) to the Church when Philip and his kingdom were at peace. He confirmed the agreement as reasonable, drawn up by religious and prudent persons, properly authenticated and sworn to, and accepted by both parties (*ab utraque parte recepta*). Frequently in confirming agreements the pope laid down that any one infringing them should be dealt with by ecclesiastical censure (this would ordinarily be excommunication).

Besides confirming agreements, we find other cases in which Innocent directed the clergy to enforce orders given by a prince—e.g., he wrote the archbishop of Giesen and his suffragans directing them to enforce the decision of the Duke of Silesia that Cracow should always be held by the eldest son of the reigning duke.

We have already referred to the Vercelli case, in which Innocent laid down that injured persons were entitled to appeal to the Pope for redress where there was no other competent court or temporal superior to do them justice. He quotes Alexius as urging this principle in an appeal to the Pope against his uncle, another Alexius, who had usurped the empire of the East. In this case political considerations, and possibly also the difficulty of enforcing an award, may have prevented his taking action. A remarkable instance of intervention, going apparently far beyond the Vercelli case, occurred in 1205, when he directed the Archbishop of Armagh to deal with a complaint brought by one Norman noble in Ireland against another. The complainant alleged that he had been compelled by force to give up his property in Ireland and leave the country and abandon all his claims there. Innocent's orders to the archbishop were to inquire, and should he find that war had been levied unjustly on the complainant, the aggressor must restore the property taken and release him from his oath. Should he disobey the archbishop's orders, he was to be excommunicated, his lands placed under interdict, and the complainant released from his oath.

Among the most noteworthy incidents of the pontificate of Innocent III is the Albigensian Crusade. The two great headquarters of Manichean forms of heresy, at the end of the twelfth century, were southern France and northern Italy, and especially the former. These forms of heresy had long engaged the attention of the ecclesiastical and of the secular authorities. As far back as 1022 a number of heretics had been condemned at a synod held at Orleans, and the matter had repeatedly come before other provincial synods, some of them presided over by popes. In 1179 the Lateran Council referred in one of its decrees to the open profession of heretical doctrines in Gascony and in parts of the county of Toulouse. The faithful were bidden protect the Christian population against the heretics. The property of heretics was to be confiscated, and it was declared that their rulers might lawfully enslave them. Those who took up arms against them were to receive some remission of the penalties of their sins, and they were to have from the Church the same protection as was given to crusaders. Two years later Lucius III at Verona, supported by Frederick I, anathematised the Cathari and other heretics, and on the advice of his bishops at the suggestion of the emperor, he directed that inquiries should be made by the clergy in every parish where heresy was suspected. Counts, barons, "rectors," and so forth were to swear, if required by the archbishop or bishop, to help the Church against heretics and their supporters. Those disregarding the order were to be punished by excommunication, and their lands to be placed under interdict. Cities resisting the order were to be cut off from intercourse with other cities, and to be deprived of their bishoprics.

Innocent held it to be one of his most important duties to deal with heretics, as his office required of him to maintain the kingdom of God free from scandals. In April 1198 he despatched a monk named Rainer to visit the south of France, and he ordered the ecclesiastical and secular authorities to help him. He ordered them in the case of obstinate heretics, excommunicated by Rainer, to confiscate their property and to banish them. Should the heretics stay on after Rainer had issued an interdict, the nobles were, as became Christians, to deal still more severely with them. Rainer had received from the pope full powers of excommunication and interdict, and the princes must not be displeased at such severity, as Innocent was determined to do all in his power to extirpate heresy. Any one who favored or shielded such heretics was also to be excommunicated and was to receive the same punishment as those whom they favored.

In the same year he confirmed others issued by his legate in Lombardy forbidding the admission of heretics to any dignities; nor were they to be allowed to take part in elections. All podestas, consuls, and members of official bodies were to swear to maintain these orders. In the same letter he confirmed the authority given by the legate to the archbishop of Milan to enforce these provisions by excommunicating any who might prove contumacious, and by placing their lands under an interdict. In a letter to the king of Hungary the pope stated the penalties he enforced against heretics (in his own territories), and asked him to banish them and to confiscate their property.

Returning to Innocent's action with regard to heresy in France, we find that for several years he endeavored to deal with the heretics of Toulouse and of the neighbouring districts through their rulers, but relations became more and more strained. In 1207, Raymond, the count of Toulouse, was excommunicated by Peter of Castelnau, the papal legate, and Innocent wrote the count, endorsing his legate's action and threatening to take away lands held by him of the Church, and to summon the neighbouring princes to take away his other lands. A few months later, 15 January 1208, Peter was murdered. The pope, acting on suspicion of his complicity, again excommunicated the count, and a crusade was started against the heretics. Innocent also authorized the seizure of his lands by any Catholic, subject to the rights of the overlord. The pope had before this made several ineffectual attempts to get Philip, king of France, to take the matter up, but Philip was not prepared to run any risks with King John of England still on his hands, and he even attempted to limit strictly the number of crusaders from his kingdom, but had to withdraw his orders in view of the popular enthusiasm. He also took exception to the pope's orders regarding the count's lands.

After the conquest of Beziers by the crusaders, they bestowed it on Simon de Montfort, their leader. This grant was confirmed by Innocent, who also gave orders that each house should pay annually three denarii to the Holy See as a sign that Simon de Montfort would maintain them in devotion to the Holy See and to the true Church. When later on he was pressed to agree to the confiscation of all the lands of Raymond of Toulouse, he refused on the ground that he had not so far been convicted of heresy. Innocent, notwithstanding his treatment of the count of Toulouse in 1208 in connection with the murder of the papal legate, yet had doubts in the matter, and was disinclined to press matters too far, but the more violent party in the Church prevailed, and at the Lateran Council of 1215 the lands already taken by the crusaders from heretics and those who had supported them, including those of Raymond, count of Toulouse, were made over to Simon de Montfort "ut eam teneat ab ipsis a quibus de jure tenenda est," thus reserving the rights of the suzerain, the king of France. Raymond was deprived of his lands, as he had failed to deal with heretics and "ruptarios." A decree was also passed regarding heretics generally, providing for the confiscation of the property of any convicted of heresy or of failure to deal with heresy. The punishment in the case of contumacy, to be inflicted by the pope, was the release of vassals from their obedience, and the lands of the rulers were to be open to occupation by Catholics who extirpated the heretics, subject always to the rights of the overlord. Provision was also made for annual inquiries by the bishops in any parish where heresy was suspected. The Lateran Council of 1215 thus ratified the action already taken in the Albigensian Crusade.

It will be observed that Raymond of Toulouse was not deposed for heresy, but for his failure to suppress heresy, and the suppression of heresy was declared a duty incumbent on rulers: neglect was punishable by the loss of their dominions. Heresy hunting was also now made a duty incumbent on the bishops of the Church.

The principles were those on which Innocent had acted throughout his pontificate, though he was much more inclined to mercy in giving effect to them than the more extreme, and possibly even than the majority of the clergy.

The exercise of direct temporal power by Innocent was confined to Italy. We shall deal hereafter with his demands based on imperial grants, and need only refer very briefly to his one material reference to Constantine's donation. This was in a sermon on St. Sylvester's Day, and we may assume, therefore, was primarily intended for an Italian audience. He told how the pope, St. Sylvester, had cured Constantine from leprosy at the time of his baptism, and how thereafter Constantine had made over to the Roman See the city (Rome), the senate, his subjects, and the whole of the West, and had then retired to Byzantium and contented himself with the empire of the East. Sylvester, from reverence for the ecclesiastical crown, or rather from humility, would not accept the crown which Constantine had offered, but used instead of a royal diadem the circular orphery. It was in virtue of his pontifical authority that the pope appointed patriarchs, primates, metropolitans, and other ecclesiastical dignitaries; while in virtue of his royal powers he appointed senators, prefects, judges, and notaries. In view of the interpretation by Innocent of the donation, it is singular that he should apparently never have made use of it in putting forward territorial claims.

Besides lands directly subject to the pope's temporal power, there were many countries in which the Roman Church had at one time or another claimed feudal superiority for the pope. Innocent was careful to claim any "census" to which he might hold the pope to be entitled, but it was principally in the case of the Sicilian and English kingdoms (after the surrender by John) that he supported his action, as justified by his feudal superiority. In both cases it was of importance to the Church that no assistance should be given by the kingdoms concerned to a hostile emperor, and we can understand Innocent's enthusiastic acceptance of John's surrender, inspired by the Holy Spirit. Later on, after Bouvines, the pope's position as overlord gave him a legal standing when he intervened between the king and his barons, and finally declared null and void the provisions of Magna Carta.

As we have seen, papal support had been forthcoming for John in 1202 when war was threatening between Philip and John, but it was now far more sustained and emphatic; and no doubt this was partly because John had become a vassal of the Roman See. Moreover, after John's surrender of his kingdom to the pope, we find not only Innocent but also the barons and John urging this as a ground for papal intervention, and the feudal relationship was clearly treated by all parties as an important feature of the situation. Louis in his statement of his claims to the English Crown referred to it, but denied that John was Richard's lawful successor, and argued that in any case the surrender was contrary to his oath and made without the advice and consent of his barons.

Important, however, as the feudal relation may have been in the case of England, it was not on it that the Pope mainly relied. Even when he declared null and void the provisions of Magna Carta, he gave his orders as vicar of Christ, and the disregard by the barons of the papal rights is only one of several grounds for the orders he passed.

Innocent was not a man to throw away any weapon which might some time or other prove serviceable, but it was on his powers as vicar of Christ that his policy seems to have been based, and as we have seen, his claim to a right of intervention in case of disputes gave him ample opportunity for the exercise of those powers.

CHARLES H. MCILWAIN

To Determine a Matter of Sin

THE IDEA [that the emperor had received the imperial crown as a gift of the pope] was greatly strengthened and extended by the dramatic and forceful exercise of papal authority by Innocent III in the earlier part of the thirteenth century, the period of the papacy's greatest actual power, though the pope himself, as was usually the case, made his contribution through his vigorous enforcement of papal "rights," rather than by any new or more advanced theory of his own in support of them. Lack of space makes it impossible to set forth here in any detail his pronouncements. Over the Empire he asserted a power that was practically without limit, especially in the matters of election and coronation, but as his interference in these cases was in part based on historical matters such as the Donation of Constantine and the "translation of the Empire," they furnish less definite illustrations of his general ecclesiastical theory perhaps than his relations with France and England. It is noteworthy that even in England, which King John had surrendered to the pope as feudal overlord, Innocent III's annulment of the Magna Carta in 1215 was not based on feudal grounds. "It is upon his ecclesiastical rights that Innocent founded his action and upon them alone." It is probably in his famous decretal *Per venerabilem* of 1202, and in his claim of the right to dictate terms of peace to France and England, that the clearest indications of his general ecclesiastical theory are to be found. "It is not alone in the patrimony of the Church where we have full power in temporal things," he says, "but even in other territories, that we exercise a temporal jurisdiction incidentally (*casualiter*) and on investigation

From Charles H. McIlwain, *The Growth of Political Thought in the West* (New York: The Macmillan Company, 1932), 231–33. Reprinted with permission of the publisher. Copyright 1932 by The Macmillan Company. Copyright 1960 by Charles H. McIlwain.

of certain cases (*certis causis inspectis*); not that we wish to prejudice another's right or to usurp a power not due us." "Three kinds of jurisdiction are to be distinguished," he says, in interpretation of the words in Deuteronomy, chapter seventeen, "first, *inter sanguinem et sanguinem*, and therefore called criminal and civil [*civile*, i.e. belonging primarily to secular jurisdiction]; lastly, *inter lepram et lepram*, and therefore known as criminal and ecclesiastical [*ecclesiasticum*, as distinguished from *civile*]; and intermediate, *inter causam et causam*, which belongs to either, ecclesiastical or civil; and when anything difficult or ambiguous arises in these [i.e. in things falling within the jurisdiction concurrently "civil" and "ecclesiastical"] recourse must be had to the judgment of the apostolic throne, and one who in his pride disdains to submit to its sentence, is ordered to die and to receive the plague of Israel, that is, by the sentence of excommunication to be separated from the communion of the faithful as one dead."

In demanding jurisdiction in the quarrel between the kings of England and France, Innocent protests that he intends no infringement or diminution of the jurisdiction or power of the king of France. "Why should we wish to usurp another's jurisdiction when we are not able to exhaust our own?" In this case it is not of the fief that the pope proposes to pass judgment, but to determine a matter of sin (*decernere de peccato*) "and of this without doubt the judgment belongs to us and we can and ought to pass it on any one whomsoever." "For we depend on no human constitution but rather on divine law, for our power is not from man but from God, and there is no one of sound mind but knows that it pertains to our office to correct mortal sin of whatever sort and to inflict an ecclesiastical penalty on any Christian whomsoever if he refuses to submit to correction."

In one of his sermons, Innocent says the Church has conferred on him both a plenitude of power over spiritual things (*spiritualium plenitudinem*) and a latitude in temporal things (*latitudinem temporalium*).

From these and from other writings of his, it seems clear that the jurisdiction claimed by Innocent III was almost illimitable and his exercise of it without parallel either in extent or effectiveness. Yet it was a jurisdiction in its nature primarily spiritual, and temporal only incidentally (*casualiter*), a power grounded on the pope's duty as vicar of God to judge of the sins (*de peccato*) of all Christians, not on his right as a temporal ruler to administer law for his subjects. Innocent then in his official utterances appears to have made no explicit claim to a direct power in temporal matters, but it remains none the less true, as Dr. Carlyle has pointed out, that "it is in the Decretal letters of Innocent III that we must look for the ultimate sources of the extreme view of the papal authority in temporal matters which was developed in the second half of the thirteenth century."

PART III

The Priest

AUGUSTIN FLICHE

The Advocate of Church Reform

WHEN WE PERUSE the voluminous correspondence of Innocent III, we are struck by the multiplicity of bulls aimed at returning clergy and laity to the practice of the Christian virtues proper to their state. Calls for ecclesiastical celibacy, condemnation of simony, considered equally pernicious in all its forms, exhortations to bishops to lead purer lives and to be more zealous in the exercise of their offices, efforts to introduce a stricter observance of the rule in monasteries and to oblige married persons to respect conjugal discipline, such are the usual themes that appear one after another without interruption. In more than one aspect this apostolate recalls that of Gregory VII with a broader field of activity.

Innocent III first undertook the reform of the Roman curia. His biographer relates that one of his first acts was to purge its personnel by removing the young nobles whose scandalous rapacity and ability to make money from everything provoked the legitimate indignation of John of Salisbury. He likewise suppressed luxury in food and clothes, which had reached unprecedented proportions, and allowed it only on great feast days.

While demanding more simplicity in daily life, he also worked especially to promote the most scrupulous honesty. Some unfortunate customs had been introduced at the papal court. False bulls were manufactured in abundance to be sent to bishops in order to persuade them to pronounce sentences favorable to those who sought them by bribing a scribe. From the

From Augustin Fliche and V. Martin, *Histoire de l'Eglise depuis les Origines à nos Jours,* X (Paris: Bloud et Gay, 1950), 156–74; 180–81; 188–93. By permission of the publisher. Translated by the editor.

first months of his pontificate, Innocent sought to stop this practice which dishonored the Roman church; he threatened suspension and excommunication, he pursued those culpable, but he obtained, it seems, only modest results; for in 1204, as well as in 1212 and 1213, he was still complaining about the use of false privileges and false indulgences, which had their origin for the most part in the curia.

Venality was also repressed. Innocent III suggested as a principle that the officials of the curia ought not receive any payment, with the exception of the personnel of the chancery whose services were poorly rewarded. It is hard to say precisely whether these orders of the pope were carried out. The court of Rome continued to have a bad press, but we ought not to attach too much credit to the reports of malcontents who did not shrink at the worst calumnies. On the other hand, we must recognize that the orders of the pope were not always carried out and that more than one official of the papal court still tried to get rich at the expense of plaintiffs or those who came to ask for a canonical opinion.

The reform of the episcopate followed that of the curia. Innocent III attached great importance to it because it was the surest step towards a reform of clerical customs. As vicar of Christ, persuaded that the religious life of Christianity was dependent on the intellectual and moral value of the bishops, he would use at all times the prerogatives conferred on him by canon law to limit the ravages of the spirit of the age among them and to compel them to practice more consistently the priestly virtues necessary for the accomplishment of their mission.

For this reason, it was necessary to look first to their recruitment. We have seen earlier that the pope had powerful levers at hand for this purpose. He could, while respecting the liberty of the electoral college represented by the chapters, examine whether the person of the elect met the conditions set down by canon law. Innocent III would not deny himself the use of this prerogative, but would use it with the sole purpose of preventing the accession to the episcopate of those who were not worthy. He methodically excluded candidates who did not fulfill the conditions of age and learning, while passing more easily over the question of birth: thus he recognized as bishop of Worcester an archdeacon of York born outside of marriage, whose consecration the archbishop of Canterbury had felt it necessary to put off for this reason, remarking that if the parents of the candidate were not married at the moment of his conception, they had regularized their union later and that he had a sufficient reason for a dispensation because of the learning of the candidate, the honesty of his morals, the purity of his life, the good reputation he enjoyed, and also because the chapter had chosen him unanimously, with the result that it would be unfortunate to deprive the church of such a pastor. The qualities of the candidate had, in this case, caused a relaxation of the rigors of the law. On the other hand, Innocent III had removed a too-youthful candidate who lacked the knowledge to be a bishop from the archbishopric of Colocza, even though he desired to please the king of Hungary, who recommended him.

Before all, therefore, Innocent III took the position that the person of the bishop ought to be above suspicion. If he was, he showed himself ready to relax the force of the canons. He would permit a subdeacon to advance to the episcopate if he had practiced celibacy strictly as was required before passing over this clerical rank. But, when he was invited by the canons of Lucca to consecrate a candidate who had been denounced to him by others as having married a widow, as an adulterer, guilty of incest, a perjurer, and also culpable of violence toward deacons, he ordered a very searching inquiry and postponed the ceremony until he would have formed proof of the falseness of such serious accusations. Nevertheless, he did not hand down a sentence of annulment without having collected all the information that would permit him to avoid injustice. At Pampeluna, a bishop was chosen who was immediately accused of simony, extravagance, carnal weaknesses, and other faults against morality; the first inquest did not bring the desired certainty because of contradictions among witnesses; the pope ordered a second before ordering deposition or absolution. Likewise, he attached great importance to the attitude of the accused, whom he considered as suspect if he put obstacles in the way of the investigation and did not come forward to exculpate himself when he was summoned.

This respect for canonical regulation was marked also by a perpetual care not to infringe the rights of the legitimate electors. It was only when an agreement was impossible in the mind of the chapters that Innocent had recourse to arbiters, whom he most often selected from among the neighboring bishops, unless, as at Milan in 1212, he was asked by the opposing factions to designate the new bishop himself. One such case had an exceptional character. In general, when an election was annulled, the procedure undertaken followed canonical forms, and the arbiters intervened only if the division among the canons persisted. At Milan, before agreeing to the demand made on him, the pope had made many attempts to conciliate the opposing parties. At Fondi, in 1199, Innocent had annulled an election as much for defect of form as for the imperfection of the candidate; he asked the chapter to choose a capable and honest person; he was met with a refusal. Although he had the right, he wrote, to provide by himself for a vacant church in the impossibility of finding a pastor, he invited the canons to return to better sentiments; he even agreed to a short delay and threatened them with suspension from their office if they persisted in their abstention. It was hard to be conciliatory and respectful of the freedom of elections at the same time.

In summary, Innocent did not seek to enmesh himself in local affairs, nor to extend the powers of the Holy See to the detriment of diocesan autonomy. He desired only to surround episcopal elections with safeguards for morality indispensable to the good recruitment of bishops and the maintenance of discipline. Without doubt, he did annul some elections for a simple defect of form, e.g., because the elect had assumed the administration of the diocese before having been consecrated. But was not the toleration of legal impediments, trivial as they could appear, creating precedents prejudicial to Christian order and to the regular march of ecclesiastical affairs? In similar cases elsewhere, Innocent did not prejudice the liberty of the electors in any way and, as we have seen, was content to allow the chapter to proceed with a new selection.

Innocent III above all distrusted candidates in whose favor the temporal power exercised too strong a pressure, and he combatted the activities of sovereigns with the most tenacious energy. Still, he gave proof of sincerely conciliatory tendencies. He admitted notably that every episcopal election should be undertaken with the *consensus* of the king and showed himself generally less intransigent than his subordinates. In 1211, he was apprised of a protest against an election which had taken place in Posnan, under the pretext that it had not been held in the right place, that the duke, a persecutor of the church, had been present, and that the canons had communicated with his chancellor, although he had been excommunicated by the archbishop of Gniezno in full synod. The canons responded that the election had been held in the cathedral according to custom, that the duke had not exercised any pressure, and that the excommunication of the chancellor had not come to their knowledge. After an examination, Innocent ratified the election with the sole request that the archbishop of Gniezno, who was favorable to the candidate, seek his agreement for the defense of ecclesiastical liberties which were somewhat threatened in Poland. We should not therefore tax him with intransigence or exclusiveness; but each time the threat was stated precisely, he sought to resist the rulers with an implacable energy.

This is not the place to dwell on his difference with the King of England, John Lackland, which had a much broader scope. It is enough to recall that it had its origin in the determination of the pope to prevent the invasion of episcopal sees by royal creatures and that, to forestall every attempt of this kind, to defend notably the See of Canterbury, Innocent did not shrink from using the interdict, which weighed heavily on the land for several years. The pope followed the same line of conduct everywhere. At Venice in 1209, he was not afraid to affront the doge in the matter of the election of the archbishop of Durazzo, who, chosen by the canons, was refused entry to his archiepiscopal see by the representative of the government, then by the doge and his counsellors, who dared to pretend that no one could become archbishop of Durazzo without their assent. The pope met the same treatment from the king of Denmark, who had tried to make the bishop of Schleswig, Waldemar, archbishop of Bremen. Waldemar was an "apostate, a useless man, a rebel, and a defaulter," whom the king had previously imprisoned as one involved in a plot against him, but with whom he was now reconciled. Innocent refused this transfer, which was also desired by Philip of Swabia. Waldemar, however, took possession of the see. The pope, far from being intimidated, entrusted the affair to the archbishop of Magdeburg, summoned the rebel prelate to Rome and, on July 4, 1209, asked Otto of Brunswick to chase him out of Bremen with his accomplices. Finally, everything was arranged: the chapter of Bremen, apprised by Rome, agreed and suggested the transfer of the bishop of Osnabrück, which Innocent was happy to authorize.

In spite of all these precautions, some intruders were able to slip in at the head of dioceses. Although Innocent watched over the regularity of elections and removed candidates who did not present the canonical guarantees of age and knowledge, the proprietary wealth of the churches more than once tempted candidates who, without being positively disreputable, lacked the priestly spirit. Thus the pope, who had never compromised the needs of Christian morality, was forced to exercise over the western bishops a surveillance that the progress of heresy rendered more necessary still than at other times, since the luxury and negligence of certain prelates was in many ways eagerly exploited by the enemies of orthodoxy. We read in one of his first letters:

It is proper that the pope should be irreproachable and that he to whom the care of souls falls should shine like a torch in the eyes of all by reason of his learning in doctrine and his example. Thus, every time someone informs us that one of our brothers in the episcopate does not exude the perfume of pastoral modesty and ruins or tarnishes his good reputation in some way, we experience deep sorrow and trouble; in order to track down such faults minutely and to correct them with the requisite severity, we force ourselves to apply the remedy of apostolic solicitude.

This bull, addressed to the bishop of Liège at the beginning of the pontificate with respect to the Archbishop of Trèves, who was under serious suspicion, contains a whole program to which Innocent III remained strictly faithful. In order to have permanent contact with the bishops, to know them better, to counsel them, to get them back to poverty, he ordered them to make an *ad limina* visit every four years, or in case of impossibility, to delegate a representative to render account of the state of the diocese. Without doubt, no echo of these interviews has come down to us, but it is relatively easy to reconstruct their tenor, for they were, by necessity, animated by the ideas which embellished the papal correspondence, where Innocent so often bared his priestly soul and tried to communicate the burning heat of his apostolic heart to his brothers in the episcopate. Above all, he recalled to them the obligation of pastoral visitation which, as he explained in a letter to the archbishop of Sens dated February 15, 1204, made possible the reform of what needed reform, the creation of what needed to be created, and the provision, in conformity to the decree of the Lateran Council, for vacant benefices, and the granting of them to worthy individuals. He made the same recommendations to the archbishop of Mainz, who, by travelling through his diocese, could acquit himself of the essential duty of his office: to nourish the flock entrusted to him by the words of Christ and the "bread of Holy Scripture." When scandals broke out in the diocese of Ratisbon, the pope ordered the bishop to visit the parishes regularly, to conduct personal inquiries, and to act zealously to remedy a disastrous situation.

It was the special duty of the pope to bring the bishops back to the exercise of their obligations if they had neglected them, and, in cases of necessity, to take sanctions against them. Innocent III acquitted himself of this mission with a paternal delicacy that did not exclude an energetic firmness. When disagreeable rumors reached his ears, he listened to them circumspectly; he informed himself about the individual who had been thus denounced, asked him to explain, and it was only if the accusations formulated took greater substance that he ordered an inquiry; this sometimes revealed slander. The pope was then the first to rejoice and was content to recommend to the prelate in the case that he should destroy suspicion and stigmatize the lies by redoubling his zeal in the exercise of his office. He did not want at any price to condemn an innocent man and took every precaution necessary so that would not happen. In 1202, a canon from Prague accused his bishop of fornication, drunkenness, also incriminating him of having sworn homage to the duke of Bohemia, received the *regalia* from him, and delivered the wealth of the church to the counsellor of the duke. Summoned to Rome, the prelate excused himself on the grounds that the trip was hard, the time for consecrating the holy oil was near, and the son of the duke must soon be baptized. The pope declared him obstinate and suspended him, in the meanwhile agreeing to a new delay and ordering the archbishop of Salzburg to look into the affair. When the inquiry proved that the bishop was not culpable, Innocent was happy to forgive him.

Even in cases of serious faults, though Innocent never shrank from enforcing the sanctions he imposed, he proceeded with the same gentleness towards individuals. He sought, above all, to arouse recognition and manifestations of repentance, as happened in the case of the bishop of Utrecht, who, accused of usury, confessed his sin to the bishop of Sainte-Croix and received absolution, which he asked for with sincere contrition, in the meanwhile promising by oath not to commit this sin again. When the guilty showed themselves more hardened, the pope ordered a detailed hearing of witnesses to proceed, as was the case for the archbishop of York, which furnished the reason for a searching investigation conducted by the bishop of Ely under the direction of Innocent. The pope insisted that they hear the abbots, princes, and "other honest individuals" who accused him, that they likewise question everyone who was likely to furnish information, and that they transmit the dossier immediately to Rome for a decision. Also, at Vichy, at Bordeaux, at Besançon, the pontiff constantly demanded the results of inquires being carried on with a careful respect for justice. At Bordeaux, the inquest conducted by the archbishop of Bourges proved, after twenty months of testimony, that archbishop Elias was "useless and unworthy." Innocent gave him two months to resign; if not, he would depose him and ask the chapter to elect a new pastor according to canonical regulation. And, as a matter of fact, Elias was replaced somewhat later by William of Geneva. At Poitier, the bishop did not respect the commands of the Holy See. He arranged to exclude poor clerics from the priesthood, despoiled others in favor of laymen, associated with excommunicated persons, and multiplied taxes. The pope ordered him to be investigated. He soon learned that these complaints where by no means exaggerated, that the prelate in question had allowed his men to whip one clergyman and to wound another seriously, that he expressed publicly his claim to be "pope in his own diocese"; he deposed him and excommunicated the clergy and laity who had supported him. We can cite other examples which give proof of the persevering effort of the pope to reform an episcopate which had for some time let itself be contaminated by the age and had given a foundation to the criticisms, in some cases justified, of the *Cathari* and the *Vaudois*.

In all circumstances Innocent was guided only by the higher interests of the church. Thus he did not limit himself to a demand for irreproachable conduct on the part of the bishop; he wanted him to be the same in his administration. There is nothing more characteristic in this regard than the bull of August 4, 1213, relative to the bishop of Brixen, who was aged, ill, and had lost the power of speech. Innocent remarked that he was, on this account, unable to fulfill one of the most essential of his pastoral duties, that of preaching. His diocese could only suffer from this, and, he added, this ought not to happen, for the bishop was made for the church and not the church for the bishop. As a result, they should ask for the bishop's resignation and, in case he refused, should use force. His preoccupation with the same subject was expressed in a letter dated October 9, 1205, to the archbishop of Mainz. This time it was a matter of the bishop of

Strasbourg's complaints that he had not been able to secure consecration in spite of his repeated requests. Innocent ordered this negligent metropolitan to proceed immediately with the ceremony, for, he said, the diocese had remained too long without a pastor, a state which was very prejudicial to it. At Trent, the bishop sought to retire because of his age, his sickness, and also his difficulties with his flock. The pope was disposed to accept his resignation, the more so because the prelate had sworn an oath to Philip of Swabia and had entrusted the administration of his church to the Patriarch of Aquila. But the bishop, with the agreement of his chapter, went back on his decision. Deeply concerned over the destitute condition of the diocese, Innocent entrusted the affair to the bishop of Treviso with a commission for him to order the chapter to proceed to an election within eight days following the deposition of the bishop, and, if they refused, he himself was to make all decisions necessary to avoid an appeal to Rome—which would only prolong a situation already drawn out too long. In the interest of a church Innocent would go even to the point of sacrificing some of his prerogatives. In 1212, the bishop of Cremona, legate of the Apostolic See, informed him that he had deposed the bishop of Vicenza, who had not come when summoned by him and that he had ordered the canons to elect a successor. Innocent remarked to his representative that he had acted a bit hastily, that he ought to have referred the matter to the pope, to whom decisions of this kind were reserved; but, because of the "great peculation and the shameful inadequacy" of the accused, he ratified the fait accompli and ordered the canons to proceed to an election within the month.

In his correspondence with the bishops, Innocent stated several times his pressing desire to improve the moral level of the lower clergy. He asked prelates above all to combat the vices that stained priestly purity and pointed out to them the means to use in restoring priests to a more worthy life. In 1198, he pointed out to those directing the church of Jutland the abuses which had been introduced into this distant and almost inaccessible land. He commanded the dean who took the place of the bishop to call synods regularly and at the same time alerted Absalon, archbishop of Lund, so that he might oversee the measures that had been taken. In England, the bishop of Winchester received full powers to reform churches and monasteries which were dependent on him, to punish clergy who practiced usury and obtained shameful profits or who lived among those governing the land, with the recommendation that he should not show himself lukewarm in correcting them. In France, a series of very insistent bulls were sent to the dioceses of Sens and Auxerre where things left much to be desired and where the archbishop of Bourges and the abbot of Cluny were ordered to come to the aid of the bishops who seemed to show signs of some softness in repressing wrongs.

The reform sought by Innocent III brought above all a very strict application of the rule of celibacy, which he desired to restore in its integrity, especially where it had not been practiced. This was the case in the diocese of Norwich, where the pope ordered that married clergy should be deprived of their benefices; in Poland, where he ordered the archbishop of Gniezno to remove them from ecclesiastical office and to suppress their revenues; in Denmark, also, he saw to their suspension and deprived them of their benefices, while interesting himself, with a scruple that did not lack delicacy, in the lot of concubines, who ought to be taken back by their fathers, brothers, or other relations. Several times also he referred to the legislation that excluded the sons of priests from holy orders, save in exceptional cases reserved to his examination. He also attacked all forms of laxness: he forbade long hair styles and lay dress, condemned without pity the worldly way of life and participation in secular affairs which could result in illicit profits, under pain of loss of benefices or income and of suspension of clerical immunity. At Paris, a priest who was found guilty of faults should be put in prison by the bishop to do penance "by eating the bread of sorrow and drinking the water of misery."

Innocent III was not content to struggle against an undisciplined way of life. Conscious of the evil of the age, he pursued the wealth of the clergy, which was often the cause of the worst evils. At the Lateran he obtained some results, but it was necessary that this progress should extend to all dioceses. Above all, it was important to put an end to the accumulation of benefices, the origin of all scandals. In a letter to the bishop of Hereford dated March 28, 1213, the pope attempted to demonstrate that it was a crime against Christian morality:

The patrimony of Christ ought to be divided equitably among those who have been admitted to his heritage and it is not proper that, while some are drunk with wealth, others are hungry and fasting. Thus by the authority of the present document, we forbid you to tolerate it that those who are sufficiently provided for with benefices should obtain churches which are under your control by law of the diocese.

Innocent did not tolerate any longer that state of affairs whereby those ministering to parishes did not have the means to live. He learned that at Verdun and at Metz, in certain churches, "the patrons gorged themselves with ecclesiastical property while the clergy were forced to fast." He did not concede that he to whom the care of souls was entrusted "should not be able to support himself with the revenues assigned to him" and ordered the chapters of the two dioceses to put down these abuses. A similar reprimand was addressed to the bishop of Ratisbon, who allowed clergy in charge of a ministry to replace themselves with vicars.

To put an end to these unhappy conditions, Innocent desired to enforce the residency requirement for priests. We read in one of his first bulls, addressed to Archbishop Walter of Rouen:

> Since it is written: *that he who does not work does not eat* (II Thessalonians 3:10), we think it is improper and undignified that some clergy do not minister to the churches whose ample incomes provide for them.

This prescription was applied especially to the chapters. The canons of Troyes had received through the mediation of their bishop and metropolitan, the archbishop of Sens, an invitation to annul an agreement whereby those who were not in residence would receive their entire incomes. Another bull, of June 6, 1198, reminded the bishop of Angoulême that he had not taken account of the protests of certain canons about decisions made in their absence and, at the same time, a dignitary of the church of Besançon had been requested, no less imperiously, to stop avoiding an obligation considered essential. Besides, the chapters ought to give good example to the rest of the clergy in all things. The canons ought not only to subject themselves to the strictest exactitude in the divine service, but their lives should be above suspicion and by their simplicity should lend no basis for an accusation of luxury.

Such was the personal action of Innocent III to lead the clergy to greater purity, disinterestedness, and outward decency. He counted on the bishops to bring about the observance of these directives and put them on guard against the subtleties which sometimes seemed to frighten them. To one of them who was very well-disposed to put down concubinage among the clergy, but who, in the absence of any accusation according to canon law, did not dare to act vigorously, he declared flatly that, when the fault was public, there was no need of accusers or witnesses and that the scandal alone was enough to provide the motive for a condemnation. To another he communicated his disposition to take action against simoniacs so that "purity and innocence would not be tarnished but the perverse simoniac would not escape the chastisement that was his due," and that because of the gravity of this fault, "in comparison with which all other crimes seem small," one could take the testimony of thieves, adulterers, and other guilty persons, while taking of course the necessary precautions. Concern about morality swept up this pope, often considered a jurist with narrow interests, more than any other problem. Scrupulous by nature, he desired only that "ecclesiastical censure should not oppress the innocent, but should correct the guilty." He wanted all precautions taken to render justice without misguiding them in questions purely formal, which risked delaying the sentence, and gave himself the duty of guiding bishops so that they would combine concern for equity with the benevolence of which a true pastor ought to give proof.

While personally exercising control with such vigilance, Innocent constantly made use of national and provincial councils, which were charged with engendering respect for the Roman legislation and adapting it to local needs. Thus, in 1200, Hubert, archbishop of Canterbury, gathered at Westminster an important assemblage in full accord with Rome, which gave effect in England to the decisions made at the Lateran Council of 1179. Such was also the case at the Council of Dioclea of 1199, which reformed the Dalmatian church; at the councils of Avignon (1209) and Montpellier (1215), the one presided over by the legate Milo and by Hugh, bishop of Riez, the other by Cardinal Peter of Benevento, where measures were taken to reform the church in the south of France and to prevent the spread of the Catharist heresy; and at the Council of Paris (1212 or 1213) which, under the direction of Robert of Courçon, proceeded to recast the laws concerning ecclesiastical discipline.

We find in the canons of these councils, among which one can find many points in common, the echo of papal interest. The Council of Paris desired above all to suppress venality among the clergy; it forbade them especially to exact a payment in money when they exercised the profession of law and had benefices sufficient for their maintenance, to fix a price for preaching, to traffic in masses and the sacraments, and to abandon their churches to become chaplains in another. The Council of Westminster did not authorize any payment for the administration of the sacraments and that of Montpellier ordered the bishops to give benefices to worthy clergy without charge. At Dioclea, simony was prohibited and the conferring of benefices by laymen was declared null.

The conduct of the clergy gave place to a still larger number of regulations. The Council of Dioclea introduced in Dalmatia and Serbia the legislation on ecclesiastical celibacy. Married priests and deacons were permitted to keep their churches if the union pre-dated their entry into orders and if their wives were vowed to chastity before the bishop. Besides violations of the law of celibacy, the dress of the clergy came in for some severe criticism. The Council of Westminster ordered them to wear black; that of Avignon, to have closed habits; that of Paris, to have nothing in their possession save what was proper; at Montpellier, precise rules were laid down proscribing bridles, gilded spurs, red or green habits, while making an obligation of the tonsure and of the hair cut in the shape of a crown. Distractions were also put under surveillance: at Paris, they forbade the clergy to have hunting dogs or falcons, abolished the feast of fools as well as dances in cemeteries and all sacred places. Canon seventeen of Avignon also forbade them in the churches and did not permit either races, cards, or love songs. We see in these various regulations the desire to avoid the possibility, as canon eighteen of the same council puts it, that the clergy should be an object of scandal and cut the figure of "the blind leading other blind."

Besides these interdictions, the councils reminded the clergy of their most positive duty concerning the cult and the sacraments. The canons of Westminster commanded them to avoid distractions during mass and to pronounce the words of the Canon distinctly, to keep the Eucharist in a proper vessel, which they should cover with a fine linen cloth to bring communion to the sick. Baptism and penance were the cause for some curious remarks. The priest was not allowed to inflict on a married woman a penance that would arouse the suspicions of her spouse nor prescribe, under the guise of penance, the offering of a certain number of masses.

For Innocent, the reform of the church should not be limited to the clergy; the laity formed an integral part of the church. For, while the clergy were bound to celibacy, the laity had to observe the indissolubility of marriage. Innocent showed himself very intransigent on this subject. Marriage is a divine institution, he reminded the bishop of Paris:

> For man, made in the image of God, placed by a divine gift above the birds of the air and the fishes of the sea and all the other living beings that move on the land, does not return sterile to a sterile dust, woman was drawn from one of his sides while he slept and designated to help him; then this commandment echoed in his ears: *Increase and multiply and fill the earth* (Gen. 1:28). From this moment the descendants of Adam began to unite in a nuptial pact. The hand of the Creator, even after the Fall, interposed its authority to such a degree that, in the words of the Gospel: *Man may not separate what God has joined* (Matt. 19:6). The sacrament of marriage cannot be considered as a human institution, because it appeared as an act of the divine authority. Thus, though it is contracted between human beings, it is in Christ that the bond is sealed, as we learn from these words of the apostle: *I tell you that it is a great sacrament in Christ and in the church* (Ephes. 5:32).

The divine law was, therefore, formal, and the pope was charged with insuring respect for it. If we attempt to disentangle the directives which emanated from the many juridical decisions delivered by Innocent III, we note above all that, in conformity with canon law as it was codified in the twelfth century, he attached an importance of the first order to the formulized consent of the espoused parties. At Modena, it was the custom, if the legitimate marriage had not been consummated and the spouse had afterwards had carnal relations with another woman, that the latter ought to be considered his wife and not she who had exchanged a promise registered in the church. The pope condemned this custom and enjoined respect for the Roman custom, according to which, "when mutual consent has been given in marriage between persons free to marry, this consent is enough, with the result that, if one of the persons thus united contracts another union later with someone else, the legal union cannot be annulled."

Practice conformed to theory. At Magdeburg, a young man married a young girl *per verba de praesenti,* then, without having relations with her, he gave her to one of his relatives. She did her best to resist, but was unable, in the final account, to escape the hateful restraint. However, she managed to free herself and asked the pope for authorization to return to her own home. Innocent thought that according to strict law, she ought to abandon him who was guilty of adultery, but he felt some reluctance at allowing her to take her place with her husband, since she had had carnal relations with a relative of his. Nevertheless, he concluded that if she could not bring herself to practice chastity, it was necessary to force her husband to fulfill his conjugal duty toward her, for he could not blame her for an adultery that he had forced her to commit and should not allow her to suffer for a crime to which she had never consented.

Such a solution was in conformity with the law and morality of the time, which the pope always sought to bring into agreement, but it could happen that law and morality would be in conflict, in which case Innocent always gave priority to morality and made generous use of his power of dispensation. Although betrothments between children before they reached the age of puberty were null in law, he considered them as valid if the young people, when they arrived at puberty, remained faithful to the engagement they had made, and he did not hesitate to annul a sentence of separation pronounced by a bishop against a woman who, engaged before the marriageable age, had renewed her promise when she arrived at the matrimonial age. The dispensations that he granted usually had as their purpose the prevention of irregular unions and the facilitation of church marriages. He facilitated marriage between Moslems related in the second or third degree, thinking that it would be dangerous not to allow them to be consecrated by the church for, if the Moslem women had to fear the loss of their husbands, one could be sure that they would put every obstacle in the way to prevent them from being converted. As to heretics, he suggested in principle that the *Cathari,* when converted, ought to be allowed to remarry, because the former marriage was not valid, but they should not be permitted to do so in the case where one of the spouses had abandoned the true faith, for he had had the sacrament, which made dissolution impossible. He noted that this was the desirable way of handling the matter, for otherwise some would find it ingenious to pretend to become heretics in order to get a divorce.

There are other more banal dispensations inspired by the same desire to prevent sin and to favor regular marriages, while appeasing the demands of canon law. A citizen of Spoleto, while he was married, had kept a prostitute whom he married after the death of his legitimate wife. When Innocent was consulted, he put no obstacle in the way when it was shown that the husband and his new wife had no responsibility in the death of the first wife and that he had not exchanged any promises of marriage during her life. The same dispensation on similar grounds was granted to an Athenian woman, who, during the life of her husband, had known another man, whom she married on the death of her first husband. A knight of Alexandria asked the annulment of the marriage of his daughter with a certain Opizon, alleging that at the time when the marriage was contracted, he had not known about the insanity of his future son-in-law. Innocent authorized of the separation. On the other hand, he upheld the marriage of a woman from Messina with a man from Limoges—who had relations with her in the course of a trip and had a son by her while his legitimate wife was living—because she did not know her conjugal status, since the man from Limoges had died and the deed had been done.

He showed himself very generous when he was dealing with a country where Christianity had been implanted only shortly before. In Livonia, he asked the bishop not to show excessive rigor, while taking account of the youth of his church. He wrote to the bishop of Tiberias that, if he had to regulate the case of polygamous pagans who were converted, he ought to vary the solutions slightly: all children could be considered legitimate, whoever their mother was, but the new converts could not keep their harem, because polygamy, once tolerated among the people of God, had been definitely condemned by the Gospel.

He was very strict when concerned with questions about a monastic vocation. A certain Hugh Vital had married a young girl in church when he was an acolyte and had consummated the marriage, then, after an argument, had left her and married another. He returned to the clergy, entered Citeaux, and was ordained a priest; then he had second thoughts and wanted to return to his wife. The pope decided that he should remain in his abbey and that they should only ask the young girl to surrender all claims to his adultery in order to preserve celibacy. The same conclusion was reached for another woman whose husband had been killed on a Crusade and who had remarried after she had pronounced a vow of chastity before the canons of St. Augustine. After having had four sons from this union, she was seized with remorse and asked the advice of the pope, who thought that, since the second marriage was imposed on her, she ought to fulfill her vow. In an opposite sense, an archdeacon made known at Rome that his father and mother had had to separate because they were related in the third degree, and that he had not known if they knew about this consanguinity when they were married. Innocent did not hesitate to grant him the benefit of this uncertainty in order that he might keep his priesthood and his office.

Kings and temporal princes of every rank had, like simple mortals, to obey the law of the church. Innocent III never sacrificed the demands of Christian morality to political advantages which would have resulted for him from a conciliatory attitude in matrimonial affairs. This is one proof among many others that the reform of the church took first place with him over every other consideration. He never wanted to pronounce the annulment of the marriage of Philip Augustus with Ingeborg; while he remained deaf to the supplications and threats that the king of France squandered on him, he did not dream for a moment of paying the price of doctrinal weakness for an agreement which could have been very useful to him in certain circumstances. Several times, he drew the attention of this prince to the responsibilities that he incurred before God. He observed the same attitude with respect to Peter the Second of Aragon, a docile vassal and faithful servant of the Roman church, protector of Christianity in the face of Islam, which he had crushed in 1212 at the battle of Las Navas de Tolosa. He had married Marie, daughter of William VIII, lord of Montpellier, who had earlier been married by her father to the count of Comminges, who had rather quickly put her away. After the birth of a son, the future king Jaime I of Aragon, Peter desired also to divorce her. He put up two arguments: first, that the first husband of the queen was still living, and, second, that he had had relations with one of her relatives. Innocent ordered an immediate inquiry, which his legates, favorable to King Peter, caused to be prolonged. Meanwhile Marie of Montpellier succeeded in informing the pope that her marriage with the count of Comminges had been concluded against the laws of the church, for the count had bonds of relationship with her. In addition, at the time of their marriage, he had already married two women and neither of these unions was dissolved by the church, with the result that that contracted with her was null. These facts were verified, at least in what concerned the second wife of the count. There was, therefore, no doubt; the marriage of Marie with Peter was legitimate and, at the risk of wounding a prince whose friend he was and who was liable to render still greater services to the church, Innocent refused to dissolve it. He wrote to the queen on January 19, 1213:

He who is our faithful witness in heaven, to whom every heart is open and no secret remains hidden, that in the marriage undertaken a long time since between you and our very dear son in Christ, Peter, king of Aragon, your husband, we have never departed from the right path and we have not deviated either to the right or to the left. We have acted, as our conscience is witness, as in all the cases brought for our examination, for, by His will, we take the place on earth of Him who, just and loving justice, judges without taking account of persons. Thus, although among other princes of this world we feel for this king, by reason of his deeds, a particular affection and we desire honors and personal advantages for him; nevertheless, from the fact that it is a question of justice, as we are not allowed to protect the poor and honor the visage of the powerful, we can not and we ought not, neither to him nor to any other, grant the lesser favor since it pertains to the sacrament of marriage, which, instituted by the Lord in Paradise before sin, looks not only to the perpetuation of the human race but represents the union of Christ with the holy church, that of God with the faithful soul, that of the Word with human nature, according to the testimony of the apostle, who in treating of marriage expresses himself in these terms: I say that it is a great Sacrament in Christ and in the Church. (Ephes. 15:22).

Once more Innocent considered himself the prisoner of doctrine before whose demands the temporal interests of the church ought to bend, so imperious were they. From this it is obvious that the theologian took first place before the diplomat. The rulers of Castile and Bohemia received the same decision as Peter of Aragon and learned that the law of Christian marriage is the same for all.

All papal interventions are therefore centered around a dogmatic idea and a fixed desire to put an end to illicit unions. The care for the restoration of the notion of Christian marriage is reconciled elsewhere with the charitable feelings that one so often meets in the acts of Innocent III. This pope, so intransigent in the matter of indissolubility, was interested in the lot of prostitutes, whom he tried to lead to a better life. We read in a bull of April 29, 1198:

Among the works of charity that the authority of Holy Scripture proposes to us, there is one of real importance, which consists in correcting him who wanders on the road of error. Thus it is necessary to ask women who live voluptuously and permit anyone indifferently and without concern to have relations with them to contract a legitimate marriage in order to live chastely. With this thought, we decide by the authority of these presents that all who will rescue public women from brothels and marry them will be doing an act which will be useful for the remission of their sins.

Innocent also sanctioned the attempts of one of the most extraordinary apostles of his time, Fulk de Neuilly († 1202), who among other pious works had dedicated himself to the relief of prostitutes, whom he received in several convents, notably that of Saint Antoine, where the preachers inspired them to lead a better life.

Along with prostitution the other sore on the society of the late twelfth century was usury. Innocent also tried to heal it. The condemnations levied by the Lateran Council of 1179 were enforced and the work was completed by certain provincial councils. In 1209, the Council of Avignon ordered a sentence of excommunication against usurers to be published on Sundays and feast days, and the invocation of the penalties set forth by the Lateran Council, if, after three warnings, they did not make restitution. It also ordered the excommunication of those who did business with Jews in their usurious practices, which was the surest way of incurring it. The Councils of Montpellier and Paris put the clergy especially on guard by forbidding them not only to practice usury but even to lend money at interest. These assemblies translated the ideas of the pope, who himself counseled that usurers should be prosecuted by attacking the most notorious first, for some well-chosen examples would cause the others to reflect and amend their lives. . . .

The increasing development of wealth and luxury, which had led Innocent to work for reform, had aroused before his accession the indignation of men who remained faithful to the ideal of renunciation that Christ had preached and to which the apostles had strictly conformed. This conception of a more evangelical life, which was the basis of the Catharist and Vaudois movements, was not the monopoly of heretics and revolutionaries. It had been taken up also at the end of the twelfth century by pious souls desirous of reacting against the return of pagan manners, without dreaming of denying dogma nor of leaving the church, which alone was able to lead them to the gate of salvation. . . .

[Editor's Note: At this point the author relates the story of the founding of the Order of Friars Minor by St. Francis of Assisi. He stresses St. Francis's connections with the Italian mystical tradition and especially with Peter Damian. He also raises the problems involved in setting up Francis's high ideal for his followers and the danger that an unlettered group of zealous men might easily slip into heresy in their preaching. With this as background, the author then treats of Francis's request to Innocent for papal recognition of his order.]

Thus, in 1210, after a year of groping, St. Francis went back to Rome accompanied by some of his friars. The bishop of Assisi, who was there, arranged an interview with Cardinal John of St. Paul for him, and he, conquered by "this man of the highest perfection," facilitated his access to Innocent III. St. Francis explained with his customary simplicity the characteristics of the rule, which were condensed in three verses of the Gospels: "If you wish to be perfect, go, sell your goods, give them to the poor and you will have treasure in heaven; then come and follow Me" (Matt. 19:21). "Take nothing for the road, neither staff, nor baggage, nor bread, nor gold, nor two tunics" (Luke 9:3). "Let him who wishes to follow Me renounce himself, take up his cross each day, and follow Me" (Matt. 16:24). Innocent III could only approve this form of the apostolate. It corresponded to his intimate sentiments and was only a variant of what he had counseled some years earlier, at the time of his meeting with Didacus of Osma and St. Dominic. Nevertheless, one reservation was imposed: the disciples of St. Francis were for the most part laymen without great learning, living by modest labor or by begging; the wandering life they led was not very favorable to the acquisition or religious knowledge that preaching presupposed and to which one could be initiated only in the cloister. But how was it possible to build cloisters given the conception of a mendicant order proposed by St. Francis? Such an objection threatened to compromise the papal adherence. But in the course of a second interview with the pope, the impression produced by the friars was so favorable, the obedience manifested with regard to the Apostolic See so entire that Innocent granted Francis oral permission to preach with the authorization to transfer it to each friar individually, each time that he would judge it necessary, but only on subjects of morality.

The basis of the Franciscan order was laid, but only under a very vague form whose inconvenience soon manifested itself. In the course of the years that followed, as the result of the increasing numbers of the "friars minor," new problems posed themselves. Since the evangelical spirit could not suffice for everything, some friars desired, in view of the preaching, to remedy their ignorance by study. Then the need for a precise rule made itself felt, without which the community risked falling into anarchy. St. Francis did not learn about it, but at Rome they were more concerned. Nevertheless, it was only after the death of Innocent III that the Roman church established an elaborate organization for the order.

It is nonetheless true that at the moment when the Lateran Council opened, to accomplish the reform undertaken by Innocent, great changes were on the point of realization. The church, faced with the assaults of heresy, had discovered the means of salvation. Tainted by the two plagues of the century, money and ease, it was turned with St. Dominic and St. Francis resolutely into the roads of poverty and learning. It desired to instruct by word and example, to ward off ignorance and to impose the law of renunciation, which was at the basis of its morality. Nevertheless, whatever may be the importance of the roles played by the founders of the mendicant orders, we should not forget that Innocent III had conceived and partially realized the reform of the church before their intervention, that he had had the great merit to foresee clearly the part that could be drawn from the movement toward poverty and the new forms of the apostolate which had taken shape at Toulouse and at Assisi. One author has written that Saint Francis "saved the Church" and "delivered Europe from the nightmare of heresy." Without doubt, he contributed, but does not the merit also belong—and perhaps still more—to Pope Innocent III?

MICHELE MACCARRONE

Innocent III Did Not Claim
Temporal Power

BESIDES THE PHRASES which are found in the letter under discussion, there are other expressions, characteristic of [Innocent], cited by those who assert that his ideas were hierocratic. Thus Arquillière hesitates over the words that turn up so often in Innocent's letters: "We who have been made princes over the whole land" and observes that with these words, Innocent "was thought to be vested with the government of the world." The phrase, as is immediately evident, is nothing else but one of the Biblical citations (Ps. 44:17) so often favored by Innocent and is frequently used in the Liturgy of the feast of SS. Peter and Paul (as well as in the Common of the Apostles, of which the office of the two saints is an extension), where it is repeated continually in the antiphons, verses, nocturnes, and minor hours, with an easy and natural arrangement. The later application to the bishops and, above all, to the pope became more common because of their succession to the apostles and was derived also from the first part of the verse of the psalm; the sons who have replaced the father as the mystical spouse of Christ are the bishops, successors of the apostles. Innocent himself, even before he became pope, spoke of this common interpretation of the phrase in the "De quadripartita specie nuptiarum" (Concerning the fourfold species of marriage), a small work which is nothing but a commentary, rich in allegory, on Psalm forty-four. In his discussion of the words in question,

From Michele Maccarrone, *Chiesa e Stato nella Dottrina di Innocenzo III* (Rome: Lateranum, 1940), 26–31; 37–42. Reprinted by the permission of the publisher. Translated by the editor.

73

he observes how the fathers of the church had once been the prophets, whom the apostles succeeded as sons: "in their place," he added, "bishops are created every day, set up by the church as princes over the whole earth." As for the particular application of the Biblical verse to the pope, it was suggested to Innocent by important precedents besides that of the Liturgy, especially by Nicholas I, who applied the words of the psalm to himself in two important documents: "By the grace of God, we have been set up in His house as princes over the whole earth," he wrote to the Archbishop of Bourges. He recalled to the emperor of the East that he had been "put as prince over the whole earth, that is to say, over the entire Church, because the earth is called the Church." The explanation which Nicholas himself gave of his citation makes it evident that he intended it in a spiritual sense, not referring to earthly dominion. The significance of the phrase in Innocent's writings is not different: he used it immediately in the first letter in which he announced his election as pope, and the verse appears natural and fitting to indicate the succession of the young Lothar to the old Celestine, as son to father. It is found thereafter in numerous other letters. It always has the same meaning as the Biblical citation. Never does it assume a hierocratic significance. We ought also to repeat that this expression is only one indication of Innocent's dependence on Biblical and liturgical texts in his style.

Alongside the words of Psalm forty-four, we can put another Biblical citation, usually invoked as an expression of Innocent's pretense to temporal dominion over the world. This is the verse of Jeremiah which is devoted to his vocation of prophet: "Behold, I have placed you over nations and kingdoms, that you may tear out and destroy, that you may build and plant (Jer. 1:10)." The nations and the kingdoms indicated in the text express the universal mission of the prophet, not to the Hebrew people alone, and to the fullness of his power. In the liturgy, the phrase is applied to St. John the Baptist—he too was called by God like Jeremiah, even from the womb of his mother—and it is uniquely placed to underline the sublimity of the mission of the last prophet.

Arquillière wonders that Innocent applied this biblical expression to his mission as pope: "in other times," he says, "Nicholas I had applied this famous passage to Michael, the Eastern emperor; Innocent has taken the place of the emperor." Nevertheless, we must observe that, while it is true that the phrase had already been applied to the emperor by Nicholas I, Arquillière has forgotten that it had already been applied to the pope in the same century by John VIII, in a letter to the Eastern emperor. In this letter, the pope claims for himself, with the words of Jeremiah, the right to correct and to reform kingdoms and peoples. Elsewhere, it was applied to the pope in a time nearer that of Innocent by Gerhoh of Reichersberg and

St. Bernard, precedents particularly meaningful for Innocent III. The verse in question was therefore commonly used to designate the mission of the priesthood, and with such a significance was found in Gregory VII, who applied the words of the prophet to the legate whom he sent to Corsica to reform ecclesiastical discipline, and in Peter Comestor, the Paris master somewhat earlier than Innocent, who explained the duty of the priest to admonish by the words of Jeremiah.

In his frequent citations of this passage, Innocent III continued such traditional applications. Dependent above all on St. Bernard, he used the strong words of the ancient prophet to vindicate his priestly rights in the Church: as was the case in the letter to the king of Dalmatia in which he recommended his legates sent to improve ecclesiastical discipline, and the citation had the same disciplinary significance in other letters. At other places in his letters, however, Innocent saw above all in this verse the vocation given by God Himself to the prophet and chose it as a parallel to that from St. Matthew which was devoted to the calling of St. Peter to the primacy by Jesus Christ. We find such characteristic correspondence in the "Responsio"; it demonstrates the fidelity of Innocent to the homiletic canons of his time. The parallel was suggested by the fact that, unlike the other prophets, Jeremiah was a priest. Still, Innocent did not go beyond the parallel. While Innocent IV, who often used the parallel of the two biblical passages, gave a precise hierocratic sense to the phase of Jeremiah; this sense was supported by a favorable medieval tradition (originated by Clement of Alexandria) which held that Jeremiah was not only a priest but the high priest, because he was the son of Elias, falsely identified with the high priest who recovered the Laws under Hosea.

With Innocent, on the other hand, the phrase preserved its traditional meaning, and even in the "Responsio" the mission of the pope, indicated by the citation from the prophet, was of a uniquely spiritual character. For the rest, we have another document of Innocent that demonstrates explicitly how he referred the words of Jeremiah to the spiritual field alone. In fact, in a letter to the citizens of Sesi, a territory ruled by the Holy See, he distinguishes the two jurisdictions of the pope clearly and applies the quotation from Jeremiah only to the spiritual one. In the Patrimony, he writes, "the spiritual jurisdiction of the Holy See is not limited by any boundary; beyond this limit, it holds power over nations and kingdoms (note the use of the verse from Jeremiah), yet even its temporal jurisdiction is extended to many." The interpretation of Innocent is therefore clearly a long way from that of Innocent IV. Even when he used the quotation in letters or sermons, he desired, by means of it, to indicate his pastoral charge which extended everywhere and comprised all men, even kings. From the affirmation of his power over kingdoms, we cannot, in fact, conclude that such power was by nature temporal. Already we have seen how the liturgy of primacy had made such terms of secular government familiar, while still referring in an undoubted manner to the spiritual power of the pope ("God gave you all the kingdoms of the world" is a statement applied to St. Peter in a response already mentioned). In two of his sermons, Innocent himself spoke of the "kingdom" which the Church ruled, but the context shows clearly that the expression was suggested by the scriptural text commented on by the pope and that every idea of temporal dominion is far removed from it.

. . . [T]he pope is usually called vicar of Christ, and this shows that for Innocent the two terms [vicar of Christ and vicar of God] are equivalent, nor can we find a preference for the second. On the contrary, we can note that the former, besides being the more frequently used, has already with Innocent the proper and exclusive meaning of pope, which it preserves even today. In fact, while the term vicar of God always stands with a quotation from Scripture . . . , the expression vicar of Christ, while often having an equal relationship to a biblical citation, is also found by itself, as a technical term to designate the pope.

Innocent therefore impressed on this phrase the significance that it preserves even today and which, as is seen in Gervase of Tilbury, was immediately accepted by contemporaries.

In addition, by giving an official approval to these words which designate the pope, he pointed out for theological speculation a new problem, that is to say, whether the pope received all the powers which Christ had while on earth and is His vicar. This problem had an immediate influence on political ideas because, given the then common doctrine that the "reign" of Christ was not only spiritual, but also temporal, it followed that the pope, as vicar of Christ, held by right not only the spiritual power but also the temporal. This, in fact, would be the conclusion of the canonists and theologians from the thirteenth to the sixteenth century and from this theological doctrine they would draw stimulus and support for the hierocratic system which pushed the parallel between Christ and His vicar to its ultimate consequences; this is precisely the reason why Bellarmine and the theological proponents of the indirect power were so vitally opposed to the doctrine of an earthly rule by Christ, from which the hierocratic concept which they were combatting seemed to derive by necessity.

The theological problem of Christ's earthly kingship has also been the subject of current research. There was an awakening of interest after the appearance of the encyclical "Quas Primas" [issued by Pope Pius XI in 1925], which instituted the Feast of Christ the King, and has recently been studied in some articles, written on the occasion of the same encyclical. In general, they examined thoroughly the scriptural basis and the passages of St. Thomas which affirm the earthly rule of Christ. However, their discussion of the theological question is limited to the controversies of the sixteenth and seventeenth centuries, disregarding the polemics, in fact, and also not examining the theologians of the twelfth and thirteenth centuries. Their evidence is abundant and entirely in agreement, in fact, and in light of them it is very clear that the doctrine of St. Thomas, maintaining in some passages of the *Summa Theologica* and the *De regimine principum* the position of Christ as an earthly king, follows the opinion current in his own time.

While not wishing to study such evidence, which would take us far afield, we observe that D'Ales is not quite correct in saying that, in the matter of Christ's rule on earth, "the evidence is open to discussion." In fact, the teaching has distant origins. From a very ancient hint in the so-called Testament of the Twelve Patriarchs, it is next found in St. Leo the Great and, above all, in Pope Gelasius, who founded his famous distinction of the two powers precisely on the doctrine of Christ as a true earthly king. "Jesus Christ," he said, "realized in himself the type of Melchisedech, king and priest, and like this ancient figure is invested with a regal earthly dignity, and not merely a spiritual one." The diffusion of this passage of Gelasius, of greatest importance for medieval political doctrine, provided the occasion for theologians and canonists to affirm the earthly rule of the Savior. Above all, among the latter we find the most frequent evidence, because the passage, literally reported in a letter of Nicholas I, was inserted by Gratian in his Decretals. Among the canonists of the twelfth century, the testimony of Huguccio of Ferrara seems to be the most interesting. Commenting on the famous extract from Gelasius, he states that Jesus Christ was indeed a temporal king and also furnishes, as an example of the exercise of this power, the chasing of the vendors from the temple and the incident of the famished crowd in the desert.

Innocent III also held the doctrine of his master and his contemporaries, and it is necessary to record his testimony, because the concept that Christ was a true king was among the most common in his writings. In general, it seems permanently linked with that of the priesthood of the Savior; and the dual dignity, royal and priestly, of Christ are expressed according to his taste by two biblical citations: "King of kings and Lord of lords" and "priest forever according to the order of Melchisedech." The royal power is always attributed by Innocent to Jesus Christ. The statement that even the pope, like Christ, unites the royal dignity to the priestly does not appear in his writings.

A mistake of E. W. Meyer has given rise to the assertion that for Innocent "the pope is King of kings and Lord of lords," while his footnote says in Latin only that the pope is vicar of Him, who is king of kings, and so forth.

Moreover Fiebach is mistaken in his interpretation of a letter of the pope, because he thinks that the pope claims to be "Lord of lords," while Innocent gives this title instead to Christ and not to the pope.

The consequence that the royal power belongs to the pope because he is vicar of Christ, who is also king, was one doctrinal development that still did not appear in Innocent. For this development, it was Innocent IV who carried it to its ultimate systematization, when he asserted that the vicar of Christ "naturally and potentially" was king, even though he did not exercise temporal power. But as the text which contains the words just cited demonstrates clearly, the Genoese pope and the other canonists of the thirteenth century add to this theory under the influence of other doctrinal elements (like the theory of the two swords) foreign to the political thinking of Innocent III, and under the inspiration of the great struggle which dominated that century. [The reference is to the controversy between the papacy and the Emperor Frederick II.] Innocent III remained aloof from this development. In his theological works, as well as in his letters, the idea of the royal dignity of the pope is not expressed.

JOHANNES HALLER

Lord of the World

FROM THE FIRST DAYS of his reign, Innocent III let the whole world know how he felt about [the power of the papacy.] In his sermon which he delivered at his consecration as bishop—he put off the celebration until February 22, the Feast of St. Peter's Chair, for good reason—he recalled the words of the Prophet: "I have put you above peoples and kingdoms to tear out and to destroy, to disperse and to reject, to build and to plant."

The conventional title of Vicar of Peter was not enough for him; proudly he called himself the Vicar of Jesus Christ, the representative of God on earth. For centuries no pope had attributed more to himself and to his office; we have to go back to Leo I to find a similar expression of self-confidence on the part of a new pope. The same tone resounded at all times through his statements; his own office, his own person were put in the foreground assiduously in a way that none of the popes to that time had done. Innocent took pleasure, so to speak, in the demonstration of his power. If, at the beginning of his reign, he conferred an important mission of ecclesiastical policy on a simple Cistercian without office and rank, he did not fail to point out that he could actually have found important personages for this work, since "all the members of the church were obedient (to him) as head." More noteworthy, we must remark how, more often than necessary, he relied on the fullness of power, the *plenitudo potestatis,* which had been given to the Apostolic See by God, and how he liked to underline his orders and instructions with a strong statement "about the forgiveness of sins." The office that he administered was not merely human. God himself spoke

From Johannes Haller, *Das Papsttum,* 2d edition, edited and enlarged (Esslingen: Port Verlag, 1962), III, 319–21; 338–57. Reprinted by permission of the publisher. Translated by the editor.

through him; he held God's place on earth, standing between heaven and earth as "Vicar of Christ, Successor of Peter, Anointed of the Lord, God of the Pharaohs, less than God, but greater than man." His empire was the whole Church, he was the bishop of all Christians; the others were only his assistants, on whom he conferred the power to represent him without surrendering anything of the fullness of his power. But not the Church alone, the world was also subject to him, for "the Lord had given Peter not only the whole Church to rule, but also the whole world." Without fear he spoke of his "principate over the whole land" (*principatus super omnem terram*); whoever opposes it makes himself the enemy of God. "The individual princes and kings have their particular domains; Peter is above all, with regard to both the limits and size of his dominion, because he represents Him to whom the whole earth and its dominion, the earth and all that lives on it, belongs." The pope is Lord and Master of all things because his office commands him to show justice to sinners and to punish their sins. Thus he becomes, by reason of his spiritual power, judge over rulers and lord of the whole world, bishop and emperor in a single person, and the one who wears the crown as well as the miter. "The King of kings and the Lord of lords"—as it was said especially on feast days—"Jesus Christ, High Priest forever according to the order of Melchisedech, had established royalty and priesthood in the Church in such a way that royalty was priestly and the priesthood was royal and, at the pinnacle of the whole, He put him whom He had designated as His representative so that—since all knees, in heaven, on earth, and under the earth, bend to him—all men may obey and follow him and there may be one flock and one shepherd."

Aside from its frequent repetition, only the proud tone of the language, which did not hesitate at extreme conclusions, putting, so to speak, a dot on the i, was new in these statements; the ideas themselves were old and well-known. We know them as the doctrine of the French church formed in the period following the Investiture struggle and since that time taught in the schools as existing truth. In Paris, Lothar of Segni had learned what Innocent III proclaimed in the full tones of his eloquence to a listening world. He said nothing new to his contemporaries; the content was well known to them for a long time; they heard in the terms, words, and citations used by the pope the voice of Bernard of Clairvaux, who had already said the same things, often with the same words, fifty years before. What Innocent presented was the knowledge of his time, and, therefore, he hardly ever was contradicted. What was new and surprising was the real logic and relentless determination with which this knowledge was now molded into a model for action. There was nothing like it since Gregory VII had struggled against the whole world and was defeated. The rule of Innocent was also one great struggle, but the ending was different. . . .

Whatever Innocent undertook in Italy and whatever his success in these matters, it was only possible because the throne of the German emperor stood empty after the death of Henry VI [1197]. For more than two centuries the fate of the peninsula had been determined and influenced by Germany; now for a long time this influence ceased because Germany was involved in the struggle over the kingship that was to last long years.

At the death of Henry VI the problem of the succession had still not been solved. The emperor's heir, Frederick, who was hardly three years old, had been elected king in Germany but had not yet been crowned. The fact that the opportunity was lost to bring the child, who was in safe-keeping at Jesi in the Mark of Ancona, immediately to Germany and to give him indisputable possession of the kingship by crowning him at Aachen was the misfortune or mistake of the Hohenstaufen party, a result of their lack of leadership, since the royal house lacked a strong personality, and the most respected princes were absent on the Crusade at the time of the emperor's death. When Constance was allowed to take her son to Palermo to crown him king of Sicily, his cause in Germany was lost. To ask the Germans to recognize as their king a child who had grown up in a foreign country under strange leadership was too much. In this situation there was no other choice than to allow the youngest brother of the dead emperor, Count Philip of Swabia, who at first acted as regent for his nephew, to secure election as king himself. After a little delay, the election was held at the beginning of March, 1198. But only a few of the princes, supporters of the Hohenstaufen, united behind this action; a second group, led by the archbishop of Cologne, once an adversary of the emperor, were already arranging another election, and it took place in Cologne on June 9. They elected Otto, the youngest son of Henry the Lion. As grandson of Henry II [of England] and nephew of Richard the Lion-hearted, he had grown up in an Anglo-Norman castle, learned French, and was a stranger in Germany. Two years before, he had received from his uncle, whom he resembled, the County of Poitou with its dependency, the Duchy of Aquitaine. He owed his election to the influence of Richard, who intended thereby to secure German support against France. The French answer was not long in coming: on June 29, 1198, a treaty was concluded between Philip II and the afore-mentioned Hohenstaufen, which obliged them mutually to assist one another against the king of England, his nephew, and their supporters. The struggle for the Roman crown threatened to turn into an Anglo-French war.

Nothing could have been more welcome to Innocent III than the fact that the forces of Germany were occupied by the struggle for the crown. This gave him a free hand to carry out his plans in Italy. But certainly in the long run, he had to hope that there would be a generally recognized emperor. His theologico-political plan for the world demanded the presence at its summit of the highest earthly power. But he also needed an emperor for his next goals. If his Italian adventure, the expansion of the states of the Church at the cost of the Empire, was to be more than a one-sided aggrandizement; he had to obtain the recognition of the Empire, which only an emperor could give. Therefore, Innocent already had decided to put an end to the struggle for the throne with a victory for one of the contenders. One can guess whom he had in mind. If Philip II was forced by the treaty with England arranged by the papal legate in January, 1199, to dissolve his pact with the Hohenstaufen, while Richard the Lion-hearted kept his freedom to support his nephew, it is obvious that the pope was hoping for Otto's victory. That he did not favor a Hohenstaufen as heir of Frederick I and Henry VI was understandable in itself; but he probably favored Otto because Richard, who supported his nephew warmly, had promised by solemn oath to return all those things earlier emperors had taken from the Roman Church.

The struggling parties did not show themselves in any hurry to secure the favor of the pope. Philip (of Swabia) took the first step by employing the bishop of Sutri, whom Innocent had sent to negotiate freedom for the Sicilian prisoners, to open negotiations. The French king took his side and voiced the strongest protest against the election of Otto as a shame and damaging to his own crown. He also offered to mediate an agreement on the old struggle over territory between church and empire in favor of the Church. Sometime in the spring, 1199, this message may have reached Rome. Somewhat later, if not at the same time, a numerous embassy from Otto appeared, with six members of the German clergy, led by the abbot of Kornelimuenster, and with a chaplain of Richard of England and a citizen of Milan. They brought the certificate of Otto's election and asked for confirmation and permission to proceed with the coronation. Innocent did not answer Philip of Swabia and he heaped wrath on the Bishop of Sutri because he had lifted the sentence of Pope Celestine against Philip. That unhappy man, a German and a former confidant of Henry VI, felt deeply the change of times: he lost his bishopric and was locked up for life in a monastery.

The pope treated Otto's embassy differently. He decided to put an end to the struggle for the crown, and he thought that he was strong enough to determine the outcome in favor of Otto. He did this especially to make his conquests in central Italy secure. He expected that Otto would not refuse recognition of the *fait accompli*. Otto needed the pope. He could not stand up against his enemies in Germany by himself, and the recent news of the death of King Richard of England put him in a position where he badly needed help. For well might he wonder whether John Lackland would aid his nephew in the same way as did his dead brother. This was all the more reason for Innocent to voice his support for Otto, who would probably be defeated and surely could not win without papal support. Innocent could also name his price. He demanded, above all, recognition of the states of the Church as they then existed and as he still hoped to make them, the Patrimony, Romagna, the Mark of Ancona, Spoleto, and the land of Countess Matilda, all of it with complete and unlimited sovereignty. In the future, only supplies for his journey for coronation would be granted to the emperor from these areas. Further, Otto had to protect the church in its possession of the Kingdom of Sicily, to recognize its legal jurisdiction in the city of Rome, to guide his relations with the Tuscan and Lombard leagues in accordance with the wishes of the pope, and to support him with money. He had to promise all of this now and to repeat it at his coronation as emperor.

This was neither more nor less than the abdication of the imperial dignity, which would disappear as an independent power in Italy and would sink to the level of a papal tool, if the conditions sought were obtained. In place of the emperor and through him, the pope would, in the future, control the political life of the peninsula. Still, the ambassadors of Otto agreed, took the oath the pope proposed for them in the name of their Lord, and put their seal on the document. On May 20, 1199, Innocent was able to tell Otto's electors that Otto could count on his support if he equalled and surpassed his predecessors in devotion to the Roman Church. He had already at the beginning of the month written to the German princes in their assembly, blaming them for not calling on his help earlier, since the question of the royal election, as he straightway explained, was principally and finally, from its origin and purpose, his concern. He admonished them not to disturb the empire any longer with their bickering, and he let it be known that, if they could not come to an agreement, he would favor the one who deserved it. Thus, in case the parties could not agree, he reserved the decision to himself as the proper judge in the case.

In public Innocent could give the appearance of being an impartial judge because his dealings with the ambassadors of Otto were secret. Within himself he had come to a decision, though he avoided every binding promise toward Otto. For the confirmation, which the legates had promised on their master's behalf, was still not forthcoming. Time dragged on. Months passed without the arrival of any news. Obviously Otto was disgruntled with the demands of the pope, and rightly so. The young Welf, had such a sense of his own dignity, despite his lack of knowledge of Germany, that the dishonoring of the crown demanded by the pope did not escape his notice. His German surroundings probably strengthened this idea in him. The excitement over the land-grab which the pope had perpetrated on the German crown could not have been a minor affair, for Innocent felt it necessary again and again to reject the charge that he wanted to destroy the empire as a pestilential lie and to point to his care for its preservation and growth. Otto and his supporters may also have been seized by the general mood; therefore their silence, which disturbed the pope.

While this stranger in the land hesitated to give his hand to the pope, there was widespread excitement among the princes of the Hohenstaufen party. After a long preparation, thirty-two spiritual and seventeen lay lords, behind whom, they said, stood many others, sent a letter to Innocent on May 29, 1199, in which they declared themselves determined to support Philip of Swabia as rightly elected to the imperial dignity as heir of Henry VI. They besought the pope in terse sentences not to snatch away the rights of the empire; they asked him to support Markward of Anweiler as regent in Sicily and stated their firm intention of bringing their king to Rome for imperial coronation in the future. The apparent sharpness of the letter was underlined by its manner of delivery; instead of a princely embassy, a judge from Piacenza brought it. Philip, moreover, was satisfied to send a prior from Strasburg.

If anyone in the Hohenstaufen party thought it could carry on the policy of Henry VI without further ado and oppose the commands of the pope, he was very much mistaken about how matters stood and the character of the enemy. Innocent answered the letter of the princes with the usual assurances of his care for the empire, but he also let them know that he had to stand up for the rights of the Church. He rejected the demands they had raised and declared shortly that the coronation of the emperor would depend on him and that he would summon the one who fulfilled the prerequisites. He delivered a long academic discussion to the prior from Strasburg in the consistory on the superiority of the spiritual to the secular power; to this he added an historical review of earlier differences with election factions up to the present time and he raised again the challenge that the Apostolic See was asked for advice so late "even though the decision belonged to it from the origin and purpose of the office: from the origin because the pope had transferred the imperial dignity from East to West, from the purpose because he is the one who confers the crown." The written answer, which he delivered to him as a conclusion, Innocent later thought unnecessary to give him at all. The attempt of the Hohenstaufen party was without result, a drop on the water.

This occurred in the fall of 1199. After that date negotiations in Germany came to a stand-still and weapons alone spoke. An unequivocal victory for Otto would have seemed very good to Innocent; he devoted himself to that end in order to get English support for him and to keep the French out of the war on the side of the Hohenstaufen. In the beginning, he had thought he could obtain his goal with a command, but he had soon learned better. Philip II proved himself to be an enemy whom Innocent could not quickly overcome.

In the beginning it actually seemed that the pope had only to speak up. We know how the king did his will in the treaty with England; he promised to give up the alliance with the Hohenstaufen. Soon after this, a more significant sign of papal superiority appeared. A bishop-elect of Cambrai, a supporter of Otto IV, was made prisoner in the territory of the king and Philip refused to release him. But when the cardinal-legate who had negotiated the treaty, proclaimed an interdict in the kingdom, Philip gave in and freed the prisoner. Encouraged by these results, the legate decided to resolve the king's marital problems. And, since Philip stubbornly refused to reinstate Ingeborg, he assembled the French bishops at the beginning of December, 1199, and pronounced an interdict over the whole kingdom. He agreed only to a postponement till after Christmas and, in Vienne, on January 15, on his return homeward, he published the interdict.

The enforcement left much to be desired. The king had already appealed to the pope and punished those bishops who obeyed the order. There were only a few; most had agreed not to observe the command of the legate. Only when Innocent caused it to be proclaimed again by two bishops from Normandy and Poitou, i.e., from the kingdom of John Lackland, did it seem to receive general observance. On this account Philip was forced to resume negotiations. And he met with surprising success. Innocent decided to reopen the case already decided by his predecessor and to investigate the validity of Philip's complaint. For this purpose, a new legate was sent, no less a personage than Bishop Octavian of Ostia, who enjoyed Innocent's special confidence. His instructions were very definite: to raise the interdict if the bishops who had been punished because of their obedience were restored, if Agnes, "the concubine," was banished from France, and if Ingeborg was restored to her position as queen. Should the king still ask for a divorce, the legate should hold court six months later on the question of the validity of the marriage, and the king of Denmark should be asked to send his representatives.

If we recognize that even the embassy itself was sent in disregard of the ruling set down by Celestine and meant a surrender of the position taken in the first place, the instruction was similar to Innocent's resolution: "to hold to truth and justice, if necessary, even to the point of bloodshed." However, the outcome was somewhat different. Cardinal Octavian, who met with the king at the beginning of September (1200), lifted the interdict as soon as the punished bishops were reinstated and compensated, and satisfied himself that Philip had given up Agnes and promised to reinstate

Ingeborg in her rights as queen for six months. The result of these events was that Ingeborg was made prisoner in a royal castle. Octavian overlooked this and also the fact that Agnes, under the pretense that she was with child—she was only in the third or fourth month—remained in France. He set the day for court for March 1201. He came to an understanding with the king which seriously violated his instructions. In his report he pointed out the danger that the church of France might throw off the obedience to Rome.

Innocent contented himself with pointing out in stern language the deviations of the legate and making him responsible for them. Whether he took the danger of a secession of the French church as seriously as Octavian is a question in itself. He had other reasons for not pressing Philip II too hard. Without the participation of the pope, Philip concluded a treaty with John Lackland in May, 1200, which, aside from serious territorial losses in Normandy, obliged the Englishman not to support his nephew Otto. This was such a setback to the papal plans that Innocent gave Octavian full power to absolve John of the oath to observe the conditions of the peace treaty. He still hoped to be able to bring English aid into the field for Otto. And if this did not succeed, he had to be concerned lest he drive the all too powerful Philip—who was already complaining of interference by the pope and his legates—into the Hohenstaufen camp.

Everything now depended on the court, which met in March, 1201, at Soissons. Bishops and nobles from France had arrived in great numbers; both parties appeared; the representative of the king of Denmark had also come. Octavian no longer was alone in the leadership; at his side was another cardinal, John Colonna, the one to whom Celestine had given the right to represent him, whom he had wanted to make his successor, a monk of stern, honorable mind. His refusal of the presents of the king caused a disturbance. The meeting began with the refusal of the Danes, on account of the relations of Octavian with the French king, to take part in the court on the grounds that it was prejudiced, and their departure for home. However, they were not disturbed by this occurrence and the trial continued for two weeks. It was expected that the king would lose the case. Then the clever Capetian surprised the world by withdrawing his request for a divorce and departing. He took Ingeborg with him, as though he was going to restore to her the position at his side that was her right, but actually to return her to her former position as a prisoner in a castle. The assembly, with nothing more to do, dissolved, and Colonna returned home in deep shame. What Innocent had warned his legates against as a hard compromise for the Apostolic See was exactly what happened: a proud beginning had met an ignominious end, and the words of the poet about the mountain that went into labor and brought forth a mouse had come to pass. But the sincere dissatisfaction, which the pope might have experienced at first, soon gave way to a keener judgment, when Agnes died in June of the same year (1201). Her death made it unnecessary for him to care for Ingeborg in the future other than platonically. His role as judge had ended when the king no longer sought a divorce; and what was the unhappy fate of the daughter of a king compared to the secular political situation which concerned the pope. In his efforts to win Philip II to his plans he was no longer hindered by the uncomfortable question of the marriage. Philip, on the other hand, had the daring to complain to the pope about the partisanship of the legate and combined with this a declaration of his willingness to undergo a further investigation if no other witnesses than his own were admitted. At the same time, he sought to have the children of Agnes made legitimate. Innocent did not hesitate before giving in, and he did not seek to continue the case. He declared the illegitimate children legitimate. Nothing more was said about Ingeborg.

In the meanwhile, Otto's situation had not improved. A few successes gained in the field by him did not change the fact that the Hohenstaufen party was the stronger in the empire. Until the summer of 1200, it seemed as if a favorable agreement of the princes on a third party, none other than Frederick of Sicily, would put an end to the dispute. Old Konrad of Wittelsbach, long-time archbishop of Mainz and, at the same time, cardinal-bishop of Sabina, returned from the East but a short while before, stoutly asserted that the decision should be made on June 29, 1200, Otto must have been very much afraid of the result, because he called on the pope for help. Now finally, the reply for which Innocent had waited a whole year came: he declared that he was ready to confirm everything that his ambassadors had promised in May 1199, in his name. The danger passed, the day of decision never came. Konrad of Wittelsbach died and Otto met with a real success towards the end of the year: in a victory at Mainz he succeeded in capturing his enemy's treasure. With Otto's last letter, Innocent now had the bond in his hand which he needed to openly espouse the cause of his candidate, for whom he had until now worked only in secret. At the turn of the year, he made his decision and, on January 5, 1201, he announced it in the consistory.

As the judge holds in his hands the acts, grounds, and countergrounds in order to discover the judgment by weighing merits, so the pope, apparently impartial, spoke here, following only the facts and pure reason "in the Name of the Father, and of the Son, and of the Holy Spirit." First he pointed out his own competence in the manner known to us: the imperial dignity is subordinate to the Apostolic See according to its origin and purpose, because it was translated from Greece by the pope and for his protection and because the emperor receives the final anointing of his coronation from the pope. Henry VI had recognized this fact with praise by asking Celestine, after the imperial coronation, for investiture with the imperial dignity in the form of a golden orb. Since there are only three aspirants: Frederick, Philip, and Otto, it is proper to make a selection from three viewpoints: what is permitted, what is fitting, and what is expedient? Thereafter, the three aforementioned persons were tested one after the other by every ingenious argument of scholastic dialectic. By these tests, Frederick was rejected first. He had no claim, his election was invalid; his recognition was unallowable and inexpedient. It went worse with Philip. More than all the others, his rule would be a danger for the Empire and the Church, because in this way the inheritance of the crown would become a custom, and it was to be feared that he would follow in the footsteps of his predecessors, who, since Henry V, had been persecutors of the Church. Otto, on the other hand, was properly elected—for it is not the number of the electors but their intention that counts—fitted by personality and descent, and he is therefore to be accepted as king and called to the imperial crown.

We can spare ourselves the effort of following the words of the pope in detail—they fill seven columns in small print—we know, however, that they do not express his true motives. What Innocent presented was in fact only a mask and the whole artful, scholastic structure of his proof was no more than jugglery. Never have terms of law been misused in a more reckless manner to cover mere cold selfishness. Innocent did not make his decision according to justice but according to the advantage of the Roman Church. His real reason for supporting Otto was his promise to recognize the conquests of the pope. Certainly the world was not to know; it must believe that the pope had made an impartial decision on the basis of justice and truth.

The verdict was made; now it must be carried out. For this purpose, the Cardinal-Bishop Guido of Palestrina, French-born, was sent to Germany as legate. He was to go by way of France and the Legate Octavian of Ostia was to follow him, if circumstances permitted. It was his duty to collect the German princes and to persuade them either to unite in recognizing Otto or to leave the decision to the pope. In this sense, the coming of the legate was announced and ordered. Innocent obviously believed that he only needed to take a firm hand for Germany to obey his will. But then new information must have arrived to let him know that he could not count on voluntary obedience. He sent the legate new instructions and ordered him not to reach any agreement with the princes to discuss the support of Otto.

His foresight proved well founded. When the bishop of Palestrina approached his destination—Ostia had to remain in France—disturbing news reached him. Otto had not been able to preserve his acquired successes. There was a decline among his supporters, his party was disbanding, and some already spoke about setting up another king. Only fast action by the pope, it was said, could rescue the situation. Otto himself later confessed that his cause would have "become dust and ashes," had not the pope stretched forth his hand with the authority of the blessed Peter. However, the cardinal hastened on his journey, and in fact, what he found on the Lower Rhine was rather discouraging. The pope's letter had brought on the worst consequences. That he or his legate should dare to summon the princes to an imperial meeting was too much. Only a handful of Otto's closest supporters accepted the invitation. In many places, the messengers stood before closed doors; in others they were hanged. Otto's cause appeared lost if the pope hesitated any longer. However, the cardinal brought out the letters he carried in which Innocent expressed his support of Otto "in our own and blessed Peter's name"; he called Otto the rightful king, ordered everyone to obey him, and excommunicated all of his enemies. This was at Cologne on July 3, 1201. Three weeks earlier, on June 8, Otto ordered a new document to be drawn up in which he promised under a golden seal to do everything that had been promised in his name in Rome before the end of the year—everything and still something more: he also obliged himself to follow the lead of the pope in his relations with France. Innocent had added this condition at the last moment in the hope thereby of overcoming the opposition of Philip II to Otto's ascent to the imperial throne. Otto resisted this to the last to no avail and, if we are not mistaken, he even attempted a little clever trickery in the drawing up of the document—it did not help him at all. If he wanted to be king and emperor, he must sign whatever the pope asked. He signed, but with the intention of not keeping the forced promises. And he remained true to this intention.

The impression of the Cologne declaration was strong, but not favorable. This interference by a pope in the electoral rights of the princes caused disgust in many circles. The word given out from Philip's side—that the freedom of the princes would perish if no one could be emperor save by the will of the pope—was not without success. Innocent saw that he had to point out again that he would not think of interfering in the princely electoral rights. He ordered the legate, Guido of Palestrina, who remained in Germany to promote Otto's cause, to proclaim his assurances on every occasion by word of mouth and in writing. Even the most noble of Otto's electors, Archbishop Adolph of Cologne, became hesitant and there was fear that he would forsake the cause. This proud count of Altena, who once had hindered the plans of Henry VI, seems also to have felt that the pope's measures were an attack on his position. Innocent talked to him cajolingly, sought to calm his concerns, and to represent his own actions as harmless: he had only shown favor to a rightful aspirant. It served no purpose; for more than a year the archbishop remained undecided until the legate succeeded in winning him over by using his own subjects. It cannot be proved that he won even a single vote of support by the word of the pope. On the contrary, a second meeting of princes, which the legate summoned, was no better attended than the first in Cologne, and the punishments he proclaimed terrified no one. The Hohenstaufen rose to their defense. It looked like a rising of the princes of the empire when thirty of them, about half spiritual and half lay, protested in a wild appeal to the pope against this unparalleled intervention, which contravened all right order. It had never been heard of that a legate had participated at the proclaiming of a king either as elector or as judge. The election was the affair of the princes, and if this was ambiguous, there would be no judge, and the princes would have to come to an agreement among themselves. Besides, the legate would have violated the form if, as a judge, he rendered judgment in the absence of one of the parties. The princes demanded his punishment. This letter was carried to Rome in March, 1202, by a noble embassy, the archbishop of Salzburg, the abbot of Salem, and a Saxon margrave. But still we must note how unskilled the Hohenstaufen were. It was understandable that they should talk about the legate as long as there was no proof that the pope supported his action. But how could they misjudge the enemy if they hoped to have any effect on him? While the princes generally entered into the discussions, they had already lost, for in this area the pope was master.

What could they hope to achieve at all, if they entered a discussion after all that had happened? What was behind this mad protest but an attempt to come to an agreement? The embassy must have been strongly impressed by the pope during the negotiations, which brought no result, since he later, perhaps with some exaggeration, could congratulate himself that they had conceded that he had the right to approve the person he should crown. In general, they were somewhat less than strong in their opposition to the pope. They used the occasion, contrary to the bellicose tone of their appeal, to obtain favors for themselves. Innocent showed himself happy to do a favor; in the case itself, he dispatched the princes with a noteworthy answer. He presented his conception of the relationship between the empire and the papacy in a closed and well-rounded argument. He had not molested the electoral right of the princes, the less so because they received it from the Apostolic See. For, by it, the emperorship, in the person of Charlemagne, was translated from the Greeks to the Germans. Therefore, Innocent argued, the pope had the right to examine the candidate he was asked to raise to the imperial dignity. For, what if the princes should elect a despoiler of churches, an excommunicated person, a tyrant, fool, heretic, or heathen? Should the pope crown him? Not at all! Then Innocent turned to the complaints against the legate. His judgment in no way, as he was reproached, interfered in the election or verdict, but only confirmed it. There was no need for an investigation in the presence of the two parties, because Philip's deficiencies were obvious. "Since we cannot under any circumstance alter our intention," we demand that Philip be cast aside, "the oath made to him disregarded, since such an oath should not be binding in favor of one who, as an outcast, is unfitted for the imperial dignity."

We know that Innocent did not invent the claim that it was the affair of the pope to examine a German royal election and to confirm or reject the results. We know that the kernel of the doctrine existed in ecclesiastical and French thought for almost a hundred years before: the translation of the empire from the Greeks to the Franks by the Apostolic See and for its protection, the conferring by the Church even of fiefs—this was often heard of. It did not go uncontradicted, but neither was it given up or disproved. Innocent drew only a logical conclusion when he saw the right of royal election as conferred on the princes by the Papal See, and another, no less logical conclusion, when he demanded that the pope give the crown only to him whom he found worthy of it. The conclusions might give surprise, but they were reasonable and the ideas from which they stemmed were old. What was new was the fact that a claim of an ecclesiastical school, which could have been accepted or rejected like any opinion, was proclaimed as a precept of public law. Whatever the church taught should be law for the Germanic-Roman empire. Certainly, this claim was no mere discovery; it developed from the doctrine that the spiritual power surpassed all worldly power and especially that the Roman Empire was dependent on the church. Innocent confirmed this reasoning by a borrowing from canon law: whoever consecrated should, as he held, examine the one who was to be consecrated. This was true also for the emperor, whom the pope must consecrate. In this sense, the answer of Innocent III to the protest of the German princes formed the conclusion of a church doctrine and its proclamation into a law which would allow no contradiction. Innocent placed the edict in a collection of decretals, which would serve the Church as a law book and, in later expanded versions, endured for centuries. We find, in the section dealing with elections, his edict on the authority of the pope in the imperial election, the decretal "Venerabilem," as it was called from the first word. Thereby, the election of the German king was made a part of canon law.

We might very well put the question whether this document—it takes for granted the general basis from which it arose—fulfilled its purpose, whether the judgment against Philip and in favor of Otto was well founded. The question whether the decretal deserves the reputation of precedent for further decisions as does the declaration of January 5, 1201— repeated in part word for word—does not allow an affirmative answer. How small is the sharp distinction between judgment and confirmation, as if a confirmation in such a case contained no judgment! How wrong the pope was in his facts about the confirmation of the elections of Lothar and Konrad III, as if the situation of things then and his treatment of the declarations of Honorius II and Innocent II had the least similarity to the present! Unofficially, the accusation was made against Philip that he himself had taken the oath of loyalty to his nephew Frederick and therefore, as an oath-breaker, could not be king. Was it right to exclude Philip because of the deeds of his predecessors? According to the German view, inheritance of the crown by the same family was natural, and royal blood conferred a claim on it. This was violated when Innocent viewed the kingship of Philip as a threat to [his goal of] preventing hereditary monarchy. Likewise, the statement that Philip was not eligible for election because he was excommunicated was dishonest. Innocent, the cardinal of 1196, who had witnessed Celestine's decision, knew that it was directed in a general way against all who had attacked the Patrimony of Peter, without naming Philip. Innocent the lawyer knew that only excommunication by name could render election impossible. Finally, as for Otto, Innocent had earlier reckoned as his special virtue the fact that, in contrast to the Hohenstaufen, his ancestors had been loyal to the church. He did not repeat this now. And for good reason. Could one praise in any way Otto's maternal grandfather, Henry II of England, the inspirer of the murder of Thomas à Becket, for his special loyalty to the church? Also, the Germans knew only too well how Henry the Lion, Otto's father, had treated churches and clergy. Among the reasons for which the imperial court banished him, the mistreatment and despoiling of churches was pre-eminent. The pope was clever not to waste any words on Otto's personal fitness. On what did he therefore base his decision in favor of Otto? Merely on the fact of his elevation, the very fact on which few in the whole world were in agreement.

Innocent III did better work elsewhere; the decretal "Venerabilem" is no masterpiece. It is presented as the just judgment of a judge and reveals itself in every line as the partisan work of a pettifogging lawyer, a web spun out of willful distortions. It was viewed in this way by many contemporaries even then. The Swabian prior Burchard of Ursberg, a clever, learned, and worldly-wise man, recorded in his chronicle the stout-hearted judgment that the pope had not rendered a just decision and had stated many senseless and false things in his letters to the princes. The actual fact was that this ceremonial manifestation seemed to make no impression at all. Not one of the German princes changed sides after this; there was no weakening of the Hohenstaufen party. Not even the bishops were concerned over the threat of ecclesiastical censure. Indeed, the pope did have many alternatives at hand in order to influence individuals: here was an individual whose life was not blameless, there one who had not obtained office properly; archbishops needed the pallium; others were engaged in court cases. But it is obvious how little the pope accomplished. When he invited one of the most guilty to Rome, he did not always know who would draw up the letters and had to have the legate fill in the addresses. The letters probably did not even arrive at their destination. In Mainz, where a double election had taken place, the Hohenstaufen party refused to accept the decision of the legate, accused him of taking a bribe, and complained about him to the pope. And when Innocent came to his legate's help, it was of no avail; the Hohenstaufen candidate prevailed. Where someone preferred to save himself difficulty by outward conformity, it was only for an advantage. Obligations accepted were not fulfilled; they were rejected or voided of application by conditions. Innocent himself seems to have felt that his actions were without success, for he showed a tendency to mete out softer punishments. There was no talk of direct action; rather it seemed that he was lacking in the necessary severity and determination. His threat to deprive the disobedient archbishop of Trier of the dignity of a metropolitan came to nothing and, in other cases, he usually did nothing. He received a strong answer from the bishop of Halberstadt, whom he tried personally to persuade to abandon Philip, to the effect that he would rather be accused of disobedience than of breaking an oath. Some had already pointed out that the pope quarrelled with the cardinals who would not agree with his conduct. Innocent felt it necessary to deny this in a wordy, preachy letter and to permit the cardinals to witness this fact with a public declaration. But he must have seen that he could not continue on his chosen path, because at the end of the year he decided to bring a year of peace to the contending parties. He did this while under serious attack so that some had little confidence that he had only the welfare of the empire in mind. Indeed, he did not hesitate to confess in view of the spread of heresy "that the spiritual sword would often be useless if the secular sword did not assist it." His command, like all earlier ones, met with no success. His policy was not even successful in his own country: in Lombardy he could not secure support for his advice and actions and recognition of Otto as king.

In the meantime, his legate was more successful than the pope, but not in the use of spiritual weapons. Guido of Palestrina knew very well how to strengthen Otto's supporters by worldly advantages and to win new ones in the same way. He restored the broken unity of the princes of the Netherlands, Otto's strongest allies, secured the support of the archbishop of Cologne by the fact that, among other things, he secured the abolition of burdensome taxes in the capital; he strengthened the alliance between Otto and the king of Denmark; thus he finally succeeded in drawing two of the mightiest princes from the Hohenstaufen to the Welf side. The landgrave of Thuringia, who once went over to Philip for a high price, returned to

Otto. The king of Bohemia agreed to desert Philip for the recognition of his royal title and the advantages offered the bishopric of Prague. For that reason, the cardinal was not afraid of the difficult trip to Bohemia. The results of these switches of allegiance were soon evident. Until the beginning of the year 1203, the forces of the two parties were about equal; Otto was recognized in the northwest, Philip in the east and south. In the summer of 1203, Otto gained a significant advantage. In the attempt to control Thuringia by force, Philip was bested and his retreat was the same as a rout. Even earlier he had viewed his situation with so little confidence that he attempted to come to an agreement with the pope. Innocent, driven from Rome by the urban unrest discussed earlier, and pressed by difficulties, agreed to secret negotiations of an unofficial sort. But they met no success, though Philip was not sparing with his promises elsewhere—freedom of episcopal elections, surrender of the inheritance of prelates, a law that would have tightened the control of the imperial ban by the pope, marriage of a daughter with a nephew of the pope, and the subordination of the church of Constantinople to the Apostolic See—because, in the points that were important to Innocent, he made no significant concessions. He would give back what had been taken improperly from the Roman church by himself or his predecessors. This was not enough for the pope; Otto had bound himself without ambiguity. Besides, the secret was not kept, and Innocent had to lie about his representatives.

Disregarding the latest success of Otto, there was still no end in sight to the struggle over the German crown, and it was too early to expect a decision by war. The decision came at another place, in the Anglo-French war, and it was against Otto and his protector, the pope.

BRIAN TIERNEY

Innocent III as Judge

IN 1202, Count William of Montpellier persuaded the archbishop of Arles
to intercede with the pope concerning the legitimization of the count's bas-
tard children. It was not that he wanted his boys to be eligible to become
priests, the usual reason for a papal dispensation *ex defectu natalium;* the
count was anxious that his children should enjoy all the rights of legitimate
offspring in the temporal sphere as well. Pope Innocent III had recently
granted this privilege to the children of King Philip II by Agnes de Meran,
and Count William hoped to obtain a similar favor.

The pope refused this request. He had just reached an agreement with
Philip about the king's matrimonial difficulties and no doubt did not wish
to provoke him anew by an officious intervention in a case that evidently
pertained to the royal jurisdiction. But Innocent III was not content to
leave the matter at that. He wanted there to be no doubt that the pope did
have extensive powers in secular affairs even though he was not choosing to
exercise them in this particular case. Hence his reply to Count William was
cast in the form of the famous decretal *Per Venerabilem;* in which Innocent
took advantage of this relatively trivial occasion to inject into the mainstream of medieval canon law a series of far-reaching pronouncements concerning the juridical rights of the pope in secular disputes. The decretal
was included first in the unofficial compilation of Alanus and then in the
officially promulgated collection of canons known as the *Compilatio Tertia.*

From Brian Tierney, " 'Tria Quippe Distinguit Iudicia. . .' A Note on Innocent III's
Decretal *Per Venerabilem,*" *Speculum,* XXXVII (1962), 48–59. By permission of the editors
of *Speculum* and The Medieval Academy of America. Quotations which appeared in the original in Latin have been translated by the editor.

Innocent ensured that no jot or tittle of his carefully chosen terminology should pass into oblivion or lack adequate canonistic exegesis when he sent a copy of this compilation to the university of Bologna with instructions that henceforward it was to be used "both in trials and in the schools." The pope's phrases were indeed discussed eagerly in the schools by generations of medieval canonists; more recently their implications have been debated with almost equal vigor by modern historians.

The decretal was full of meat. Innocent's apparently innocuous, incidental comment that the king of France recognized no temporal superior provided a canonical basis for a whole theory of the independence of national kingdoms from the empire, which in turn has given rise to an elaborate controversy among modern historians about the origins of national sovereignty in Europe. As for the immediate occasion of the letter, the pope held that authority to legitimize for spiritual functions necessarily included a capacity to legitimize in the temporal sphere as well "because for spiritualities greater care and authority and worthiness are required." This also gave rise to an important canonical controversy. But the greatest significance of the decretal for students of medieval political theory lies in the fact that, having made these points and having protested that he had no wish to usurp the jurisdiction of another, Innocent went on to give a more general explanation of the pope's right to intervene in secular affairs:

Motivated, therefore, by these reasons, we did the favor asked for by the king, drawing justification from both the Old and New Testament, because we exercise temporal jurisdiction not only in the patrimony of the church (over which we have full power in temporal affairs), but also in other regions, in certain cases, we exercise this power incidentally.

The Old Testament proof was a passage from Deuteronomy (17:8–12) "If thou perceive that there be among you a hard and doubtful matter in judgment between blood and blood, cause and cause, leprosy and leprosy; and thou see that the words of the judges within thy gates do vary: arise and go up to the place which the Lord thy God shall choose. And thou shalt come to the priests of the Levitical race and to the judge that shall be at that time . . . And thou shalt do whatsoever they shall say." The New Testament was cited (Matthew 16:19, "Whatsoever thou shalt bind on earth it shall be bound in heaven") to demonstrate that in the new dispensation the apostolic see was evidently the "chosen place" of God, and the pope himself the judge who presided there. And so Innocent reached his conclusion:

There are, to be sure, three distinct kinds of cases: first between blood and blood, for which reason it is called criminal and, also, civil. The last between leper and leper, for which reason it is known as ecclesiastical and, also, criminal. In the middle between case and case, which is referred to both, the ecclesiastical and the civil; when there is something difficult or ambiguous in these matters [in quibus], it must be referred to the Apostolic See: whoever in his pride refuses to observe this sentence is condemned to death, that is, to be separated from the communion of the faithful by the sentence of excommunication like one dead.

The interpretation of this passage is of crucial importance for the whole much controverted question whether Pope Innocent III was essentially "dualistic" or "hierocratic" in his theory of the relations of church and state. It was already well established that in the strictly ecclesiastical sphere all "hard and doubtful matters," the so-called *causae arduae,* were to be referred to the apostolic see for decision. The question is whether Innocent was simply extending that claim to the sphere of secular jurisdiction or whether his words were intended to convey some other meaning. It happens that the two outstandingly superior textbooks on medieval political theory in current use offer distorted interpretations of the pope's words and that the distortion has not been discussed, nor the passage adequately analysed in any of the recent specialist works on Innocent's political theory. A note of correction therefore seems in order.

A. J. Carlyle saw in *Per Venerabilem* only a claim that "in cases of conflict between the spiritual and the temporal jurisdiction, the spiritual power is to decide." C. H. McIlwain similarly supposed that the "third judgment" referred only to those matters that were "in the first instance concurrently within the jurisdiction of both temporal and spiritual courts." With his usual discernment however, McIlwain added that this was not the only possible interpretation of the passage. "If the words 'in these' . . . refer back to all three kinds of jurisdiction, then the interpretation above is wrong, and Innocent IV later added practically nothing to the claim of his predecessor."

Innocent III's grouping of clauses does suggest that he intended the "in quibus" to refer particularly to the third type of judgment. But it seems quite certain that he did not intend to exclude the first two types of cases from papal jurisdiction, and there can be no reasonable doubt that, in the third class of cases, he intended to include all lawsuits, whether ecclesiastical or secular, and not merely those cases that had an ecclesiastical as well as a secular aspect.

As to the first point, one has only to consider the nature of the first two types of judgment. One of them was "ecclesiasticum et criminale." That is to say it had reference to criminal cases that fell within the jurisdiction of the spiritual courts, such as heresy or sacrilege. Obviously the pope was not intending to exclude himself from the role of judging such cases; the very essence of the papal position was to be supreme judge, *iudex ordinarius omnium,* at least in spiritualities. The other class of criminal cases mentioned, "inter sanguinem et sanguinem," was defined as "criminale . . . et civile." That is to say it referred to crimes like murder or assault normally cognizable before a secular judge. But Innocent could not have intended to exclude matters of this kind from the sphere of papal judgment for, in the decretal, *Novit* (1204), he explicitly claimed the right to intervene in such cases *ratione peccati* [on account of sin]. A crime of violence was also a sin, and all cases involving sin pertained to the papal jurisdiction according to Innocent.

The ambiguous definition of the third class of cases ("inter causam et causam quod ad utrumque refertur tam ecclesiasticum quam civile") offers greater difficulties of interpretation. The first argument against the view of Carlyle and McIlwain that Innocent's words referred only to cases where the spiritual and temporal jurisdiction overlapped is an *argumentum ex silentio.* It did not occur to any contemporary canonist that the pope's phrases could possibly have the meaning attributed to them by the modern historians. The point is of some significance, for several of the early commentaries on the *Compilatio Tertia* were written by canonists who are known as convinced dualists, e.g., Laurentius Hispanus, Vincentius Hispanus, and Johannes Teutonicus. These men were all interested in defending the essential autonomy of the secular power against the hierocratic views of contemporaries like Alanus and Tancred who maintained that supreme spiritual and temporal power was united in the pope. If Innocent's words could have meant to a contemporary merely that the pope was claiming jurisdiction when some "ambiguity" arose concerning a case which was "concurrently within the jurisdiction of both spiritual and temporal courts," either Laurentius or Vincentius or Johannes would have been delighted to point out the fact. None of them did so. Laurentius, the only one who referred specifically to the words of Deuteronomy in his glosses on *Per Venerabilem,* did maintain that the text was not necessarily a vindication of Alanus's extreme hierocratic doctrine of papal power, but he adopted a different line of argument to establish his point. . . . The distinction Laurentius made was not between secular cases and mixed cases but between appellate jurisdiction and ordinary jurisdiction. Alanus, on the other hand, maintained that the pope was "the ordinary judge . . . both as far as spiritual matters and temporal affairs."

The argument that ecclesiastical courts could exercise jurisdiction in mixed cases (the so-called *ratio connexitatis*) was, of course, not unfamiliar to canonists of the early thirteenth century. Indeed one may doubt whether Innocent would have thought it necessary to invoke Peter and Paul and an Old Testament prophet to establish such a relatively modest claim. We can demonstrate further that he conveyed a different meaning to contemporaries by considering some comments on the *ratio connexitatis* itself. From about 1215 onwards it became a common practice among the decretalists to present lengthy lists of all the cases in which papal jurisdiction could be exercised in the temporal sphere. Such lists invariably mentioned the *ratio connexitatis,* and they invariably mentioned the decretal, *Per Venerabilem.* But they did not cite *Per Venerabilem* in support of the claim to jurisdiction *ratione connexitatis;* it was always cited as the basis of a quite different claim. Thus Tancred wrote (citing Laurentius in the first part of his gloss):

This is one case in which the ecclesiastical judge can concern himself with matters of secular jurisdiction, namely when no superior is to be found. Another is when the secular judge neglects to render judgment or do justice. A third is when any matter is difficult and ambiguous and the judges differ, as below in the title *Qui filii sint legitimi, Per venerabilem.* La(urentius). Fourth, when it is a matter of land subject to the jurisdiction of the church. . . . Fifth, if it is according to custom. . . . Sixth, in all ecclesiastical crimes. . . . Seventh, when any case is referred to the church through denunciation by reason of crime, as above in the previous title, *Novit.* Eighth, when the secular judge is suspect and accused. . . . Ninth is the reason of connection, for an ecclesiastical judge can judge concerning dowry by reason of the fact that he has jurisdiction in matrimonial cases, as above in the title *De dote post divortium, De prudentia.*

This gloss was copied with little variation by Goffredus Tranensis and Bernardus Parmensis, and its substance repeated by Innocent IV and Hostiensis. Each of them cited the decretal *De Prudentia* on the law of dowry to illustrate the *ratio connexitatis,* while each cited *Per Venerabilem* in support of the much more vague and far-reaching claim to a jurisdiction in secular cases whenever the issues proved "ambiguous" or "difficult" or when the judges were at odds with one another.

Finally, when the canonists did come to gloss in detail the words "Tria quippe distinguit iudicia" ["There are, to be sure, three distinct kinds of cases"] their interpretations regularly explained the third judgment as referring to cases which were either secular or spiritual, not both secular and spiritual at the same time. Innocent IV described the three judgments in this fashion:

Sanguinem [Blood]. A judgment is between blood and blood when the accuser says it is proved that the defendant has shed blood, that is, has committed any civil crime, let us say homicide, adultery, theft or anything of that sort. *Inter lepram et lepram* [Between leper and leper]. When the accuser says, "You are infected with the leprosy of heresy," that is, with any ecclesiastical crime, let us say simony, sacrilege, or anything similar, and the accused denies it. *Inter causam et causam* [Between case and case]. When the plaintiff says, "You owe me [a sum] from a loan or contract," or some similar civil action. Or, again, [when the plaintiff says] "You are bound to pay tithes to me" or "I have the right of patronage in this church," or some similar civil and ecclesiastical action, but the defendant denies it. For in all these matters, if anything shall be difficult or ambiguous recourse is to be had to the apostolic see.

There were thus really four types of cases involved—criminal actions, which could be either ecclesiastical or secular, and civil actions, which could likewise be divided into ecclesiastical cases or secular cases. The lack of symmetry in Innocent III's exposition in which both types of civil suit were lumped together under one heading arose simply from the structure of the text of Deuteronomy that he was expounding.

Hostiensis and Abbas Antiquus reproduced almost verbatim the comment of Innocent IV and a very similar explanation was given by Boatinus Mantuanus. I do not think that there can be any question here of a "hierocratic" distortion of Innocent III's original meaning. No other meaning had been suggested. The mid-thirteenth-century canonists were merely giving concrete examples to illustrate an interpretation that had been taken for granted by their predecessors. The principal reason why a modern reader might suppose that the third type of jurisdiction was intended to apply only to mixed cases lies in the fact that the immediate occasion of the decretal was a matter of legitimization, which did fall into this category. But, in the paragraph that we have been considering, Innocent III had turned aside from the issue of Count William's offspring to offer some general observations about the nature and extent of papal jurisdiction. It was not the habit of the canonists to relate such observations solely to the subject matter of the decretal in which they occurred; rather they sought to educe from them general rules of law, as in the comments of Tancred just cited. Innocent III himself was of course well aware of this decretalist technique. In general, it seems to me, the argument that Innocent's true meanings were misunderstood or distorted by the canonists of the next generation should be viewed with extreme caution. The pope was himself a trained canonist and a legislator of genius. He knew exactly what legal implications the canonists would find in the terms he chose to use, and we must surely suppose that he had a shrewd understanding of the effects they were likely to have on the long-range growth of canonical thought.

A new period in the study of Innocent's political ideas began with the publication in 1940 of Maccarrone's *Chiesa e stato,* the first work that seriously attempted to analyze his thought within its canonistic framework. Subsequently major contributions by Mochi Onory, Kempf, Stickler, and Tillmann have clarified our understanding of many doubtful points. It seems arguable, however, that all of these writers have been unduly influenced in their exegesis of *Per Venerabilem* by a natural inclination to defend Pope Innocent III against the charge of seeking worldly power as an end in itself. They are anxious, that is to say, to establish that the great pope was not actuated by motives of gross worldly ambition, but that all his interventions in the political sphere were inspired "by motives of a spiritual order" (a favorite phrase of Mochi Onory). Let us acknowledge at once that

Innocent's intentions were probably of the best. It is, heaven knows, no mean task to try to build the City of God on earth. But it also remains true that, after his pontificate, many theologians and some popes did become committed to a doctrine of papal temporal power that was repugnant to the consciences (as well as the interests) of most medieval princes and prelates, that this papal claim produced a destructive tension in medieval Catholicism, and that Innocent III's decretals played a significant part in its development. The problem of whether he had good intentions is one issue, primarily psychological; the problem of what exactly he did claim in the secular sphere is another, primarily canonical. Both are important, but to endeavor to solve the second problem merely on the basis of a conviction about the first leads only to confusion.

This seems especially the fault of Mochi Onory. Above all he failed to see—and this is true of Maccarrone too—that there was a radical difference between a papal claim to exercise indirect power in temporal affairs and a claim to exercise direct power in certain exceptional circumstances which the pope himself undertook to define. It was quite consistent with the dualist theory to emphasize that an exercise of spiritual jurisdiction by the pope might sometimes, indirectly, produce effects in the temporal sphere. A sentence of excommunication launched against a king for some specifically ecclesiastical offense like sacrilege might, for example, have political repercussions. But it was surely not consistent with the dualist position for a pope to claim that he could exercise jurisdiction in secular cases whenever the case happened to be a "difficult and ambiguous" one (as was claimed in *Per Venerabilem*) or whenever the temporal judge was negligent or suspect or the office of emperor vacant (as Innocent suggested in the decretal *Licet:* "If he gives up his power, if he neglects, is doubtful, or is a suspect judge. . ." as Hostiensis put it, summarizing Innocent III's doctrine.

It is hard to see how a pope could claim to judge secular cases even in such circumstances, or to enforce his sentences with coercive sanctions, unless he supposed that the nature of his office was such as to include jurisdiction over the purely temporal issued involved. Helene Tillmann is the only modern writer who has emphasized the important distinction between indirect power and direct power exercised *in certis causis,* but even she obscured its full implications by maintaining that the papal claim was rooted in the medieval doctrine of necessity. Innocent III certainly did know the Roman law tag, "Necessitas legem non habet [Necessity has no regard for law.]," and could have used it as the basis of a claim to temporal jurisdiction in exceptional circumstances. But the fact is that he did not choose to do so. The legal doctrine of necessity, if applied to the transfer of cases between secular and ecclesiastical courts, might have had uncomfortable consequences. It could after all have worked both ways. No thirteenth-century pope would have conceded that the emperor could judge a spiritual case (on the ground that "necessitas legem non habet") whenever the ecclesiastical judges found the matter "difficult and ambiguous" or when the papacy happened to be vacant. Innocent III, therefore, preferred to base his claim on the quite different ground that he was the vicar of one who was a priest after the order of Melchisedech—and Melchisedech was of course both priest and king. On this theory the pope could judge secular cases when he considered it appropriate to do so simply because regal jurisdiction inhered in his office (and, correspondingly, the emperor could not judge spiritual cases because he possessed no spiritual jurisdiction).

Friedrich Kempf avoided this conclusion in his discussion of *Per Venerabilem* by stressing the voluntary nature of the jurisdiction involved. He did not argue that Innocent was claiming merely *iurisdictio voluntaria* in the most technical sense of that term (as opposed to *iuirisdictio contentiosa* [jurisdiction involving a real legal problem], but he did maintain that, in *Per Venerabilem*, Innocent asserted the right to judge a secular case only when all the parties in the case voluntarily selected him as an arbitrator. There seems nothing in the decretal itself to support such a view. Its tone is quite different—"cum aliquid fuerit difficile vel ambiguum ad iudicium est sedis apostolicae recurrendum cuius sententiam qui superbiens contempserit observare mori praecipitur. . . ." Kempf also argued that *Per Venerabilem* must be interpreted in the light of Alexander III's decretal *Cum Sacrosancta,* and so understood in a dualist sense. In this earlier decretal Alexander replied to a series of questions from the archbishop of Rheims. The last one enquired whether an appeal from a secular judge to the pope was valid and the pope replied: "even if the (appeal) is valid according to ecclesiastical custom, we do not think it valid according to the strict meaning of the law." Kempf sees in this a definitive acknowledgment by the papacy of the autonomy of secular jurisdiction. Alexander did not, however, make any pronouncement at all in his decretal on the essentially theological issue of the inherent temporal power which might, or might not, be attributed to the papacy on the basis of such scriptural texts as Matthew 16:19. He indicated only that, as a matter of law, there was no adequate basis in the existing canons for a general right of appeal (though the custom of a local church sufficed to make the appeal valid). It was quite open to a future pope, who held on theological grounds that Christ had conferred on the papacy a supreme temporal jurisdiction, to enact such canons as he thought necessary to define the circumstances in which that jurisdiction would in fact be exercised. That is exactly what Innocent III did.

A. M. Stickler has insisted that the very occurrence in canonistic works of lists of "exceptional" cases in which secular jurisdiction would be exercised directly by the pope proves that, even in mid-thirteenth century, the canonists acknowledged in principle the autonomy of the secular power; and he suggested that the presence of such lists in the writings of extreme hierocrats like Tancred and Hostiensis reflects an unresolved tension in their thought. It is true that some dualist writers did hold that the fact of papal jurisdiction in secular cases being exercised only occasionally and in exceptional circumstances constituted an argument in favor of their own point of view. But their position was a very uneasy and illogical one, and it was natural enough that, after a generation's discussion of Innocent III's legislation, a major shift had occurred in canonistic thinking from the prevailing dualism of the late twelfth century to the dominant hierocratism of the mid-thirteenth. As we have argued, some of the "exceptional" cases were consistent with a dualist position, but some were not. On the other hand, the detailed definition of specific cases in which papal jurisdiction would be exercised directly in temporal affairs was entirely consistent with the most extreme hierocratic theories. Any court that claims a supreme appellate jurisdiction needs to define the circumstances in which it will in fact entertain appeals. It is quite possible to possess jurisdiction legitimately without exercising it in all cases; it is not possible to exercise jurisdiction legitimately in any case without possessing it. We may add that the listing of these exceptional cases occurs not only in the works of the canonists (whose technique of presenting scattered comments on a given topic in widely separated contexts could easily lead to inconsistencies), but also in the orderly exposition of the hierocratic theme by a systematic philosopher like Giles of Rome, who evidently saw no inconsistency in this procedure. Giles maintained that all power, spiritual and temporal, was vested in the pope, that sometimes he wielded his temporal authority directly but more commonly permitted it to be exercised by secular rulers. He went on to mention seven specific cases (based on the canonical exceptions) where the pope actually exercised the universal temporal jurisdiction that pertained to his office, one of them being the "hard and doubtful" matter referred to in the decretal *Per Venerabilem*. Once again there is no question here of a hierocratic distortion of the pope's original meaning. Innocent himself had indeed spelled out precisely the same doctrine towards the end of *Per Venerabilem* itself: "Paul also, that he might expound the plenitude of power, wrote to the Corinthians saying, 'Do you not know that you shall judge angels? How much more the things of this world.' And so [the pope] is accustomed to exercise the office of secular power sometimes and in some things through himself, sometimes and in some things through others."

Innocent did not consider it appropriate or desirable to exercise his jurisdiction over spiritual affairs and over temporal affairs in precisely the same fashion, and he pointed this out in *Per Venerabilem*. In the ecclesiastical sphere he was *iudex ordinarius omnium;* in the temporal sphere he had no intention of burdening the papal curia with a mass of petty feudal litigation that, by legitimate custom, belonged to the courts of secular rulers. He did want to ensure that the temporal jurisdiction of the papacy could be invoked whenever a secular case had political implications involving the peace and good order of Christendom, and his various decretals provided a canonical basis for appeals in all such cases. Again, Innocent did take it for granted that, under the pope, secular rulers had a permanent and necessary role to play in the governance of Christian society, and that this role was a part of the divinely ordered scheme of things. He assumed that two hierarchies of administration were necessary for the government of the Christian world but, in his view, both hierarchies culminated in the pope. If this constitutes dualism, as some modern students of Innocent's thought seem to suppose, then all the medieval popes and all the most papalist of medieval theologians were dualists. It did not occur to Innocent III or his successors that it lay within their competence simply to abolish the offices of all secular rulers and themselves assume the exercise of all temporal power. But it also lay quite outside their competence, in the ecclesiastical sphere itself, to abolish the office of bishop and rule all the affairs of the church through papal delegates. Either innovation would have grievously perturbed "the general state of the church," which was not permitted to a pope or any human legislator.

The recent work on Pope Innocent III has been much concerned with relating his ideas to their medieval background. This is all to the good. It needs to be emphasized that the theory of papal power he propounded bore little resemblance to modern positivist theories of sovereignty and still less to modern totalitarian theories of despotism. We shall, however, eventually come to a full understanding of Innocent's position, not by minimizing his plainly stated claim to temporal power, but by relating that claim to the complex of doctrines concerning natural law, counsel and consent, *status ecclesiae,* and customary rights that medieval popes, as well as their critics, took for granted.

KENNETH PENNINGTON

Innocent III and Canon Law

HISTORIANS HAVE traditionally acknowledged the importance of Innocent III's pontificate for the development of the medieval church. They almost unanimously concur that his pontificate represented the apogee of the medieval papacy. Law, they assert, was one of the key elements which Innocent used to construct papal government, and Innocent is generally regarded as one of the great lawyer popes of the Middle Ages. Further, historians have credited Huguccio, one of the most important canon lawyers of the twelfth century, with molding Innocent's mind while he was a student at Bologna and have found in Huguccio's work the inspiration for some of Innocent's policies as pope. This paper will examine the evidence upon which these two assertions rest.

Both medieval and modern historians of canon law have assumed that Lothar of Segni learned canon law at Bologna from Huguccio, who taught at Bologna until 1190 when he became bishop of Ferrara. He remained at Ferrara until his death in 1210. We have two letters which Innocent wrote to Huguccio while he was bishop of Ferrara, although, peculiarly, the tradition that Innocent had been Huguccio's student did not arise from these letters. The first letter, which Innocent wrote early in his pontificate, noted that Huguccio was learned in law and commended him for consulting Rome in legal matters in spite of his legal erudition. The second letter, written in 1209, was in answer to Huguccio's question concerning the nature of the water which had issued from the side of Christ while he was hanging on the cross. Innocent's letter in reply to Huguccio's inquiry was formal and devoid of any personal touches. Innocent could have recalled his

Reprinted from the *Bulletin of Medieval Canon Law*, ns, 4 (1974), 70–77. With permission.

student days at Bologna in these letters. When he wrote to King Richard I of England and the cathedral chapter of York about providing a prebend for Peter of Corbeil, Innocent noted that he had been Peter's student. However, Innocent gave no indication in these or any of his other letters that he had ever studied law with Huguccio.

The tradition that Innocent had studied law under Huguccio arose from a letter with did not concern Huguccio personally. Innocent had written to the bishop of Mantua that two sacred orders could not be conferred on one day, or on two consecutive days if fasting had been carried over from one day to the next. This decretal was contrary to the opinion which Huguccio had expressed in his great *Summa* on Gratian's *Decretum,* and Innocent referred to Huguccio's opposing opinion in his letter without explicitly naming him. However, later canonists pointed out to their readers and students that Innocent was refuting Huguccio's opinion in this decretal.

Hostiensis, for example, in the middle of the thirteenth century commented on Innocent's letter: "It can be presumed that Innocent held Master Huguccio in great reverence because through the foregoing words it seems that he did not intend to reprove Huguccio's opinion—even though Innocent immediately did so." Later in the fourteenth century, the Bolognese canonist, Johannes Andreae (d. 1348) compressed Hostiensis' gloss and wrote: "Innocent did not want to reject the opinion of his master Huguccio explicitly, which, nevertheless, he does reject in the end." Johannes Andreae was that first canonist—so far as I can find—who said that Innocent had been a student of Huguccio, and all later historians have cited this text to prove that fact. However, Johannes clearly based his gloss on Hostiensis' text, although he reproduced it carelessly. There is no earlier evidence that Innocent studied under Huguccio, and the tradition must, therefore, be relegated to the garden of historical mythology. Johannes might have been recording an oral or an unknown written source at Bologna, but I think that the evidence points to a corruption of Hostiensis' gloss rather than an independent tradition.

This leads us to the larger question of whether Innocent III ever formally studied law. Innocent did study at Bologna. But did he study law there? Historians—having hitherto accepted the story that Innocent studied under Huguccio—have used the anonymous *Gesta Innocentii papae III* as further proof that Innocent studied law at Bologna. Consequently, they have interpreted the imprecise remarks of the *Gesta's* author to mean that Innocent went to Bologna to pursue legal studies after he had finished studying theology at Paris. Historians have applauded Innocent's good sense. They feel that he was a mediocre theologian at best, and law was better suited to his talents. The section in the *Gesta* on Innocent's early education is worth quoting in full:

He pursued scholastic studies first at Rome, then at Paris and finally at Bologna, and he surpassed his contemporaries in both philosophy and theology, just as his works which he wrote and drafted at various times show. Before his pontificate, he completed the books, *De miseria conditionis humane, De missarum mysteriis* and *De quadripartita specie nuptiarum.* During his pontificate he wrote books of sermons, letters, registers and decretals which manifestly make evident how much he was learned in both human and divine law.

The first sentence of this passage has been cited as evidence that Innocent studied law at Bologna, but one may note that the *Gesta*'s author said nothing about studying law. Innocent, he said, pursued *scholastica studia.* In the thirteenth century "scholastic studies" commonly meant the study of the liberal arts or theology, but we do have an example in which Innocent himself used the term "scholastici" to refer to law professors. However, the *Gesta* concluded the sentence by stating that Innocent excelled in philosophy and theology: the second half of the sentence specified the kinds of "scholastic studies" in which Innocent had been engaged. If Innocent did not study law at Bologna, what could he have studied there instead of law? He may have studied theology or the notarial arts; we know that both disciplines existed in late twelfth-century Bologna. Obviously, Innocent may have "read" law at Bologna—that was the usual reason for studying there—but there is not any certain evidence in the *Gesta's* account that he did so.

In the last sentence of the paragraph, the *Gesta*'s author declared that Innocent was learned in 'both human and divine law.' To be sure, if he had not studied law, by the time in which the *Gesta*'s author wrote (ca. 1210), Innocent would have acquired a substantial knowledge of law just from sitting in his consistory three times a week. But the specific phrase, "learned in both human and divine law" is typical of the sort of accolades with which medieval biographers were prone to describe their subjects, and does not suffice as evidence to attribute legal training to Innocent. The phrase itself is too vague.

Not only the *Gesta* but also lawyers characterized Innocent's intellectual gifts with words of extravagant praise, but I do not think that their encomia constitute a proof that Innocent was trained as a canonist. Vincentius Hispanus, for example, said that Innocent was "pater eminentis scientie et perspicacissimi ingenii." Vincentius used almost the same wording to describe Pope Gregory IX in his prologue to the *Gregoriana,* although he explicitly stated that Gregory was learned *in utroque iure,* a phrase which he did not use to describe Innocent III. Hostiensis called Innocent the "pater iuris" several times in his legal works. Thirteenth-century canon law was shaped and formed by Innocent's decretal letters, and Hostiensis, as well as many other lawyers, knew how important Innocent's pontificate had been for the development of ecclesiastical law. The title "pater iuris" was certainly appropriate for Innocent, but such a title would not, it seems to me, prove legal training any more than the *Gesta*'s statement that Innocent was "learned in both human and divine law."

The one positive piece of evidence that Innocent studied law is the enormous collection of decretal letters which were written during his pontificate. Many of these letters display sophisticated knowledge of Roman law and legal concepts, while demonstrating great skill in deciding individual cases. Only a trained lawyer or lawyers could have drafted these letters. We can even be sure that Innocent had a hand in many of the cases which the letters report, for the *Gesta* tells us that Innocent judged many of the "more important" cases at the Curia, although he did not judge personally all the cases which came to Rome. Innocent's letters show not only an awareness of the problems which concerned the canonists at Bologna, but often—as in the letter to the Bishop of Mantua referred to above—demonstrate a knowledge of individual canonistic opinions. However, as Christopher Cheney has pointed out, we can never be sure when Innocent's decretal letters reflect his own words or thoughts:

> We must squarely face the facts that there is no positive proof of the pope's [Innocent's] drafting of any particular letter, and that we cannot hope to distinguish certainly between those which he wrote and those written by high officials of the Curia who shared his views and his intellectual background, and acted under his instructions. Nor must we assume that the most eloquent or the most profound letters were necessarily those which the pope himself composed.

Further, we may suppose that the officials at the Curia would have put forward most of the varying canonistic opinion in their arguments, and Innocent's decretals would have reflected their knowledge as well as his own. Innocent, in short, like later popes who were not lawyers (e.g. Honorius III) may have produced his letters with the help of curial officials, perhaps never even seeing many of them, and his decretals cannot provide us with absolute evidence that he had studied law.

A persuasive argument, although *ex silentio,* that Innocent never studied law is that he never wrote a legal treatise of any kind even though he wrote a number of works after he left Bologna. He composed three theological tracts—mentioned in the section of the *Gesta* quoted above—before he became pope. These works are of pedestrian quality and are purely theological, very similar to contemporary theological tracts which were produced in Paris. There is hardly any trace of legal learning in them. Even in subject areas where Innocent could have employed legal arguments, such as in *De sacro altaris mysterio* or *De quadripartita specie nuptiarum,* he used no direct legal sources. Is it possible that Innocent could have studied law for any length of time without there being a definite reflection of this interest and learning in his works? If he was as learned in law as historians have maintained and his letters seem to indicate, why did he not write any legal tracts? In a work like *De miseria humanae conditionis*, we would not have expected Innocent to display his legal erudition. But when he discussed the species of human matrimony in *De quadripartita*, his analysis was strictly theological rather than legal. The law concerning marriage had been rapidly changing during the last half of the twelfth century, particularly under the impact of Pope Alexander III's decretals. If Innocent was trained as a lawyer, it is certainly curious that he did not allude to the pertinent canonical texts when he discussed marriage.

Finally, there is the problem of the length of time during which Innocent could have studied at Bologna. Helene Tillmann has determined that Innocent probably left Paris for Bologna in the summer or fall of 1187. At this same time (October–December, 1187) Pope Gregory VIII made Innocent a subdeacon. Innocent could have gone back to Rome then, but if he stayed at Bologna and held his office *in absentia,* he undoubtedly did go to Rome by September of 1189 when Pope Clement III raised him to the cardinalate. Thus, even by the most generous estimate, Innocent could have studied at Bologna for only two years; hardly enough time for him to have become a highly skilled canonist, even if he had studied law.

In conclusion, there is no evidence that Innocent III was the student of Huguccio or any other canonist at Bologna, and historians should be chary of interpreting Innocent's thought through the medium of canon law alone. If, however, Innocent was either not or only partially trained as a lawyer, this fact in no way denigrates his accomplishments. Like King Henry II of England, he had a keen sense for administration, which would not have been more acute even if he had studied canon law. But we might deepen our understanding of his pontificate if we looked at Innocent as basically a theologian rather than as a lawyer. A man's thought is shaped by his background, and Innocent's statements on Church and State might be better understood if they were seen as pastoral exhortations and theological expositions rather than as a lawyer's shrewd formulations. Many of the ambiguities of Innocent's pontificate which have exercised the pens of historians might be made clearer if we viewed Innocent as a pastoral theologian who was more concerned with resolving specific problems within his flock than in establishing legal precedents for future popes. In fact, many of his most important ideological innovations—the concepts of *ratione peccati* and *consequenter* and the use of Old Testament figures like Melchisedech as models for the thirteenth-century papacy—have few if any antecedents in the writings of the canonists. The paradox is, nevertheless, that Innocent's pastoral approach to crucial problems both within and outside of the Church had profound legal ramifications. Thirteenth-century canonists modified the prevailing dualistic theories of the twelfth century when they attempted to explain Innocent's decretal letters which concerned Church and State in legal terms. Innocent's views, whether intentionally or not, shaped canonistic thinking for the rest of the thirteenth century.

Was Innocent III a lawyer? We may never know how much legal training Innocent had with absolute certainty. What can be said is that the positive evidence which supports the traditional view that Innocent was a Bologna-educated canonist is very slight.

WILHELM IMKAMP

Innocent III as Theologian

SUMMING UP, we can see that the most important statements [of Innocent III] on the papal primacy have essentially an ecclesiological basis. Even if Innocent was not unaware of the eschatalogical significance of the papal image, he had to be aware that papal primacy was part of the actuality of the struggling Church. This fact becomes evident in the way he used terminology referring to the Church as a body [corpus]. Rather than the unity of the militant and triumphant Church with Christ as its head, we have a differentiated and structured unity of a struggling Church under its head, the successor of Peter. Through the corpus terminology applied to papal primacy, the eucharistic dimension in its eschatalogical aspect retreats into the background. Arguments characterized by christological terminology now move to the foreground. The strongest statements about papal primacy take a "christological detour," as is evident in the "caput-kephale" [head] interpretation as well as in the evaluation of the "head" metaphor behind Pope Leo I's formulation of the papal plenitude of power. Many statements on the primacy read just as though they were transposed from Christology. In this context, we note, therefore, that Leo's formulation on the plenitude of power does not belong in a precise canonistic conceptual framework—"de primatu Romani pontificis" [On the primacy of the Roman pontiff], but has its origin instead in a christological notion related directly to the idea of a vicar [that is, the pope as vicar of Christ. Ed.]. Consequently, the meaning of primacy cannot be precisely determined. In this central issue of the argument over the primacy, Innocent shows that he is more theologian than canonist.

Wilhelm Imkamp, *Das Kirchenbild Innocenz' III (1198–1216)* (Stuttgart: A. Hiersemann, 1983), 324–26. Translation by editor. I would like to thank Kenneth Pennington for assistance with the translation.

If the title "mater" [mother] applied to the church, developed from the notion of bridal fertility, we notice a certain hesitation about applying it to the whole church; this hesitation may have had its origins in the fact that "mater" is primarily a title that expresses the primatial status of the Roman church. Innocent used the title far more often in this sense than with reference to the whole church. If the study of the corpus terminology refers first of all to the person of the pope, "mater" applies to the description of his office. The title can, therefore, be used without distinction for the "ecclesia romana" [Roman church] as well as in reference to the "sedes apostolica" [apostolic see]. Innocent appears to make a distinction between two meanings of the motherhood of the Roman church. The first refers to the Roman church as the mother of all the other churches and, on this account, their head. As "mater omnium Christi fidelium" [mother of all the faithful of Christ], she stands in a direct relationship to each Christian believer and is, therefore, identical with the "ecclesia universalis" [universal church]. "Mater" is, therefore, never thought of as a description of a relationship originating from historical circumstances, but rather as an expression of a difference in rank, whereby, certainly in the immediate context, the fruitfulness not only of the the distinctions in rank among churches but also in the sacramental relationship between the individual Christian and his church can be shown. Precisely along this pathway lies the possibility to identify the "ecclesia Romana" [Roman church] and "ecclesia universalis" [universal church]. The corpus terminology, in its approach to the papacy, leads to a description of the plenitude of power in the person of the pope; the development of the "mater" title expresses most effectively the primatial status of the Roman church. Innocent next expressed the bond between the pope and the Roman church, using the image of spiritual marriage. The ecclesiastical meaning of this image, whether applied to a bishop in relation to his church or as a basis for the papal reservation of (episcopal) translations [transfers from one diocese to another], as Innocent especially developed it in the first year of his pontificate, was originated or developed by Innocent out of the image of the marriage of Christ with his Church. There was, also, up to Innocent's time, with few exceptions, no image for the episcopal or papal representation as Christ. Originally, the basis for comparison was the indissolubility of the marriage bond between man and wife. The application by the decretists of terminology from the law of marriage to the bond between a bishop and his diocese would be taken up and further developed by Innocent. First, spiritual marriage between the bishop of Rome and the Roman church would be put expressly in the broad context of spiritual marriage developed in the "De quadrapartita specie nuptiarum" [On the fourfold type of marriages]. The image of spiritual marriage, symbol of the relationship of the pope to the Roman church as the bearer of primatial power, which it brings as a dowry to this marriage, leads the other churches to the pope—as Sarah once led her handmaid to Abraham—in order that they might receive from him the "debitum providentiae" [debt of providence]. In this way a special emphasis would be put on the orthodoxy of the pope as the motive and the ultimate basis for the "debitum reverentiae" [the debt of reverence] that the Roman church brings to him. This orthodoxy is so steadfast according to Innocent's personal conviction, which he bases on a passage in Luke, 22:32 ["but I have prayed that your faith may not fail; and once you have turned back, you must strengthen your brothers"], that the Roman church must never dismiss the pope on account of "fornicatio spiritualis" [spiritual fornication]. In these ideas of Innocent, we can see a little of what would later emerge as infallibility. Naturally, he adhered to many artificial and forced applications of the terminology of the law of marriage as it related to the tie between the pope and the Roman church. We should not overlook, however, that on this point the pope revealed his special originality. Indeed, the analysis of the position of the bishop of Rome within the framework of his image of the Church reveals our author as both theologian and canonist. The plenitude of power of the pope would be expressed in christological terms, the position of the Roman church summed up in the old and meaningful title of "mater." The bond between pope and church would finally be drawn precisely out of marriage law with the help of canonistic categories, in such a way that papal primacy would be brought closer to the personal infallibility of the Roman pontiff.

The primacy of the bishop of Rome had a broad ecclesiological foundation and fitted harmoniously with Innocent III's image of the Church.

BRENDA BOLTON

Innocent III and the *Humiliati*

MANIFESTATIONS of popular religion both in conscious and less conscious opposition to the official hierarchical church were frequent by the early thirteenth century. Such movements, generated by a new and exciting interpretation of apostolic life among the laity, often expressed particular social and economic needs. This evangelical awakening emphasised urban and fraternal Christianity and was welcomed by those in the towns who were untouched by the ministrations of the local clergy. Strong religious sentiment led them to practice a literal and christocentric piety through corporeal works of mercy and personal experience of poverty. Real spiritual devotion was no longer confined to monastic enclosed communities but was centered on the domestic family unit, in which women too played a valuable role. Yet this spontaneous expression of lay piety represented a threat which could not be ignored. It was also a challenge which Innocent III met, during the seventeen years of his pontificate, by attempting to harness the untapped reserve of religious enthusiasm and vitality and to divert it into an orthodox channel which affected not merely acknowledged heretics but many of his own clergy.

One such group of enthusiasts were the *Humiliati* of Lombardy whose wide popular appeal led to the establishment of their houses in Milan, Como, Lodi, Pavia, Piacenza, Bra, Brescia, Bergamo, Monza, Cremona and Verona. Legend places their origin in the eleventh century but they are first named officially in the general condemnation of 4 November 1184 by which Lucius III anathematised a whole group of sects classed as heretical.

Reprinted from G. J. Cuming and Derek Baker, eds., *Popular Belief and Practice* (Studies in Church History, 8) Cambridge: Cambridge University Press, 1972, 73–82. With permission.

The *Humiliati* of Vibaldono near Milan appear to have been reinstated in 1186, although their request for permission to preach was refused. In 1198 or 1199, two leading members of the *Humiliati,* James de Rondineto and Lanfranc de Lodi, came to Innocent to seek approval and recognition of their way of life. His treatment of them merits detailed consideration as it contrasts with his predecessors' failure to face the very real problems posed by these popular religious fraternities. He asked that they should present a short statement or *propositum* to indicate their willingness to devote themselves to a life of Christian piety. Some characteristic features of the movement may be established by an examination, not only of their *proposita,* but also of Innocent's letters concerning them, and of chronicle evidence.

By 1200, the *Humiliati* seem to have organized themselves into three groups, which are referred to as orders. The first and second orders, led by *praepositi* and *praelati* respectively, were composed of unmarried men and women living separate and ascetic lives in religious communities according to a form of rule unrecognized by authority. The third order comprised a group of laymen living at home with their families and practicing strict evangelical precepts. These were the Tertiaries who caught the eye and imagination of several chroniclers. One couplet runs:"Sunt in Italia fratres humiliati, Qui jurare renuunt et sunt uxorati." The *Chronicle of Laon* substantiates the importance to them of family life, prayer, preaching and mutual support and emphasizes their refusal to swear an oath. Burchard, abbot of Ursperg, refers scathingly to them as *rudes et illiterati,* while Humbert de Romans considered them aptly named since they led a humble life of manual work. Their *propositum* indicates that they ate and prayed in common, dressed soberly and sought to lead lives of apostolic purity and piety. They felt that their *raison d'être* was preaching, but this had been forbidden to them by Alexander III and Lucius III, a prohibition strictly enforced on a local level by diocesan bishops. The third order is addressed as *societas, fraternitas,* and *universitas,* possibly indicating that its members already formed some loose association or rudimentary guild organization.

That Innocent was conscious of the fundamental importance of the growth of religious sentiment is apparent from the *arenga* of his letters to the *Humiliati.* His policy was to establish the *distinctio* between irrevocable heretics and believers, and thereby to draw a line between heresy and orthodox piety. Whereas he insisted on condign punishment for heretics, likening himself to a doctor forced to amputate a malignant limb to save the body, he maintained that the cure is all important, the method by which it is achieved far less so. The regeneration of clerical elements within the church was a matter of great urgency and Innocent's contact with the *Humiliati* showed him that such movements, carefully controlled, could be of use. There was much to be gained by adopting the more successful of their methods and thus bringing them back like lost sheep into the fold. His attitude towards them was therefore cautious but conciliatory: he did not wish to punish the innocent and was prepared to overlook minor deviations.

On 6 December 1199, he wrote to Adelard, bishop of Verona, to warn him that the *Humiliati* in his diocese were being indiscriminately excommunicated and classed with Cathars, Arnaldists and Poor Men of Lyons. He ordered that measures against them should cease. Those of their views which were apparently orthodox should be reconsidered, and even when they appeared to stray from orthodoxy, they should be given the benefit of absolution if prepared to acknowledge such error and to submit. At much the same time he was confronted by their request for recognition. He felt that the *Humiliati* could be a useful weapon with which to fight heresy. However, he declared himself unable to grant their request without deep thought and considerable investigation, because the character of their life, although analogous to that of other pious associations, was vastly different from that followed by any existing religious community. So he established a special commission, composed of the bishop of Vercelli, a regular canon from the community of Mortara, and the Cistercian abbots of Lodi and Cerreto. This was to receive, examine, and pronounce authoritatively on the *proposita* of the *Humiliati*.

Innocent originally planned to bring the *Humiliati* within the church by uniting them in a single rule, a *propositum regulare,* although he made it clear that he did not intend to discipline the community with the characteristic obligations of either monks or regular canons. But the evidence collected by the commission, after two years of complicated and detailed investigation, appears to have pointed to the impossibility of placing the community under one rule. In 1201, their *proposita* received papal confirmation in three documents. Separate letters were sent to the Tertiaries and to the second order, while the first order received a privilege similar to that granted to religious institutions. The movement appears already to have had a definite form and known leadership since Innocent addressed some of the *praepositi, praelati,* and *ministri* by name. Seemingly the task of the commission had been merely to indicate future lines of development, not to lay down totally new forms.

All three documents deal with the *Humiliati's* rejection of oathtaking. In common with the Cathars, they based this rejection on the Epistle of St. James. Innocent realised that such an interpretation of the New Testament was theologically dangerous, for the *Humiliati* were implicitly putting themselves in the same category as clerics, for clerics did not swear, and thus for the *Humiliati* to imitate them in this would be to behave heretically. Using extensive biblical justification, he attempted to compromise with all three orders by requiring them to recognize oaths in urgent cases but freeing them from the obligation to take those which were unnecessary and worthless.

The question of tithe payments could not be resolved in one formula common to the whole movement. Each document, therefore, contains instructions appropriate to lay or clerical elements. The Tertiaries, as laymen, could neither possess tithes nor refuse to pay them to their diocesan bishops. The second order was free from payments on its own lands and from its animal husbandry, but was still obliged to pay tithes when due to the church. The first order was granted remission according to the formula *sane novalium* and, with diocesan permission, was allowed to possess tithes for its own use.

A unique provision for the Tertiaries allowed them to gather every Sunday in a suitable place at which those "wise in faith and expert in religion" could preach as long as they ignored theological questions and dealt only with exhortations to a pious and earnest life. Episcopal licence was necessary for this but the bishops were expressly commanded not to refuse. Such qualifications do not affect the importance of this provision. Although Innocent took care to distinguish between the preaching of ordained priests and that of pious lay groups, he was prepared to modify the fundamental law that no one might preach without ordination. The *Humiliati,* preaching on their experience of Christian life, were thus allowed an existence within the church.

The situation was difficult for a juridical mind such as Innocent's; the *Humiliati* did not represent, at least from the church's point of view, a homogeneous entity, since the movements contained both lay and clerical elements, living only partially in *vita communis.* The Tertiaries received papal approval of their *norma vivendi* but, possibly because of their married state, were never accepted into the church as *religiosi.* Innocent's original proposal for a single *propositum regulare* came nearest to fulfillment in his treatment of the second order. Its *institutio regularis* was approved by the Holy See and conceded to the unmarried laity the jurisdictional status of *religiosi.* The first order was specifically confirmed as a religious community and its obligations and privileges were recognized in its *ordo canonicus.* Its members were to be tonsured and were granted the right to wear a habit *ut laicos litteratos,* presumably similar to that worn by Italian civil lawyers. They were to be cloistered, but an instruction was given that if anyone tried to leave, he was not be be restrained. They were allowed to build their own churches with episcopal permission but were not to prejudice those already in existence. Although their rule contained elements of Benedictine and Augustinian monasticism, they were specifically to follow the liturgical customs of the canonical congregation of Mortara from which the bishop of

Vercelli came. The form of visitation and the relationship between the houses were based on the Cistercian pattern. The letter to the first order contains elaborate details and instructions. The four superiors of the order, the *praepositi majores* of Rondineto, Vibaldone, Vigalono and Lodi, were to visit each other in turn. Furthermore, together with the four leaders of each of the other two orders, they were to consult together at least annually in a general chapter which was to deal with matters of business and religion. Laymen were specifically excluded from *spiritualia* although they had parity with clerics in temporal affairs. Any one of the *praepositi majores* could be deposed by the other three, and provision was made for a new election conducted by an arbiter from the community, assisted by one lay and two clerical electors. After a three-day fast, the whole community of brothers and sisters was to vote, and the successful *praepositus* then sought the confirmation of his diocesan bishop. His appointment was for life or until deposition.

The composition of the movement, its place in the general pattern of heresy, lay piety, and the formation of new orders are open questions, although some tentative suggestions may be made. The first order of priests appears to have been mainly aristocratic. Its members provided leadership for the movement and possibly recruits to the *praelati* and *ministri* of the second and third orders. Guy de Porta Orientalis, *minister* of the Tertiaries, is described as *vir nobilis* and *capitanei*. In Lombardy there was a strong tradition of alienation among the lesser nobility, especially the *vavassours* who were usually excluded from any positive role in either political or ecclesiastical affairs. Just as some had supported the Patarines of the eleventh century, so others may have been tempted to join the *Humiliati* among whom they could more easily achieve the eminence denied to them by the church. The houses of this order were well endowed with lands and possessions, possibly given by aristocratic patrons. Perhaps this order also contained priests who had broken away from the church.

The movement appears to have had a strong lower-class base. Pious lay fraternities sprang up at a time of considerable urban expansion. They reacted not only against the pressures of anonymity and overcrowding, but also against the increase of wealth in direct contradiction to the primary demand of the Gospels for poverty. Some of the Tertiaries were evidently artisans, for Innocent showed concern that they should not be required to fast if they were at work. To avoid any preoccupation with riches they were instructed to observe Christian precepts and to give to the indigent all income in excess of their own needs. But even at an early date, they may have given the impression that they were far from poor since, in 1214, Innocent urged the Lombard towns not to tax their communities too heavily. By the middle of the thirteenth century they were established in a profitable wool industry, partly worked on a domestic basis but also involving the second order who, after the canonical hours, hurried away to their separate cloisters to exercise this skill *pro communi commoditate.* They seem to have turned gradually from humble manual work to a quasi-capitalistic organization, the existence of which the movement's chroniclers, John de Brera and Marcus Bossius, both writing in the fifteenth century, made vigorous attempts to justify.

Even after their recognition by Innocent in 1201, the *Humiliati* still encountered strong resentment from the secular church. In 1203, at Cerea in the diocese of Verona, they were not only expelled but saw their goods granted away by licence from the archdeacon. Although they were referred to as heretics, there is no evidence that they were not completely orthodox. Innocent always took great care to provide that, on the particular matters of preaching, church-building and tithe payments, permission should be sought from the diocesan bishop. The secular clergy could not understand why Innocent accorded favors to these repentant heretics whom they regarded as tares among the wheat. To attack heresy with such recently converted men and women seemed to them to be equivocal and to create a dangerous precedent. But Innocent was well aware of the deficiencies of his clergy. In 1199, he had overruled the bishop of Metz and had allowed a group of laymen to read the Scriptures in the vernacular "lest these simple people should be forced into heresy". He recognized the positive contribution of Christian example which such groups could provide, and attempted to defend them against the hatred and fear of the secular clergy.

The *Humiliati* were, in many respects, remarkably similar to the Franciscans. Both movements lived according to the *forma primitivae ecclesiae,* surrounded by lay Tertiaries and communities of women. Both were deeply mistrusted by the secular church. The *Humiliati* even shared some of the friars' success. Jacques de Vitry, visiting the heretical city of Milan in 1216, was able to report that the *Humiliati* were *alone* in resisting and, indeed, in actively working against heresy through conventicles and at least 150 conventual groups. But there were vital differences between the two: the *Humiliati* had no outstanding leader and no Cardinal Protector to defend them against their enemies or to vouch for their orthodoxy. The *Humiliati* were bound by a compromise rule which was an amalgam of diverse elements. The friars had the advantage of entering the church several years later with a rule that was entirely their own. Possibly the *Humiliati* were becoming rich and less attractive to the idealistic recruits who sought to experience real poverty.

Between 1200 and 1215, there was a proliferation of religious groups, penitential, pious, charitable and military, in places as far apart as Languedoc and Livonia. Innocent examined each one with the care that he had accorded the *Humiliati*, taking some within the church as *religiosi* and authorizing others to preach under the immediate vigilance of the diocesan bishop. His action may have provided a stimulus to episcopal preaching but it also seems to have provoked a strong response from the secular clergy. In 1215, at the Fourth Lateran Council, it was decreed that there were to be no new religious orders. Furthermore, anyone wishing to re-found a religious house had to make sure that the rules and institutions were those of an approved order. This may mark the victory of the "conservative" bishops rather than the policy of Innocent himself. It is difficult to understand why he should have undergone such a complete *volte-face* unless considerable pressure was placed upon him. The bishops, fearing the contamination of their people and the exposure of clerical deficiencies, sought to create a situation in which heretics would, in future, stand out sharply from the rest of the flock. The Lateran Council crystallised the pattern which had become apparent after 1201. It was preferable that groups of clergy and laity living in common should be persuaded to adopt the traditional rules of regular canons or hospitallers than that new rules should be created. Episcopal pressure seems to have led to the affirmation of a new principle. After 1215, canonical legislation to regulate and discipline new orders was brought within the competence of the Holy See.

No community was ever again organized on quite the lines laid down by Innocent for the *Humiliati*. He had shown flexibility by retaining the essential form of the movement when it would possibly have been easier to absorb the first order into an existing rule and to ignore the third. He had demonstrated his practical concern by allowing the Tertiaries to preach and by rewarding the devotion not only of men but of women. Yet he sowed the seeds of their destruction as a primitive evangelical movement. Outside the church, they were valuable critics, and their emphasis on communal work and the family unit put them in a strong position to convert. Once they had shown that they could win adherents, Innocent, with his love of institutions, disciplined, regulated, and absorbed this spontaneous lay movement into the church. After 1201, they were forced into a diocesan structure which led to the ultimate vitiation of their early form. In some respects, they antedated the friars but their movement lacked the clarity, precision, and leadership which would have made it a decisive force for the future. By 1214, Innocent himself was aware that they were no longer the eager representatives of a literal and christocentric interpretation of piety, although their movement continued to attract recruits for some long time after. But this is not to underrate Innocent's achievement: from an undifferentiated *corpus* of religious sentiment, he enabled distinctive and valuable movements to emerge and ensured that they were perpetually harnessed in the service of the church.

JAMES M. POWELL

Innocent III and the Crusade

THE FIRST MAJOR testing ground for the crusade program of Innocent III lay in France in the period between 1213 and the opening of the Fourth Lateran Council in 1215. As we have seen, Innocent placed considerable emphasis on the support of the French monarchy to ensure the success of the crusade, but the situation in that country was far from favorable. Not only was it divided by the Albigensian Crusade, but large segments of the northern French aristocracy were embroiled in a conflict over the succession to the county of Champagne and the impending war against King John of England and Emperor Otto IV. The appointment of Robert Courçon as legate balanced that of Cardinal Nicholas of Tusculum. The cardinal had been sent to England in October 1213 to negotiate with King John about the conditions for raising the interdict that had been imposed by Innocent because of the king's refusal to accept the appointment of Cardinal Stephen Langton as archbishop of Canterbury. Although Robert's legation was primarily concerned with the crusade, his powers were not defined so narrowly as to exclude these questions. Nor could they be, for without a successful resolution of these conflicts the work of the crusade would be impeded. Therefore, the legations of Robert and Nicholas were not separate, but were part of a two-pronged papal effort aimed at restoring peace in France and England and thereby promoting the crusade. Moreover, in the work of Robert we get a first glimpse of the way in which recruitment for the crusade was integrated into the papal peace program. Although there is considerable uncertainty regarding details, the assumption of the cross by leading nobles from opposing groups demonstrates the close relationship between

From James M. Powell, *Anatomy of a Crusade, 1213–1221* (Philadelphia: University of Pennsylvania Press, 1986), 33–47. With permission.

the two programs. The enrollment of prominent nobles in the crusade made it possible for the legates to exert pressure on them in the cause of peace. Obviously, such tactics, if carried too far, could arouse opposition from those who saw them as intrusions into the secular sphere. The legation of Robert Courçon revealed both the potential and the risk in this approach.

Robert Courçon, cardinal priest of St. Stephen, was one of the more important intellectuals of the late twelfth and early thirteenth centuries. English by birth, he was closely associated with the schools of Paris, where Innocent III himself had studied. Robert was a member of the circle of Peter the Chanter at Paris, a group of masters who had profound concern for the moral transformation of both clergy and laity. Like so many appointed to be crusade procurators by Innocent III, Robert had participated in numerous cases as a papal judge delegate, in the course of which he became acquainted with some of the leading figures among the French clergy and aristocracy. Innocent made him a cardinal in 1212. Robert was already well known to the pope, both for his commitment to the reform of the church and his effectiveness as a judge.

Nevertheless, the legation of Robert Courçon has proved controversial both to his contemporaries and to modern scholars. There has been a general tendency to view it as a failure and as damaging to the crusade. Some have maintained that it ended in Robert's recall in disgrace. On the surface, at least, it would seem that Innocent III simply picked the wrong man for the job and came to regret it. But the reality is much more complex. There can be no question that Robert's legation aroused considerable opposition and that the pope had to intervene when the efforts of the legate threatened negative results. Robert was not afraid to use his legatine authority to the fullest and on one occasion this brought him into direct conflict with the pope. But whatever errors of judgment he made, he loyally and vigorously pursued the policies laid down by Innocent himself. In particular, the pope could not have asked for a more meticulous servant with respect to the crusade. A letter of Pope Honorius III, written immediately following his accession to the papal throne, demonstrates that most of the leading members of the French crusade contingent were recruited under the direction of Robert Courçon. Subsequent correspondence shows that strong ties continued to exist between the cardinal and the French crusaders long after the end of his legation in 1215. These facts suggest that, whatever shortcomings Robert had, the effectiveness of his legation cannot be judged by a simple yardstick of success or failure.

Robert Courçon's work was preparatory to the Fourth Lateran Council. It involved the reform of the church, the establishment of peace, and the promotion of the crusade. These three areas were, in fact, closely related to one another. Both the reform of the church and the papal pacification program were of vital importance to the ultimate success of the crusade: the first by preparing the Christian community to be a worthy receptacle of divine favor, and the second by removing a serious impediment to the recruitment of crusaders. But Robert's reform efforts evoked opposition from at least some clergy as an intrusion into their affairs. His efforts to promote peace were partly at the root of complaints made by the aristocracy and the king. Finally, some could not understand why crusade preachers would administer the crusade vow to so many persons who would be useless in combat. The chroniclers of the age viewed all of these initiatives with suspicion and mistrust, raising against them the traditional charges of greed and dishonesty that were the defense of local men against intruders. William the Breton spoke for a large number of his contemporaries when he wrote:

Robert Courçon, legate of the Apostolic See, and many with him, were preaching through the whole Gallic kingdom. And they signed many indiscriminately with the cross, children, old men, women, the lame, the blind, the deaf, lepers: thereby impeding the work of the cross rather than aiding the work of the Holy Land. Moreover, in their sermons, by which they seemed to want to please the crowd more than was necessary, they defamed the clergy, saying disgraceful things and lying about their life to the people, and so they sowed the seeds of scandal and schism between the clergy and the people. For these reasons, and on account of certain other complaints, both the king and the entire clergy appealed to the Apostolic See against the legate.

When the legate journeyed to Limoges, he enquired into the fitness of the abbot of St. Martial. The local chronicler, Bernard Itier, responded by accusing him of simony. At Laon, the chronicle maintained that he attacked "the dignity of prelates and the customs of important churches."

Historians have generally taken these charges at face value, or at most discounted them as exaggeration, but they have failed to emphasize the myopic quality of the charges, which often showed little concern for the great issues that engaged popes and kings. Nevertheless, the complaints of these chronicles are real, whatever the limitations of their authors. The views they represent are the local perspective on the major issues of the day. They provide a valid insight into the difficulties faced by Robert Courçon, regardless of how deficient they are in explaining the nature of his problems.

The councils held by the legate, his visitations of religious houses, and his decisions about local officials of the church represented to many an unwanted and unnecessary intrusion into local affairs. What was especially resented was that the legate and his associates denounced clerical abuses in their sermons in order to enlist the support of public opinion for the cause of reform. The series of councils Robert summoned—beginning at Paris in June 1213 and moving to Rouen the following February, thence to Bordeaux, Clermont, and Montpellier, and climaxing in Bourges in May 1215—reiterated concerns that had already been formulated at the Third Lateran Council in 1179 and were preparatory to the decisions to be made at Lateran IV. The condemnation of usury aroused both royal and baronial opposition, but the chief resistance to the legate among the clergy resulted from his involvement in a number of ongoing disputes within the French church. Of these, the most vitriolic involved the Order of Grandmont, founded by Stephen de Muret and profoundly influenced by the reform currents of the twelfth century.

The divisions between the lay brothers and the clerics on the issue of poverty that split the order had broken out in the 1180s and had been the subject of numerous appeals to and decisions by the popes, including Innocent III, who had rendered a detailed judgment in 1202. The crux of this controversy involved the division of control over the order between the two groups, with the *conversi,* or lay brothers, in charge of temporal affairs. Rome received a continuing stream of complaints from the clerics to the effect that the *conversi* were using their powers to injure them. It was on an appeal from the *conversi* charging the clerics with abuses against poverty that Robert Courçon was drawn into the dispute. He summoned the prior of Grandmont, the head of the order, to appear before him to answer the charges. When that official refused, stating that he was forbidden by the rule of the order to leave his house, Robert suspended him from office. In the meantime, the prior had appealed to the pope, who had assumed jurisdiction in the case, and he succeeded in bringing the thunder of Rome down on the head of Robert Courçon on the grounds that he had intervened in a case that was already before the papal court. Innocent arranged that the questions before Robert should be transferred to the archbishop of Bourges and two other prelates, who had previously served as judges delegate in this case. The pope was clearly under the impression that his legate had deliberately overstepped his bounds. On the other hand, given the delay in responses and the difficulty of communication, it is entirely possible that the prior of Grandmont, a man of great experience in such matters, had succeeded in outflanking the legate by his appeal to Rome and then entrapping him in a fait accompli. Whatever the case, matters could not have gone better for the prior or worse for the legate.

Examples of disputes involving Robert Courçon's legation could easily be multiplied. Baldwin notes that Robert suspended at least ten canons of the cathedral of Laon "for having acquired their prebends by simony." He prohibited the monastery of Montieramey, in the diocese of Troyes, from accepting candidates below eighteen years of age, but Honorius III permitted this practice once more in 1218. At Vendôme he initiated proceedings against simoniacal canons. He condemned clerical rebels against King John at Poitiers, as well as members of the clergy who kept concubines and dressed in too secular a manner, an action repeated by Cardinal Guala, who became legate in England in 1216. He proceeded against violations of clerical dress at Treguier and abuses against chastity at Rouen. Marcel and Christiane Dickson have detailed numerous other examples, mostly of a routine sort, in which Robert's legatine office involved him in the affairs of local churches and monasteries. Many of these cases were not controversial, but the investigation of the fitness of the abbot of St. Martial at Limoges did arouse resentment, as the chronicle of Bernard Itier testifies. Still, even granting the ineptitude of the legate in his handling of the Grandmont affair, the reaction of the French prelates in May 1215 at Bourges, where their opposition broke into the open, seems to have been triggered at least as much by concerns expressed by Philip Augustus that the legate had exceeded his mandate by interfering in matters touching the interests of the crown as by complaints about his reform activities.

Robert Courçon's mission involved two issues in which the French monarchy and aristocracy were vitally interested: the Anglo-French conflict and the succession to the county of Champagne. His correspondence with King John from 1213 to 1215 indicates that he worked to end the war between England and France and to secure Anglo-French support for the crusade. Robert was also charged to enquire into the grounds of consanguinity between Phillipine of Champagne and Erard of Brienne in order to prevent their marriage, by which Erard aimed to strengthen his claim to the county against Blanche and her son Theobald.

Some time before May 1214 Philip Augustus wrote to Innocent III raising a number of issues on which he differed from the legate. This letter unfortunately has been lost, but it is possible to reconstruct the major lines of Philip's argument from Innocent's reply and other sources. Innocent's letter to Philip dealt specifically with the question of the legate's jurisdiction over usury, but it is clear that this was not the only or necessarily the main issue raised by the king. Innocent informed Philip that the other questions he had raised would be taken up in the forthcoming council. The pope defended the actions of the legate with respect to usury, but he obviously was seeking to avoid other more controversial problems. Their nature may be surmised from a letter of Odo of Burgundy to the king and from a temporary negotiated settlement reached by the legate and the representatives of the king on Philip's orders.

As early as June 1213, prior to Robert's arrival in France, Philip had sent Innocent III's letter concerning the crusade (probably *Quia maior*) to his council for examination to see if its provisions infringed upon royal rights. The response of Odo of Burgundy to the king has been preserved. The provisions singled out for special attention by Odo were those by which the persons and goods of crusaders were taken under the protection of the church until the crusaders' return or death and those relating to crusaders' debts and the papal prohibition of usury by the Jews. Regarding these questions, Odo wrote: "It does not seem just or reasonable or licit for the Lord Pope or others to establish something in your kingdom, without the agreement of yourself and your advisers, whereby you and your barons and your subjects should lose the service and the due justices of their men." The advice was hardly exceptional, but was almost certainly the basis for Philip's objections to the pope. Philip's letter was, therefore, directed against *Quia maior* rather than the legate, except to the degree that he was the zealous agent of the pope in carrying out its provisions.

In response to the pope, Philip ordered the bishops of Paris and Senlis, together with the legate, to enquire into the manner in which the church traditionally regulated the rights of crusaders in France in order to establish a norm until the issues could be determined at the council. This enquiry shows that the king was concerned with an even broader range of problems than those revealed in the letter of Odo of Burgundy. The questions dealt with included the obligation of crusaders to pay taxes to the crown before their departure on crusade, their service in feudal and royal armies in this same period, and the jurisdiction of secular and ecclesiastical courts over crimes committed by crusaders. These were very sensitive areas for the king at a time when he and his principal advisers were preparing for war against King John and his ally, Emperor Otto IV. The pope was confronted with a difficult situation, in which Philip's support of the imperial candidacy of Frederick of Sicily against Otto, which he favored, could be jeopardized by conflicts over papal crusade policy. Nevertheless, rather than give up that policy, he temporized. Philip took advantage of the pope's decision to reach a temporary agreement with the legate that would give him a free hand with the French crusaders during the critical period leading up to the Battle of Bouvines in July 1214.

This analysis sheds new light on the interpretation of the sources concerning the recruitment of French crusaders during the legation of Robert Courçon. Thomas C. Van Cleve, for example, echoed the charges levelled by the chroniclers against the recruitment policies of Robert's legation, but his statement that they were most successful "among the masses, the unfortunate, and the weak," deals only with that innovation of the Innocentian crusade program that disturbed the accepted view of the suitable crusader. However, as noted earlier, the letter of Pope Honorius III dated August 7, 1216, provides a substantial list of crusaders from the leading ranks of the French aristocracy, who could only have been recruited during the legation of Robert Courçon. A detailed discussion of these individuals throws additional light on the connections between Robert's involvement in peace negotiations and his recruitment of leaders for the crusade.

The key figure mentioned by Honorius was Odo, duke of Burgundy, one of the major advisers and supporters of Philip Augustus of France. He commanded the rear guard of the French army at Bouvines. Other major supporters of Philip addressed by Honorius included Milo, count of Bar; Henry, duke of Brabant, the son-in-law of the king; Drogo de Merlo, the constable of France; Simon of Joinville, seneschal of Champagne; and Hugh de Lusignan, count of La Marche. Hervé de Donzy, count of Nevers, was allied to King John but had also taken the vow from Robert Courçon. In the aftermath of Bouvines, Robert worked to bring about a reconciliation between the count and the king, acting at the behest of King John. Following the death of Odo of Burgundy in 1218, Hugh of La Marche and Hervé of Nevers emerged as the leaders of the French crusaders.

Evidence that so many important royal supporters had taken the crusade vow from Robert Courçon, with the possibility that they had done so before the Battle of Bouvines, suggests a reason for Philip's concern about the mission of the legate. If Robert had used their crusader status to impede their participation in Philip's army, he would have deprived the king of some of his most important commanders, not to mention the many lesser vassals who would have withheld their services. A further reason for Philip's reservations about the mission of the legate arose from the fact that Robert had entered into direct contact with King John to promote peace and to obtain joint Anglo-French participation in the crusade as early as September 1213. This evidence confirms the direction in which the legate was working. He was committed to a juncture of the peace program with the recruitment effort. Such a policy imperilled the aims of Philip Augustus. Under the circumstances, it is not surprising that these efforts produced something of a crisis. Perhaps in this instance, too, Robert had moved beyond the point that Innocent himself would have desired. After all, the pope shared with Philip a desire to defeat Otto IV and establish Frederick II on the German throne. Innocent had no choice but to recommend compromise to his legate in the interest of these broader designs.

With the agreement reached between Robert and the bishops of Paris and Senlis, the way was open for the continuance of his legation in France into the fall of 1215, when he departed for Rome to participate in the Fourth Lateran Council. In the months following the Battle of Bouvines, King John used the offices of the legate to carry on negotiations with the French court. Robert played a significant role in the peace arranged by the two kings in the fall of 1214. In December 1214 he participated in a council at Montpellier. He may have spent the early part of 1215 in Flanders working in conjunction with Oliver of Paderborn, the crusade procurator for that part of Germany. It was in May 1215 that Robert summoned a council to meet in Bourges. Once again he ran into controversy, this time with the French hierarchy. The seriousness of this dispute may be judged from the fact that the bishops appealed to Rome and that Robert was unable to proceed with the council. The loss of the register of Innocent III for this period, however, has left us with only the notice of an agreement between the pope and the church of France on the subject of the acts of Robert of Courçon. The full nature of this problem can only be explained, as we shall see below, by events at the council. What is certain is that it did not impede the continuance of Robert's work. It is to the period following this dispute that his important work in reforming the statutes of the University of Paris belongs. Likewise, he received notice of the excommunication of Erard of Brienne, who was continuing to lay claim to the county of Champagne. Robert was still busy on that front. We know that Milo de St. Florentin and other supporters of Erard took crusade vows at some point as part of an effort to force a settlement of his conflict with Blanche. Despite this pressure, Erard remained recalcitrant and never himself took the vow. But his case illustrates in a specific way the attempt by the legate to employ recruitment as an instrument to secure peace. Robert returned to Rome for the celebration of the Fourth Lateran Council, where his views exercised considerable influence. There is no substantial evidence from this period or from the pontificate of Honorius III that he had returned in disgrace or that the substance of his work was repudiated by the papacy. Rather, his mission provided an experiential base for the decisions regarding the crusade reached at the Fourth Lateran Council.

The council—which met between November 11 and 30, 1215—was the largest and most comprehensive assembly of the ecclesiastical hierarchy ever held in the Middle Ages. Innocent's effort to secure attendance resulted in the presence of about four hundred archbishops and bishops, eight hundred abbots, and numerous theologians and heads of chapters and religious communities. Its ecumenical character was established by the attendance of the primate of the Maronites and Deacon Peter, representing the Melkite archbishop of Alexandria. The Latin patriarchs of Jerusalem, Antioch, and Constantinople were present with many of their suffragans. Almost all of the archbishops and bishops appointed as crusade procurators were present, save for the archbishop of Lund. In his opening sermon, Innocent used the image of the Pasch to establish the relationship between the crusade and reform. Innocent interpreted the Pasch in terms of a corporeal passage for the liberation of the Holy Land, a spiritual passage to achieve reform, and an eternal passage to glory. There was, moreover, a special urgency in his words. He seemed unsure that he would live to see the consummation of his plans for the crusade. His theme—reflected in his choice of a quote from the Gospel of Luke (20:13), "I have desired with a great desire to eat this pasch with you before I suffer"—took on more personal tone later in the sermon when he said, "I do not refuse, such being the will of God, to drink the chalice of the passion, if . . . it is handed to me." Further on, he became even more specific: "Certainly, I would prefer to remain in the chair until the achievement of this enterprise." The work of the council was more than the culmination of his plans; it was the culmination of his life.

The tendency among modern scholars to compartmentalize the various aspects of the council's work into doctrinal, political, ecclesiastical, and crusade categories obscures to some extent their interrelationships, their existence as part of a total fabric. Decisions made in one area had definite ramifications in others. Thus, several political issues taken up at the council had particular relevance to the crusade. The most important of these were the conflict between King John and the English barons, which also involved Prince Louis of France, that between Otto IV and Frederick II over the imperial throne, and, less clearly but still at least indirectly related, the matter of the Albigensian Crusade and the status of Raymond, count of Toulouse, and Raymond Roger, count of Foix. Innocent III was already committed to King John, having excommunicated the barons and rejected the Magna Carta. He had also supported the candidacy of Frederick II. Finally, he was the prime mover in the Albigensian Crusade. In all of these matters, the promotion of peace as a prerequisite for the success of the crusade was never far from his mind. On none of these fronts had his previous efforts been fully successful; it was for this reason that they were brought before the council.

The actions taken at the council regarding England were an extension of the efforts undertaken by Innocent's legates. In September 1214, following Bouvines, King Philip and King John had exchanged letters of truce arranged through the efforts of Robert Courçon, whose name appears in the witness list of John's letter with the attestation that the truce was sworn in his presence. Despite this success, John's war with his barons, who were increasingly supported by Prince Louis of France, was a serious cause for concern. When King John took the crusade vow on Ash Wednesday in 1215, he took on not merely the status of a vassal of the Holy See but also the protection due a crusader. Innocent judged the actions of the barons to be directed against the interests of the crusade. The baronial war threatened not only King John but also the recruitment program for the crusade. The chief action of the council was the rejection of the appeal of the barons against John and their excommunication. But, as Christopher Cheney has said, there can be "little doubt that the pope was already aware of the negotiations between the English rebels and the French court" aimed at enlisting the support of Prince Louis in their cause. The excommunication was also, therefore, an attempt to forestall this alliance. Innocent made this clear in the letters that he wrote to King Philip and to Prince Louis himself to inform them of the action taken by the council. The pope also acted quickly to appoint Cardinal Guala as his legate to England to replace Nicholas, who had returned to Rome. Despite the failure of the effort of the Council to restrain either the barons or Louis, Innocent continued to work for peace in England.

The conflict over the imperial throne also had direct ramifications on the crusade. Like King John, Frederick II had taken the crusade vow. Although some historians have continued to argue that his action was undertaken without the knowledge of, and even contrary to the will of, the pope, the weight of evidence now strongly supports the view that Innocent not only knew of but had, through his representatives, even worked toward this goal. Of course, there were obvious advantages for Frederick, as for King John, in taking the cross. He obtained the protections of a crusader against his enemies and gained status in the eyes of the church. But the pope also gained. The crusade vow provided a lever that might be used against Frederick should he prove reluctant to depart on crusade. Moreover, his service on the crusade could at least temporarily serve to reduce tensions between the church and the empire.

The relationship between the Albigensian affair and the crusade was twofold. On the one hand, the continuation of the war against heretics in the south of France posed a threat to the recruitment of French crusaders for the East. Innocent had dealt with this problem by suspending the indulgence for the Albigensian Crusade. Nevertheless, the leaders of the war against the heretics continued to view themselves as crusaders. Secondly, Simon de Montfort and his supporters were not willing to permit the counts of Toulouse and Foix to recover the lands they had lost to the crusaders. They were able to bring considerable pressure to bear on the pope, first to place these lands in the care of Simon until a decision could be rendered by the council, and then, at the council itself, to force the pope to accept the overwhelming vote of the bishops to make this arrangement permanent. In particular, the bishops argued that any effort to dispossess the count of Montfort would harm the crusade against heresy. But the pope also had to be concerned about the effect of the continued war and the disruption of the Midi on his projected expedition to the Holy Land. Although this aspect of the problem is not dealt with in our sources, it may well have been a factor inclining the pope toward the restoration of the counts of Toulouse and Foix. But the decision of the council to support the claims of Simon de Montfort closed this approach to the pope and ensured that the Albigensian Crusade would continue to engage substantial forces.

Behind these political issues lay Innocent's concern for the success of the crusade and his quest for internal peace in Europe, because these very issues were among the most serious causes of conflict in Europe at this time. By bringing them before the council, Innocent was attempting to build a broader base of support for their solution. His efforts were only partially successful. He had planned to bring all of the contending parties together at the council to resolve their remaining differences and thus to free them to devote all their energies to the crusade. It seems clear that he was willing to make some compromises in order to achieve his goal, but the fathers at the council were in no mood to permit him to barter away any of the gains that had been made against the Albigensian heretics or even to listen to proposals from the adherents of Otto IV. While the final decisions reached in these matters were generally consistent with Innocent's aims, they did not represent any dramatic breakthroughs toward the settlement of the conflicts. In France, England, and Germany, the situation after the council remained much as it had been before. The task of resolving the conflicts was once more one of slow and tedious negotiation.

Innocent did succeed in gaining the support of the council for a detailed plan for the implementation of the crusade that committed the clergy to a significant role in financing it. This approbation gave Innocent and his successor a necessary lever to enforce the financial commitments made by the clergy. The constitution, *Ad liberandam,* appended to the seventy decrees approved at the council obtained the force of law. For the first time since its inception, the crusade possessed a body of legal regulation that incorporated virtually all aspects of its program, as well as spelling out the obligations of various segments of the Christian community to support it. That this legislation had been approved in the council accorded with the most fundamental views of the period regarding use of the machinery of representation and consent to secure a binding commitment of the Christian community.

The parallels and differences between *Ad liberandam* and *Quia maior,* viewed in the light of intervening experience, not only confirm some of what we have learned from the study of the mission of Robert Courçon, but also demonstrate the incomplete and tentative character of the crusade plan outlined in 1213. Of course, much in *Ad liberandam* repeated what had been stated earlier or dealt with the more immediate task of fixing a date for the beginning of the expedition. If fixed that date for June 1217 and announced Innocent's intention of meeting with the leaders of the crusade going by sea in the environs of the ports of Brindisi and Messina in order to arrange for a sound organization of the army. Similarly, he planned to provide a legate for those who would travel by land. *Ad liberandam* specified a broad range of exemptions from taxation for crusaders during the period of their preparation for departure and while they were actually on crusade, and it forbade the collection of interest on their debts. But an agreement reached with the French hierarchy at the council limited the effect of this provision along the lines desired by Philip Augustus. This was the chief import of the reconciliation reached between the bishops and Robert Courçon at the council. The pope again called upon secular rulers to force the Jews to remit interest on crusader debts and enforced this with a prohibition of Christian business with them until they had complied. He also asked rulers to arrange a moratorium on debts to the Jews. He repeated his call for the kings, feudal aristocracy, and communities to provide expenses for a suitable number of combatants in place of those unable to go in person, with the provision of an indulgence according to the quality of their support, specifically referring to his previous encyclical letters, and thus to *Quia maior.* There were also clear precedents for the prohibition of trade in arms with the Moslems and for efforts to ensure the safety of the crusaders from piracy on their journey.

The most important new element in *Ad liberandam* related to financing the crusade. The pope had omitted any reference to a crusade tax from *Quia maior.* Instead, he had ordered the placement of casks for the collection of freewill offerings in the churches. *Ad liberandam* does not specifically mention the latter, though their continued presence and use can be assumed from a statement at the very end confirming a partial indulgence to all who would contribute to the crusade. It details, instead, both the freewill offerings of the pope and the cardinals and the taxes to be paid by the clergy. To set an example, Innocent pledged thirty thousand pounds, in addition to arming and fitting out ships for the Roman crusaders. He also allotted three thousand marks to the crusade that remained from alms given earlier for the support of the Holy Land. At the same time, the council unanimously agreed to a tax of a twentieth on clerical incomes for three years, with a provision that the pope and cardinals would pay a tenth. Innocent had thus succeeded in laying the financial cornerstone of his policy. But a reading of the text suggests that the final result was the product of rather intensive negotiations to ensure that the pope and cardinals would pay a just share. Still, the approval of the council gave force, especially by its inclusion of specific ecclesiastical sanctions, to the collection of the tax and promised thereby that it would be more effective than the tax the pope had enacted on his own authority in 1199.

Innocent's crusade plan of 1213 does not emerge in *Ad liberandam* precisely as it was expressed in *Quia maior.* There is no direct mention of the pope's advice to administer the crusader vow without respect to the suitability of persons as crusaders. While the conciliar constitution contains a provision for the redemption of the vows of such persons, it seems reasonable to suggest that the criticism levelled at the explicit effort to recruit them as crusaders had had an effect. Even more telling is the fact that canon three of the council reinstates the crusade vow for those engaged in the war against heretics. Innocent's effort to subordinate the Albigensian Crusade to that in the East was thus repudiated by the council. Is this one of the matters that came out of the conflict between Courçon and the French bishops and which was referred to in the nonextant letter described in an index of the pope's register for his eighteenth year? Very possibly this is the case. Courçon had visited southern France and had been involved with the Albigensian Crusade during his mission. Given the evidence that Innocent's views regarding the crusade differed from those of the French hierarchy, it is at least worth considering that Courçon's problems with the French bishops, which came to a head at Bourges in May 1215, arose in part from his effort to pursue the pope's policies vis-à-vis the Albigensians. In this connection it is interesting to note that Robert Courçon made contact with Count Henry of Rodez, the only important member of the southern French aristocracy to participate in the Fifth Crusade. Had Innocent been able to develop his approach unimpeded by the council, there would likely have been others. More important, he was forced to make concessions to the French hierarchy and to Philip with respect to the exemptions of crusaders from taxation. It is, therefore, not at all surprising that Honorius III did not again send Robert Courçon to France as legate following Innocent's death and that Robert's popularity remained high among the French crusaders.

Finally, Lateran IV expanded on the peace program briefly mentioned in *Quia maior*. In 1213, Innocent had viewed the peace program in traditional terms; the crusade was a substitution for unjust war and violence in western society. *Ad liberandam* also stresses the necessity of peace to the success of the crusade but goes on to fix precise terms for its enforcement. Peace is to be observed for four years. Bishops are charged with persuading those in conflict to make peace, or at least to conclude truces. The penalties for violation are the strongest available to the council. Those who refused to make peace would be excommunicated and their lands place under interdict. If they persisted, the bishops were to denounce them to the secular arms as disturbers of the work of the crusade. The experience gained during the period from 1213 to 1215 had made very evident how difficult it was to secure an end to internal violence.

In spite of these changes, the essential program of Innocent III not only emerged intact but was strengthened by the action of the council. Certainly this was the case with both the crusade tax and the peace program. His theology of crusade remained largely intact, though some features no longer figured prominently in *Ad liberandam,* such as the administration of the vow to unsuitable crusaders. But *Ad liberandam* was not to be regarded as a repeal of *Quia maior* or of previous papal letters concerning the crusade, as its text makes clear in referring to the grant of the indulgence to all contributing to the crusade in proportion to their gift. Despite significant setbacks, the program laid down in 1213 could continue.

ELIZABETH T. KENNAN

The Political Crusades

POLITICAL CRUSADING in Europe, that is conquest of territories or forceful assertion of power in the name of conversion and under the strictures of canon law, had a multifarious history in the twelfth and thirteenth centuries. We are all aware of the ambivalent motives of armies which conquered the lower Elbe and penetrated the Iberian peninsula, recruited and reinforced by plenary indulgences. There is no confusion about the human mingling of zeal and ambition which produced them. What is at issue is the reaction of two thirteenth-century popes to this state of affairs which both inherited, and the effect which their actions had on the course of papal history.

Innocent III and Gregory IX, two of the shrewdest lawyers produced by the medieval church, two of its most tenacious politicians, men related to one another and to the powerful Conti family of Campagna, these are the popes traditionally held responsible for diverting the great crusade into the narrow channels of European political warfare. On the whole, no one has jibbed at this attribution. Attempts have been made, particularly on Innocent's behalf, to justify the pope's motives and to palliate accusations of personal ambition. But no one has doubted that political crusades resulted from individual papal decisions. Papal theocracy, powerful and impatient, is accused of taking up the crusade to assert its own dominion in Europe.

The crusading issue is complex, for it involves at least two levels of papal intervention. In the first, the pope unambiguously calls a crusade as a preliminary to military action against an identifiable political enemy: Mark-

Reprinted from G. F. Lytle, ed., *Reform and Authority in the Medieval and Reformation Church* (Washington, D.C.: The Catholic University of America Press, 1981), 15–35. With permission.

ward of Anweiler or Frederick II. In the second, the pope may only encourage or simply tolerate crusades such as those in the Baltic, the Rhineland or the south of France, which bring tangible advantage to a third party.

Of the two, crusades against Italian rivals are easier by far to penetrate. Quite simply, there were no such crusades until 1240. It is quite true that Innocent III offered an indulgence in 1199 when, responsible for the protection of the infant Frederick II and for the maintenance of his claims to the kingdom of the two Sicilies, the pope failed to contain an invasion of German adventurers bent on the destruction of the boy and his regency. In November, when that army had conquered all of Apulia and was poised to sail to Palermo where the boy was undefended, Innocent proclaimed a phantom crusade against it. He first promised indulgences to any who would fight the Germans and then, almost as an afterthought, harried the Sicilian Moslems to his cause by threatening a crusade against them. But, once having asserted his position unequivocally, he dropped all further references to crusading and proceeded conventionally to assemble a ramshackle army and to play politics and time against the Germans.

It is possible that Innocent's momentary crusade in 1199 was inspired by the actions of his legate to the invaders, Cardinal Hugolino. In a dramatic confrontation at the monastery of Casimari that summer, Hugolino had by sheer intransigence faced down an attempt to bully the legation into ceding Frederick's rights to the insurgent Germans. Surrounded by a mob of German soldiers demanding political concessions from the papal emissaries, Hugolino alone among the cardinals coolly produced his instructions and refused to capitulate. His bravado won the day. Markward of Anweiler was frustrated in his attempt to falsify the papal position in Sicily and the legation was released. Hugolino's heroics at Casimari seem to have made a deep impression on the curia. The *Gesta Innocentii*, the official record of Innocent's pontificate, lionizes him for fortitude:

(The cardinals) were desperately confused and did not know what to do. But Hugolino, Cardinal Deacon of S. Eustachio, having taken up the spirit of fortitude, brought out the bull of the Lord Pope . . . and he said, "Behold the mandate of the Lord Pope. We cannot make it otherwise."

The lesson in the *Gesta* is clear: against hopeless odds, intransigence alone is a defense.

This is the lesson which Innocent seems to have been following in November. Faced with almost certain defeat and, temporarily, lacking resources for a counter offensive, he signified his intransigence with the promise of a plenary indulgence. The crusade went no further than that, nor, apparently, did he intend it to.

In fact, Innocent seems already to have developed a distrust of crusades which involved territorial conquest in Europe. In the same year, a German missionary party from the archdiocese of Bremen applied to Rome to undertake a crusade to Livland in the eastern Baltic where they proposed to establish a bishopric. Expeditions of this sort were, of course, nothing new in the Baltic: from Charlemagne to the Second Crusade, German hegemony in this area marched with conversion.

By 1180, however, German influence in the Baltic had been largely replaced by Danish. As early as 1171 the Danes obtained an indulgence from Rome to encourage them and their allies from Sweden and Norway in an attack on the heathen in Estland. This first offensive slipped by degrees into a Baltic war with commerical overtones. New Danish expeditions were sent in the 1180s and 90s and Estland was still subject to combined Danish-Swedish raids as late as 1226.

So strong was the spiritual hegemony of Denmark in the Baltic by the end of the twelfth century that when the Bremen expedition formed in 1199 its leaders sought Danish permission before setting out to Livonia. Once that permission was granted, the newly minted Bishop of Livland, the German Albert of Bremen, signed 500 men with the cross. *Then* he travelled to Rome apparently confident that the enabling indulgence was a matter of form.

He must have been somewhat chagrined by Innocent's response. Instead of carte blanche to conquer Livland for the faith, Innocent granted a carefully restricted commission. German crusaders were empowered to protect Livonian neophytes from heathen neighbors resentful of their conversion. That is all. They were permitted only to fight a holding action, more suitable to a garrison than an army. It could hardly have been an appealing charge to northern German adventurers and in 1202 the crusading army in Riga was replaced by a new military order, the Brethern of the Sword, especially created by Albert for his garrison. Behind their stockade, the Christian mission to Livonia entered a period of prosperity.

Innocent's intentions for the Baltic were further clarified in 1206–7. In the earlier year the Cistercian abbot of Lekno had travelled to Prussia, then in the hand of indigenous Pruthenians who were heathen, to seek release of some brethren held captive there. Perhaps it was his surprise at a mild welcome which made him travel next to Rome and volunteer to evangelize the Pruthenians. Innocent welcomed the suggestion, commissioned him, and provided for other Cistercians to accompany him. Throughout the rest of his pontificate, Innocent nurtured that mission, deputizing the Archbishop of Gniezno to regulate it, preventing the Cistercian General Chapter from recalling it, and, finally, creating a Cistercian bishop of Prussia from amongst its ranks to maintain it.

In fact, the only thing which Innocent did *not* do for the Pruthenian mission was to create an army to advance it. By contrast, he pressed hard for peaceful conversion using the least forceful of agents, contemplative monks. In contrast to earlier treatment of Baltic peoples he spoke of the Pruthenians in the mildest of terms, as recipients ripe for the Gospel.

And, to some extent, he seems to have been right. By 1215 the Cistercian bishop of Prussia, whose name was Christian, could claim startling success. Not only had a number of Pruthenian nobles converted, they had furthered the mission by a significant grant of land. In 1216 Christian travelled to Rome for a confirmation of that grant. But in his absence, a heathen reaction swept away most of his congregation. The issue of force was now raised.

Christian appealed to Rome for a crusade. The new pope, Honorius III, responded with crusading bulls for service in 1217, 1218, and 1219. In part his formula was an old one: crusaders from Poland and later from Germany already pledged to defend Jerusalem could convert their vows to service in Prussia. But beyond this formulaic beginning, Honorius, like Innocent III in 1199, severely limited the crusading commission. Crusaders were to be responsible exclusively to Bishop Christian. They were to do nothing to detract from potential (peaceful) conversions among those still heathen, and they were not so much as to set foot on land held by the newly baptized. Throughout, Honorius's intention was to make the crusaders the instruments of the mission, not its successors.

Whether because of these strictures or because the fluctuating host of a crusading army is not an efficient defense, the first Pruthenian crusade failed. Repeated calls for recruits had to go out and in 1224 Christian, like Bishop Albert of Livonia, abandoned the crusade for a garrison of knights, this time drawn from the military order of Calatrava dependent on the Cistercians.

Although 1224, unfortunately, did not mark a permanent end to crusading in Prussia, still it does clearly mark the end to an important phase of the mission effort in the area. Innocent III in 1199 and again in 1207 created a new Baltic policy based on restricted use of force, and, in Pruthenia, no force at all. When hostility from the unconverted made war necessary, it was a stockade war which both Innocent and Honorius prescribed. Crusaders were not to win territory but only to protect lives. Within the limits of the possible, these crusades were apolitical.

In the light of their Baltic policy, therefore, it is ironic in the extreme that Innocent and Honorius should be held responsible for the most political all European crusades, that against the Cathars in the territories of Toulouse and Trencavel. In the 1220s, Guilhem Figueira, poet and long-time imperial propagandist, made the case against Rome:

Rome, truly,
I know without doubt
That under a false pardon
You deliver the nobles of France
To the torture of hell . . .
Rome, may God give me no part
Of the indulgences
Nor of the pilgrimage
That you make to Avignon . . .

The poet was writing after Louis VIII's invasion of the Midi in 1226, in the name of crusade against the Cathar heretics. But it is in Rome, not in Paris, that he lays the blame. That he should do so is witness to the miscarriage of Innocent III's policies in the Albigensian war.

Military action against the Cathar heretics in Toulouse certainly presented opportunities for political exploitation. And it is true that Innocent repeatedly proposed the use of force against these stubborn enemies. But he did not, initially, envision a crusade. From the promulgation of the canon *De haereticis* in 1184, civil authorities had been bound to join the church in suppressing heretics and were liable to both civil and ecclesiastical penalties in case of failure. It was under this canon that Innocent first attempted to generate military action in the south. In June 1204, he invoked the aid of Philip II in enforcing confiscation and exile on barons who collaborated with heretics. This was to be less a war than a police action. In a letter of the following winter, the pope explained that royal intervention was necessitated by the failure of his Cistercian mission to win even the attention of the heretics. The cutting edge of the spiritual sword, he argued, must be honed by application of the temporal one, and the powers who protected heretics admonished by the loss of their gods. But, because of the great merit of such disciplinary action, the letter concluded, for his efforts the king deserved pardon of sins equal to that won by fighting in the Holy Land.

Technically, then, Innocent appears to have offered Philip a crusade to Toulouse in 1205. But the pardon was to be for the king alone. Innocent assumed that the Cistercian mission would continue and would still bear the burden of extirpating heresy. Philip's role was to restrain those who hindered the missionaries, and did not, in fact, exceed the duties envisioned by *De haereticis*.

In November, 1207, however, Innocent spoke with a different tone. By this time, attempts to reform the local clergy had stalled in the mechanism of jucidial appeals and in the general lethargy of local councils. The elaborate mission of Cistercians and Spaniards mounted to convert the Cathars was bankrupt and close to despair. In the face of their heroic attempts at evangelization, the numbers of the faithful actually declined, while the Cathars became more defiant and more violent. In the frustration of this deteriorating situation, Innocent proposed a full crusade. He wrote to the French king not of disciplining magnates but of suppressing monsters. There was no mention now of conversion or of support for a missionary effort. The heretics were no longer conceived even as capable of salvation. Instead, they were to be prostrated by war and subjected to truth. The king who fought them was to receive an indulgence and his realm was to be taken under papal protection for the duration of the war.

The murder of Peter of Castelnau, papal legate to the south of France in the ensuing months, of course, crystallized the pope's determination to bring this crusade against the Albigensians. In the series of letters of 1208 resulting from that murder, Innocent bitterly denounced the violence and depravity of the heretics and their protector, Raymond of Toulouse, whom he accused personally. The church's loss was now public and the crusade general.

But even in the fury of 1208 and 1209 when Innocent was fulminating against Raymond of Toulouse, he still took precautions to insure that this crusade would be fought for the aims of the church and not for those of its soldiers. He carefully avoided accepting the leadership of Peter of Aragon who had considerable interests in the area. Instead, he insisted on an army from the north which, at the outset, would have no policital interests to pursue. To lead it, he concurred in the choice of Simon de Montfort, a satisfyingly minor baron who could be bullied by papal legates—and who was.

As the war progressed, Innocent struggled to contain the political ambitions of the crusaders. The bulk of the army presented few difficulties; they were highly transient, spinning out a bare forty days in the Midi to qualify their indulgences. But Simon de Montfort learned to ally himself with the local hierarchy and even with the papal legates against the pope. Innocent could do nothing when Peter of Aragon enfeoffed him with the country of Carcassone after the fall of that city. But when the Council of Montpellier attempted to bestow on him the full territories and jurisdiction of the count of Toulouse, the pope refused to contenance it. In the face of heavy pressure from his own legates and from the bishops of southern France, he insisted that Simon could be no more than custodian of the Toulouse possessions. Permanent rights would have to rest on the outcome of Raymond's trial, to be held in conjunction with the Fourth Lateran Council.

In the event, Raymond of Toulouse was found guilty of heresy at the Council and a substantial portion of his lands transferred to de Montfort. But Innocent had succeeded in insuring that the transfer occurred through the offices of a disinterested ecclesiastical court, and not through conquest or gerrymandering. And, he had set a precedent in maintaining the integrity of a European crusade. As pope he called the crusade; through his legates he supervised the fighting; by a general ecclesiastical council he regulated the division of spoils. Insofar as possible, local political interests were kept under heavy restraint.

By the time Guilhem Figueira was writing his vilification of Rome, all these precedents had been overthrown. On the death of Philip Augustus in 1224, the new king, Louis VIII, moved to intervene in the Midi. The crusade he envisioned, however, was to be royal and not papal. In a remarkable letter he requested Pope Honorius III to resign the Albigensian crusade into his hands. The pope was to issue letters patent without further adjudication, stripping the heir to the house of Toulouse of all his possessions and consigning them unconditionally to the monarch. To direct the spiritual aspect of the crusade, Honorius was to create for the French Archbishop of Bourges a special legatine mission empowered to preach the crusade and to adjudicate all matters related to it. From his decisions there was to be no appeal allowed to Rome. But, lest the pope be entirely excluded from the crusade, Louis asked him for 60,000 livres a year to finance it!

In 1224 Honorius III was not willing to sell out. He opened negotiations with the young Raymond VII of Toulouse and allowed his discussion with Louis to drift. But in 1225 he began to relent. The legate he sent to France in that year, Romano Frangipani, cardinal deacon of St. Angelo, cooperated with the French king in staging a series of local councils designed to give an aura of plausibility to the royal plans for a crusade. Councils at Paris, Melun, and Bourges took up the Albigensian business and presumed to adjudicate the conflicting claims of Amaury de Montfort and Raymond VII of Toulouse. In January, 1226, a council at Paris, with the legate presiding, signed Louis with the cross, bestowed an indulgence on him and his army for a war against the heretics, and gratuitously promulgated excommunication against any magnate who might oppose him.

It was nothing short of a French coup d'etat. The crusade which Innocent had struggled to preserve from dynastic ambition had become the cover for the royal conquest of the Midi. Amaury de Montfort was forced to resign all his father's possessions into Louis's hand. Raymond's rights were held confiscated by the French council. And, in all this, the pope weakly concurred. The crusade which followed was a parade of confiscation.

In abdicating control over the second phase of the Albigensian crusade, Honorius III set a dangerous precedent. It was now clear not only that European crusades could admirably suit political ends, but that the papacy might be willing to allow them to do so. And, as Guilhem Figueira's broadside on this very phase of the crusade demonstrated, Rome would harvest the blame for local profiteering.

Local interests were quick to see a lesson in the crusading successes of the Capetian house. Within a year both the archbishop of Bremen and the bishop of Utrecht were experimenting with crusading indulgences to solve the military problems of their own jurisdictions.

In Bremen, the Stedinger, a cohesive group of peasants living along the lower Weser, had long resisted episcopal taxes and protested unfavorable leases. In the 1220's, they violently rejected all attempts to collect ecclesiastical dues. Archbishop Gerhard II, hardly a man to allow his rights to wither by default, responded with military force. In the winter of 1229 he sent his brother, Hermann von Lippe, with an army of knights down the Weser to break Stedinger independence. Instead, the archbishop's army was crushed and his brother killed. Gerhard determined not only on victory but on revenge. In March 1230, he convoked a synod at Bremen which condemned the Stedinger as heretics and placed them under ban on excommunication. Six months later he travelled to Rome to seek Gregory IX's permission to preach a crusade against them.

Gregory's reaction was guarded. He first requested the provost of Munster to attest the legality of the excommunication and the validity of charges of heresy against the Stedinger. Once satisfied on these points, he wrote to the bishop of Luebeck and two prominent Dominicans in the archdiocese of Bremen, asking them to intervene and recall the Stedinger from their errors. When nothing came of his peaceful initiative, he requested the bishops of Luebeck, Ratzeburg, and Minden to investigate the charges of 1230 once again. Not until October 29, 1232, two years after the original request had been made, did Gregory authorize a crusade. He empowered only the three bishops who had investigated the case to preach the crusade, and authorized only a partial crusading indulgence. In January 1233, he extended permission to preach the crusade to five more bishops in northern Germany. Not until June did he issue a general license to preach the Stedinger crusade and grant a full indulgence, equal to that won by fighting in the Holy Land.

Even authorizing it, Gregory seemed to have reservations about the crusade in Bremen. In March 1234, while the crusade was very much in progress, he approached his legate, William of Modena, asking him to settle the discord in the archdiocese. In August 1235, he cancelled the crusade. But by that time, the Stedinger army had been massacred and the survivors forced to capitulate to the archbishop. The political ends of the war had already been served before the pope intervened to stop it.

In Utrecht there had been civil war since 1225. Although alliances were diverse, the principal antagonists were Egbert, prefect of Groenigen and Rudolf, leader of the tribe of Drenther who lived to the south and west of Groenigen. Egbert was supported by the bishop, Otto II. When the Drenther besieged Groenigen in 1227, the bishop himself came to the city's relief. In July he led his forces out to meet Rudolf, having first granted them an indulgence for fighting. Perhaps he had some intimation of the outcome, for his troops were massacred and he himself martyred with peculiar brutality.

When the lords and clergy of Utrecht met to assess losses after the battle, they decided to seek an experienced warlord as the next bishop. The man they chose, Wilbrand, bishop of Paderborn, recommended himself to them for his service in the war of Lombardy and Sicily. Gregory IX must have approved their choice and their reasoning, for he translated Wilbrand from Paderborn to Utrecht. The new bishop committed himself as his constituency expected, to the defeat of Rudolf and the Drenther.

As much as the lords of Utrecht expected victory from their bishop, they did not provide him with an army. Support from the surrounding nobility though occasionally brilliant, was still occasional, and Wilbrand found himself forced to recruit troops among the old allies of Groenigen, the Frisians. In 1228, he enticed a group of them into service by exhortation and by "an indulgence of the lord pope." Their campaign, part of a complicated six-pronged attack, was successful, and by the feast of St. Martin, the Drenther were forced to sue for peace, while the armies disbanded.

Peace was not to last, however, and by August of the following year, Rudolf had retaken the strategic castle of Corvodia and the bishop was obliged to renew the fighting. After a year of inconclusive campaigning, perhaps pushed by a council of war at the cathedral in 1230, Wilbrand mounted a major effort to gather new forces for a decisive confrontation. He went personally, and apparently on his own authority, into Frisia, proclaiming an indulgence and preaching a crusade against the Drenther. The Frisians responded with a religious fervor which, considering their previous service for the bishops of Utrecht, could only have been naïve. Not only did free men fall in to fight "as true pilgrims" and "most special defenders" of their church, the people sent them off amidst an outburst of intercessions and processions.

In preparing so great a display for his crusading troops and raising such expectations, Wilbrand may have overspent his spiritual capital. The army was promptly defeated and that defeat struck not only at the military posture of the bishop, but at the spirituality of his see. All of Frisia was aroused over the issue of the bishop and his indulgence and there was some question whether he could make it back to Utrecht in safety. The scars of that disillusionment must have been deep, for when the Dominicans came to preach the crusade against the Stedinger in the hinterland beyond Groenigen in 1234, they were stoned.

The crusade against the Drenther was ominous in the extreme. It is impossible to know from the extant records whether the papacy had even been informed of these indulgences. Although the first two are described as "papal" in the Utrecht chronicles, this adscription may have been formulaic— or simply convenient. The indulgence of 1230 seems to have been initiated entirely by the bishop, though he certainly had no legal right to do so. He may have claimed authority from canon sixty-two of the Fourth Lateran Council, which recognizes the power of bishops to grant indulgences, but, in fact, that canon has only the most limited application: short-term remission of penance on the occasion of jubilees or consecration of new churches. There is nothing here which would justify an episcopal indulgence, especially a plenary indulgence, for military service. Canon three of that same council does provide that those who take part in a crusade against heretics are eligible for plenary indulgences. But, in Utrecht, there was seemingly no effort to establish that the Drenther were heretics. The *Gesta* of the bishops of Utrecht simply treats them as political enemies, though uniquely savage ones.

The Utrecht indulgences, then, represent another coup of papal prerogatives. The crusade which, until this time, had been initiated solely by the pope, was now usurped by no grander a figure than the bellicose bishop of Utrecht. In 1230 he called a crusade without any consideration of the legality, to say nothing of the righteousness, of his action. The Drenther were charged with no heresy. No papal legate supervised the fighting. No disinterested ecclesiastical court pondered the denouement. Wilbrand's indulgence was a gimmick. It worked a total, perhaps, of three times. But the third time it brought him into bitter disrepute with his own people.

As in the Low Countries, so in the Baltic, crusading in the 1230's became a tool of political aggrandizement. But here the breakdown of Innocent III's original policy was sharper and more poignant.

Within a year of the failure of the Pruthenian crusades, the Teutonic Knights, looking for a base of operations, approached the Polish Duke Conrad of Masovia for territorial concessions in Prussia including the lands around Chelmno on the Vistula. From Frederick II they subsequently received rights to whatever else in Prussia they could conquer.

In an attempt to forestall an invasion by the Knights with its explicit territorial ambition and its disregard of conversion, Bishop Christian seized the moment when the Teutonic Knights were in Jerusalem with Frederick II to form his own military order, the Knights of Dobrin, to take over from Calatrava. In 1228 and 1229 this tiny force (a total of about 15 men) began to establish themselves in southern Prussia. But time ran out.

In 1230 Gregory IX made peace with Frederick II and began receiving reports on the Baltic from his new legate, William of Modena, close associate of Hermann von Salza. The Knights used the moment to press their claims to Prussia. In an astonishing coup, Hermann von Salza persuaded the pope to abandon Innocent III's first principle in managing a European crusade: Gregory confirmed the territorial claims of the Teutonic Order at the same moment he authorized them to undertake a crusade in the lands affected. In his letter of January 18, 1230, the pope acknowledged:

Recently, our esteemed son, Hermann, Master of the Teutonic Order of St. Mary, proposed in our presence, that the noble Conrad duke of Poland had conceded the castle at Chelmno with its appurtenances and certain other castles in the terrritory of the Pruthenians to your Order in pious liberality, adding whatever of their lands you and your assistors could take. We accept that agreement with no little satisfaction, in the hopes that the faithful living near those boundaries who are daily exposed to the danger of death might receive timely aid from you. Wherefore . . . we urge you in the Lord to seize that land from the hands of the Pruthenians and we prescribe this for you and those who help you for the remission of sin . . .

For the remainder of the year 1230, the Knights worked to buttress their claims to Prussia. Further concessions were garnered from Conrad and even from Bishop Christian, and these, in turn, confirmed by Gregory. On September 12, Gregory repeated the terms of his January concession; five days later he issued an order to the Dominicans in Northern Germany, Poland and Pomerania, to preach a crusade against the Pruthenians.

It is impossible to know whether conditions had changed in Prussia over the course of 1229 and 1230. Was there new hostility between the heathen and the converted Pruthenians which would give substance to claims that the baptized suddenly needed military protection? Bishop Christian, as he made grants of land to the Order in 1230, did allow that their presence would be a useful shield. Beyond this, there is little indication of new Pruthenian warfare. More important than the military posture of these Baltic tribes, however, is the fact that Gregory himself made no attempt to investigate local conditions before he proclaimed the crusade. He was, perhaps, lulled into this laxity by the confidence of his papal legate in the Knights. More likely, however, his willingness to acquiesce in the extraordinary demands made on him by Hermann von Salza is a mark of his extreme anxiety to patch matters up with the imperial party in the wake of the treaty of San Germano. However that may be, his newfound relationship with the Teutonic Knights cost him the reversal of twenty-five years of papal policy in the Baltic. The bull which authorized the Knight's crusade stigmatized a people who had long been considered ripe for the mildest possible evangelization with ferocious and uncontainable barbarity. It then authorized their extermination.

Once the crusade was initiated, Gregory continued an active interest in it though he never investigated its local ramifications. His role was limited to recruiting on behalf of the Knights. For several years he issued a stream of bulls empowering and urging Dominicans to preach the crusade. But for reports on affairs in the fields, he relied solely on his legate, William of Modena, who continued to work closely and collaboratively with the Knights. Gregory had virtually no contact with Bishop Christian after 1231 and, indeed, when the bishop was captured in 1234, he may have believed him dead.

The crusade was devastatingly effective. In 1234 at Sirgune a combined army of Poles, Germans, and Pomeranians crushed Pruthenian resistance. The Knights were free to follow up their territorial claims. Dominicans, assigned to the crusade as its official preachers, moved in with them to replace the Cistercian mission. From 1234 to 1240, there was no mention from Rome of Bishop Christian. But, the bitterness of Gregory's last years must have been increased by a violent indictment of the Teutonic Knights and their Prussian crusade brought in 1240 by that bishop, now discovered to be merely captive and not deceased. Gregory reported Christian's comments in a letter to the bishop of Meissen:

We hear from our venerable brother, the bishop of Prussia, that the . . . (Teutonic Knights) remaining in Prussia will not permit the Pruthenian catechumens who wish to be admitted to the grace of baptism to be signed with the Christian symbol. . . . They have not been afraid to afflict those neophytes who have been baptized and who were bound by a vow of fidelity to the same bishop with a variety of tortures unless they obeyed them. Because of fear of tortures many others were forced to return to the errors of unbelief. . . . Beyond that, when the bishop was in captivity (from which the Knights did not take opportunity to release him), the same brothers with (other) newcomers invaded the episcopal church and the entire land of the see, and the city and castle of Sanctir in a hostile manner, and they despoiled them of all the chattels found there; they detained the episcopal rights, the tithes and purveyance and other rights pertaining to the episcopal table by violence; they abused whatever they could usurp for themselves against law and permission in the parochial churches and chapels . . . and in the institutions of priests and clerics, for the dereliction of that episcopal office.

It is a measure of Gregory's abdication of responsibility for this crusade that he had no way of knowing whether Christian's accusations were true or false. His letter to the bishop of Meissen asked him to do justice in the case, but it also asked him to ascertain the facts. The possibility must now have appeared to Gregory himself that he had allowed an unregulated crusade to wreak havoc on the legitimate mission of the Church in Europe.

From the vantage of the ruined Prussian crusade, we can finally consider what might be called Gregory's personal crusading adventure. And in this the first salient feature is his hesitation to employ a crusade, per se, against his enemies in Italy. In 1227 and 1228 provocation must have seemed great. Frederick had not only broken his own pledge to crusade in 1227 and jeopardized the fate of the other crusaders by lingering at Brindisi, but when he did sail for the Holy Land he left sealed orders creating Rainald of Urslingen imperial vicar for Ancona and the Mathildine lands, and stripping the pope of all rights in these sectors of the patrimony. In the late autumn, 1228, Rainald launched a two-pronged attack on Ancona and Spoleto, thereby opening a second front in Frederick's challenge to the papacy. Frederick, excommunicated since October 1227, threatened the pope's leadership of the Church as well as his special relationship with the Latin Kingdom when he sailed for Jerusalem in defiance of Gregory's orders. Simultaneously, his agents moved to shatter that territorial base which Innocent had so carefully constructed for the papacy in central Italy. Yet Gregory resisted Frederick's challenge by traditional means: a massive propaganda campaign was mounted against the emperor's person, and mercenaries were sent into the Regno to offset Rainald's invasion of the patrimony.

Gregory IX just barely waged a conventional war against Frederick and his lieutenants in 1228 and 1229. He considered the emperor, in his defiance of papal tutelage and his outright attacks on papal independence, an enemy of Christendom. And he certainly made the most of excommunication in his own counter attack. Not only was the anathema to provide a theatrical setting for stating his case against Frederick, it was also the occasion for releasing the emperor's subjects from their obligations to him. More daring still, Gregory encroached on the great crusade in 1228 by diverting funds from the clerical tenths designed to support it to pay for his campaigns in Apulia. Yet, despite these confusions of spiritual and secular means, Gregory never actually granted an indulgence for his war in Sicily. With a crusade already in progress in the East and Frederick himself in possession of Jerusalem, such a stroke must have seemed a monstrosity, and perhaps especially so to the man trained in Innocent's curia.

Defeat of the papal army in 1229 and a new conciliatory mood in the imperial camp made it possible in 1230 to negotiate a peace between Gregory and Frederick which lasted the strains of nine years of Italian politics. In 1239, however, under the pressure of an escalating campaign for Sicilian hegemony in northern Italy, that peace finally snapped. When it did, the pope once again attacked his imperial adversary with an intense onslaught of propaganda. Frederick was excommunicated as a signal for the papal engagement against him and agents were sent from Rome throughout the West to announce and re-enact the anathema. At the same time, Gregory made tentative overtures to secure the election of a new emperor. In quick succession, all of the imperial party in Germany was excommunicated and placed under interdict. But it was not until Frederick had invaded the papal patrimony and marched within striking distance of Rome itself that Gregory initiated a crusade against him.

Accompanied by a barrage of political mythmaking, Frederick moved into Ancona and Spoleto late in 1239, taking papal strongholds in his stride. Pausing at Viterbo, the pope's traditional sanctuary, he flaunted his control over the last of Gregory's sanctuaries and published his intention to stop next at Rome. With insulting flamboyance, he challenged the Romans to open their city to him and join him in making it, once again, the imperial capital of the world.

His challenge to Gregory could not have been more pointed. He held the papal patrimony and was on the verge of destroying papal rule in Rome. The pope, who had heard reports of Frederick's excesses in the north, might well have feared for his life. He certainly despaired for the independence of his office. Yet he was virtually a prisoner in Rome; German possession of his strongholds meant that there was nowhere to flee. He had no army; his allies in Lombardy were cut off; many of the cardinals seemed about to desert him; the Romans were on the point of defection.

Gregory responded with a gesture that was resonant of the event in 1199. In an event made famous to our generation by the prose of Ernst Kantorowicz, he rallied the Roman people to the relics of Sts. Peter and Paul and declared a crusade against the Hohenstaufen. The antidote to helplessness was once again intransigence.

Political crusades in the pontificates of Innocent III and Gregory IX, then, were invariably signs of papal weakness. When such crusades were fought at a distance from Rome they were almost impossible to control. Innocent III spent a great deal of ingenuity and even more determination to counter the centrifugal forces of the first Albigensian Crusade and bring it home to the Fourth Lateran Council for judgment. Gregory IX, with similar misgivings but considerably less forcefulness, tried to regulate the Stedinger Crusade, but failed. In managing a crusade from Rome, papal legates were more often a hindrance than a help. The legates at Albi in 1210 tried to give the whole of Toulouse away to de Montfort. It was the papal legate Romano Frangipani, who bestowed the second Albigensian Crusade on Louis VIII. William of Modena covered for the Teutonic Knights in Prussia so consistently that Gregory IX never heard of Bishop Christian's appeals for ransom.

Worse than the legates were the bishops who had their own political goals to pursue in crusading. The bishop of Utrecht's utter disregard for Rome, of course, is an extreme case. But the archbishops of Narbonne and of Bremen pursued their own ends under the guise of hierarchical obedience. In the light of their undeflected self-interest, the doctrine of *plenitudo potestatis* loses much of its sheen.

In the end the European crusades brought bitterness indeed. They were worst of all, of course, for the victims: the heathen of the lower Vistula, the peasants of the Weser, the converts, real and potential, of the Pruthenian mission. But not all the victims were direct targets of the crusaders: Raymond of Toulouse was disinherited as was, ironically, Amaury de Montfort whose father's spoils from the first Albigensian Crusade did not last even a generation. For Christian, bishop of Pruthenia, held from 1234 to 1240 at a ransom which the Teutonic Knights neglected to pay, the Prussian crusade must have been Kafkaesque.

But the ebb of the European crusading movement was bitter, too, for the papacy. It left exposed in its wake the outlines of a pervasive contempt for the power of Rome. Louis VIII manufactured his crusade to annex Toulouse and then informed the pope. The archbishop of Bremen requested a papal crusade but conducted his war against the Stedinger without regard for papal misgivings. The bishop of Utrecht seems to have acted as if the plenary powers of the papacy did not exist. And the Teutonic Knights manipulated the pope with nice calculation to the abandonment both of his training and of his principles. By 1240 the double-bladed sword of the crusading movement had been repeatedly lifted out of the pope's hands by others grasping for place and profit. The question now was whether it might not prove as dangerous to its maker as to its victims.

PART IV

Innocent III and Secular Rulers

CHRISTOPHER CHENEY

England and France

THIS PART of our study is concerned with the pope's relations with King Richard I and King John, and with some episodes of papal relations with the English hierarchy which were influenced by the kings. Innocent III's dealings with the kings were partly of the nature to be expected between two heads of State. From the point of view of an Angevin king of England, indeed, the connection seems to have been treated as the relations of two independent powers. But just as the Roman Church, *mater et magistra* of all churches, demanded universal conformity with its dogmas and discipline, so the pope, as pastor and priest, justified a concern with the internal affairs of the king of England's lands, with his treatment of the clergy, and with the personal conduct of the king himself. And even in the realm of international diplomacy the pope, while he sometimes occupied the role of an Italian temporal prince, had interests which transcended those of the Patrimony of St. Peter and mundane politics. His diplomacy was directed, in theory at least, to the common good of Christendom: peace, the union of the Churches, the Crusade. This being so, it is extremely difficult to separate one strand of policy from another.

If politics is the art of the possible, it still remains true that to gain all that is possible it may be necessary to aim at getting much more. The medieval papacy consistently asked for more, immeasurably more. This made its claims look unrealistic. The didactic preambles to many of Innocent III's letters made generalized claims to the authority of Christ's vicar, on the strength of which the pope proceeded to some particular demand for absolute obedience. But the basic strength was doctrinal and log-

Reprinted from C. R. Cheney, *Innocent III and England* (Stuttgart: A. Hiersmann, 1976), 271–74. With permission.

ical, not political. Doctrine and logic required the pope to write as though all Christians would rush to obey or submit at once when censured. To many this seemed exorbitant. Christians did not always carry compliance so far, and the pope knew it. So one problem which the historian faces is that of the relation between the pope's demands and his expectations in political matters. A further problem is that of the response his orders received. The sanctions which Innocent III disposed of when he uttered these orders were both spiritual and material: how can we hope to estimate their force?

Alongside the papacy in the world of politics stood the monarchy, always acting on the principle that its political authority extended over clergy as well as laity. To assess the strength or weakness of monarchy with the eyes of political philosophers is irrelevant. If the Angevin kings could not refute the logic of the papal position, they found an assortment of theoretical props in tradition and law sufficient to satisfy themselves. Most of the laity and many of the clergy were ready to calm scruples, if such arose. We have to estimate the force of incompatible principles of secular and ecclesiastical government in an area where all parties were obliged in practice to compromise. The organs of clerical and lay government had evolved in such a way over the past forty years as to admit of a measure of willing cooperation between the Angevin kings and the popes. The kings allowed English prelates to attend Roman councils and—with occasional exceptions—put no obstacles in the way of appeals from local church courts to Rome. They even acquiesced, to a point, in papal taxation of the clergy.

Previous chapters have shown how the crown might influence elections of prelates and limit the activities of church courts, although papal doctrine treated these things as the domestic business of the hierarchy. These were matters of 'ecclesiastical liberty' on which the papacy had to compromise in practice although it would never accept the lay principle. The attitudes of pope and king at the diplomatic level could not fail to be affected gravely by episodes in which the king challenged the right of the pope to control the clergy in his dominions. But each side had to recognize the interest of the other in their subjects. These matters of disagreement might arise irrespective of political alignments of the king and the pope. For the pope did not pursue one end only, did not only claim a place like that of a lay ruler in what one may term the European state-system. And his multifarious, sometimes incompatible, aims made upsets with the monarchy frequent and made it difficult for the clergy to see how they stood in relation to their two masters. The local clergy seldom regarded the king as the pope did. And quite apart from prejudice or predilection they could not forget that the royal government dispensed patronage and had the power to help and to harm in many ways.

Occasions for clashes of interest between the English king and the pope were frequent in Innocent III's pontificate. These have not unnaturally led to a supposition that this pope was determined from the first to humiliate the Angevin monarchy and that this determination coloured all his dealings with England. In a learned study published in 1904, Else Gütschow concerned herself above all with the disputes between king and pope. Her picture is of a deliberately pursued struggle between the two powers for overlordship of the English Church. The pope was consistently anti-Angevin, regarding Kings Richard and John as nothing but enemies of the Church. Gütschow practically stopped her survey in May 1213 with the dramatic collapse of King John's resistance to Rome, and treated his 'abdication' as a final and complete defeat. So it was possible for her to give a consistent and plausible picture. But when the years 1213–16 come into view and the details of normal Anglo-papal relations of earlier years are seen as well as the diplomatic 'incidents', the picture is different. The most striking episodes do indeed illustrate the principles on which papal claims rested; but those claims were not consistently pressed and provide an inadequate guide to the motives and actions of Innocent III in his dealings with the English king and the English Church. Particular episodes in which pope and king confronted each other—important as they were—are no more significant than the occasions when incompatible principles and mutual distrust were forgotten or set aside through force of circumstances.

The pope's dealings with England were part and parcel of his efforts to exercise his vicariate throughout the Christian world. There were times when royal encroachments on the liberties of the English Church alarmed the English clergy more than they excited the pope. He might well hesitate before taking a hard line with the king of England about his offenses against the local church when he saw him as the prospective leader of a crusade. He was moved to be patient when the affairs of the Empire loomed large in papal diplomacy and English support for the house of Welf was needed. Even minor troubles of the papacy in other parts of Europe led Innocent III to need cooperation from England in the enforcement of his censures. In 1198 he incited King Richard to penalize merchants of Piacenza for their city's outrage upon the papal legate. In 1200 he commanded the archbishop of Canterbury to refuse all intercourse with King Sverre of Norway, whom the pope had excommunicated as an oppressor of the clergy and of the poor, a murderer, and a usurper.

When our survey of the pontificate from end to end is completed, it will appear that Innocent III's policy was affected but not wholly determined by those views of his on papal authority which have received so much attention from lawyers and theologians. In politics he was a pragmatist. He responds to a situation as the moment requires or the opportunity offers. At all times he is ill-informed about England and can only make the best of the reports (usually out of date) with which he is fed by interested parties. Other parts of Christendom concern him more. The business of the Empire, the conquest of Constantinople, the heresy of the Albigensians—these were some of the preoccupations which usually pushed English affairs into the background.

Little need be said here of the policy of King Richard and King John. Their attitude to the papacy and Pope Innocent III was basically distrustful, as might be expected of sons of Henry II. Their interests were not the same as his. They had less concern with him than he with them. They were neither interested in his spiritual welfare nor affected directly by his territorial ambitions, but they could not be blind to his skill and influence as a diplomat and they were jealous of his authority over the English clergy. The letters they addressed to the pope (composed by skilled clerks) are usually bland and obsequious in tone; but the kings could be cruder in their expressions when they wrote to officials of the Curia or the pope's delegates. When delay or prevarication would not secure their ends they were capable of downright contradiction and stood on their dignity. There is little sign that they were personally affected by threats of ecclesiastical censure, but they were aware of the ways in which the pope's displeasure could be exploited by their enemies. So they treated him circumspectly, and King John's excommunication from 1209 to 1213 was unique.

JOHN C. MOORE

Sardinia and the Papal State

STUDENTS OF THE Papal State are understandably inclined to concentrate on those geographical areas in central Italy, from the Campagna to Ravenna, that were to become the more or less permanent Papal State of modern history, even though everyone acknowledges that papal claims and the reality of papal control within this region fluctuated widely throughout the centuries. Tuscany, southern Italy, and Sicily were sometimes claimed by the popes but not ultimately incorporated into the Papal State, and these areas also receive due attention from historians of the Papal State. But papal claims also extended to other areas less frequently discussed, among them Sardinia.

Sardinia has not seemed very important to scholars of the Papal State. In their fine studies, Daniel Waley and Peter Partner scarcely mention Sardinia, and it does not appear in the index of either of their books. Waley characterizes a papal claim to Sardinia (and Corsica) in 1159 as a mere protest rather than "a serious statement of papal intention." But in the fluid situation in Italy during the pontificate of Innocent III, the pope clearly thought it possible to bring Sardinia under his control, just as he thought that much of Italy could be dominated. This paper is intended to describe Innocent's efforts to establish his authority in Sardinia and to show how Pisa frustrated those efforts. Because Sardinia was tied to Pisa, because Pisa was part of Tuscany, and because Tuscany was claimed by emperors, popes, and the Tuscan cities themselves, the pope's efforts in Sardinia can only be understood within a broad diplomatic and political framework.

The histories of both the Papal State and Sardinia in the early Middle Ages are obscure. Under the late Roman Empire, central Italy and Sardinia

Reprinted from *Speculum*, 62 (1987), 81–101. With permission.

were part of the empire ruled by Constantinople, and the popes owned vast estates in both areas. As Byzantine authority weakened, the popes of the late seventh and eighth centuries began to develop the idea of an autonomous state under their control, and this idea was confirmed, in whole or in part, by their royal Carolingian allies. At what point the popes first claimed Sardinia is unclear. The first known instance of Sardinia's being included in a Carolingian donation is that of Louis the Pious in 817, but this reference is problematic. On the one hand, the document is a confirmation of existing possessions rather than a donation of new territories, suggesting that Sardinia had been included in eighth-century donations. On the other, some scholars believe that Sardinia (and Sicily) are later interpolations, since earlier documents refer only to Corsica where this one refers to Corsica, Sardinia, and Sicily.

If the popes did in fact control Sardinia during these early centuries, papal authority there did not survive the Moslem attacks of the eighth, ninth, and tenth centuries, and the island was thereafter ruled by four princes called "judges" (titles dating from late Roman government), who presided over the "judgeships" of Cagliari, Arborea, Torres or Logudoro, and Gallura. In the eleventh century Genoa and Pisa launched their offensives against the Moslems, and they were soon in competition with each other throughout the Mediterranean, from the Balearics to Constantinople. Much of that competition was focused on Corsica and Sardinia.

In the complicated world of the volatile and quarrelsome judges of Sardinia, marked by incestuous marriages, invasions, kidnappings, rapes, and murders, the Genoese and Pisans found alliances where they could. Sometimes they paid large sums to the judges for the privilege of exploiting Sardinian lands. Sometimes the judges borrowed so heavily from the Genoese and Pisans that they were forced to surrender their lands for direct exploitation. The stakes were high. Sardinian ports provided commercial and military stop-off points on the routes to Sicily, Africa, Majorca, and Catalonia; domination of those ports permitted Pisa and Genoa to threaten the shipping lanes of each other. Besides its strategic importance and its value as a market, Sardinia was a major source for grain, wool, pelts, hides, salt, and silver.

In the course of the twelfth century, Pisan influence in Sardinia grew. Acting as mediators between Genoa and Pisa, popes from the eleventh century on strengthened the position of Genoa in Corsica and of Pisa in Sardinia. In the 1090s Urban II made the bishop of Pisa papal legate for all Sardinia. In the 1130s Innocent 11 added archiepiscopal authority over two Sardinian bishoprics, plus primatial honor in the province of Torres. In 1176 Alexander III added primatial honor in the provinces of Cagliari and Arborea as well, though ten years earlier he had called on the Genoese to defend Sardinia from the Pisans. About 1190, the Pisans drove the Genoese from Cagliari altogether and installed as judge their own candidate, Guglielmo di Massa. Guglielmo was to remain there as the Pisan client—albeit one not easily controlled—until 1214. The Pisans also extracted a promise of submission from the judge of Torres, Comita I. They were unable to prevent their two client judges from waging war over the judgeship of Arborea that lay between them, but Pisa extracted some benefit even from that, since the bishop whom Guglielmo drove from Arborea was Genoese. By the end of the century Pisa had permanent "captains" installed in at least five Sardinian ports, and there was a sizable Pisan colony in Cagliari by 1212.

The ambitions of Emperor Frederick Barbarossa added another unpredictable ingredient. At one time he permitted his vassal Count Guelf to call himself "prince" or "rector" of Sardinia; at another he sold to the judge of Arborea the title of "king of Sardinia"; then he granted "the entire island of Sardinia" to Pisa as a fief, before later sponsoring a compromise, dividing the island between Pisa and Genoa. Even the king of Aragon had a hand in Sardinia: in 1186 he promised to help Genoa defend his relative, the queen of Arborea, from attacks by the Pisans.

Amid these competing interests, papal claims enjoyed little success. Popes Lucius II (in 1144), Adrian IV (in 1159), and Alexander III (in 1162) had asserted that Sardinia was a possession of the papacy, but to little effect. In 1188 papal legates successfully mediated a "perpetual peace" between Genoa and Pisa concerning Sardinia, but the peace did not last long, and its text said nothing about papal lordship of Sardinia. With the accession of Innocent III, however, came new opportunities. The death of Henry VI in 1197 and the anti-German reaction that swept through Italy enabled Innocent to reestablish the Papal State, and he claimed Sardinia as part of that patrimony.

Much of Innocent's energy during the first years of his pontificate went to driving German rulers from Italy and Sicily and establishing his authority over Queen Constance and her son Frederick. At the same time, though, he turned his attention to Tuscany. In February 1198 he wrote to the archbishop of Ravenna, stating his intention to restore "the Exarchate of Ravenna, the March [of Ancona], and Tuscany to our demesne, to which they belong." He did not mention Sardinia, but his claim to Tuscany was closely related to the question of Sardinia. If Tuscany, including Pisa, would become subject to him, he would have little trouble gaining control of Sardinia.

The claim to Tuscany and Pisa was ambitious. Tuscany is commonly spoken of as having two parts, the duchy to the north and an area to the south, ultimately incorporated into the Papal State, called Roman Tuscany, papal Tuscany, or the Tuscan patrimony. In the thirteenth century the northern border of Roman Tuscany usually included Radicofani, Aquapendente, and Lake Trasimeno, and its principal cities were Viterbo, Orvieto, and Perugia. Waley and Partner treat Innocent's claim to papal Tuscany as being reasonably well founded in law and in tradition, but they see his claim to the duchy of Tuscany as unrealistic and unfounded. Taken together, tradition and the Carolingian donations provided a weak foundation for Innocent's claim to ducal Tuscany. On the other hand, Innocent could find in the *Liber censuum* a description of a Carolingian donation that included all of Tuscany. Given the inclination of the Hohenstaufen to ignore altogether the terms of the donations, Innocent can hardly be blamed for making expansive claims. Hohenstaufen depredations and the new opportunities presented by Henry's death surely made Innocent's claims seem justified and realistic, even if they were to prove unrealizable.

The city of Pisa presented additional complications arising from its independent role in Tuscany, often in support of the emperors and in opposition to the popes. The death of Emperor Henry VI on 27 September 1197 had ended imperial domination of Italy, and about six weeks later, on 11 November 1197, the principal cities, barons, and bishops of Tuscany— but not including Pisa—entered into a formal agreement. The Tuscan League thus formed offered cooperation with the papacy, but certainly not submission. It was nevertheless approved by two cardinals present, Pandulf and Bernard, and it was in fact the product of papal policy. Cardinal Pandulf had worked in Tuscany throughout the previous summer to create a league to oppose the Hohenstaufens, and even the death of Henry VI did not lead the pope or the cardinals to press for Tuscan submission to the pope. Celestine's hopes were so modest at the time that rather than pushing for Tuscan and Pisan submission to the pope, he merely wanted Pisa to join the league, in alliance with the papacy. When Pisa refused, he placed an interdict on the city.

But the accession of Innocent brought a dramatic turn in papal policy. In early February he wrote a sharp rebuke to the legates, saying he found the agreement neither useful nor honorable, especially since it failed to acknowledge that the duchy of Tuscany belonged to the Roman church. He declared that the agreement was not binding and informed the rectors of the Tuscan League that they could form no valid agreement without papal approval.

Innocent's repudiation of the cardinals' commitment has been interpreted in a variety of ways, none of which seems entirely satisfactory. An uncomplicated and I think accurate explanation is as follows. The papal claim to all of Tuscany dates from the eighth century. Although certainly neglected, it was not forgotten; Celestine III included it in the *Liber censuum* in 1192 and mentioned the claim again in the last month of his life. He did not insist on Tuscan acknowledgment of papal lordship over the Tuscan League, seeing the league as the best he could do at the time, but neither did he abandon the claim. In fact his command that Pisa join the league suggested that he was claiming secular rights in the area.

Immediately after his election, even before his consecration, Innocent repudiated the league approved by Celestine and his legates and reasserted the ancient claim to all of Tuscany. He arranged to lift the interdict on Pisa, since he could hardly punish Pisa for rejecting a treaty which he himself was rejecting. The cardinals were to reopen negotiations with the Tuscan League, trying to get acknowledgment of papal secular lordship (this last point was not stated explicitly, but was presumably the oral message Innocent said he was sending with his messenger). Then the Pisans were to join the league or have the interdict restored.

For several months Innocent courted the Tuscan cities, including Pisa, but before his first year was out he learned that Celestine and his legates were right, that the Tuscan cities were not going to accept him as ruler. He accepted essentially the same terms the cardinals had settled for a year before and threatened Pisa with interdict if the city did not join the league. As was true with Celestine, Innocent's order to Pisa suggests that he had not abandoned altogether his claim to secular authority over Pisa and the Tuscan League, but he was never again to claim it explicitly, as he had done in 1198.

Although Innocent gave up his attempt to dominate all of Tuscany, he was not to give up on Sardinia. He never clearly justified his claim to Sardinia; but even more than his claim to all of Tuscany, it had a firm position in papal history. There were the claimed Carolingian donations. In the late eleventh century Pope Urban II had argued from the Donation of Constantine that *all* islands belonged to the papacy, an idea that was to surface occasionally for centuries thereafter. And several twelfth-century popes had claimed Sardinia for the papacy. Innocent was not characteristically unscrupulous in advancing papal prerogatives, but he commonly pressed them as far as he possibly could. He was usually able to find justification for any action he thought really important, and he could have argued plausibly that the papacy's legal claim to Sardinia was better than anyone else's. As it happened, however, his claim was buttressed more with assertions than with legal arguments, and no one explicitly challenged the validity of those assertions.

So far as we know, Innocent's first direct involvement in Sardinia was quite restrained and did not result from his own initiative. On 11 August 1198 he addressed a letter to several prelates in Sardinia, reviewing a controversy between the canons of Oristano and their archbishop. What seems to lie behind the letter is the invasion and occupation of the judgeship of Arborea by Judge Guglielmo of Cagliari, with Pisan support, in the 1190s. The archbishop of Oristano was Genoese and had fled from Guglielmo and his Pisan supporters. The canons of Oristano and other clergy of Arborea came to terms with Guglielmo and stripped the archbishop of all his possessions. The archbishop argued, Innocent said, that the judgeship of Arborea was held from the Roman church, and that Guglielmo could not take it nor could the canons of Oristano confer it without papal consent. Innocent referred the matter to the Sardinian prelates since he could not discover the truth himself, but he did not reaffirm for himself the papal claims on Cagliari or Sardinia as a whole. This surprising restraint is presumably to be explained by the fact that the letter was written at a time when Innocent was still hoping for Pisan and Tuscan submission, and he did not want to antagonize the Pisans by challenging their position in Sardinia. The archbishop of Oristano asserted that papal rights were being violated, but Innocent himself did not then pick up the theme.

A sign of growing papal interest in Sardinia came two years later, in October of 1200. The archbishop of Pisa maintained that his authority over Sardinian churches meant that the impending election of an archbishop of Torres required his approval. Innocent replied that he had searched the text of the relevant privileges and could find no basis for the archbishop's claim. Innocent warned him not to interfere in the election in Torres and told him to forward to Rome the papal census owing from Sardinia.

In November or December of the same year (1200), Innocent adopted a much more aggressive tone toward Sardinia. His letter was apparently prompted by a letter of Guglielmo di Massa, who had written to the pope to enlist his help in settling a difference with the judge of Torres. Innocent took the occasion to rehearse a variety of charges against Guglielmo, dating back over a decade, and he ordered Guglielmo to appear in Rome with the judge of Torres to settle all the matters at hand. Innocent asserted: "No one doubts, and you yourself recognize, that all of Sardinia belongs to the lordship, right, and property of the Apostolic See." At the same time he told the three metropolitans of Sardinia to investigate all the matters mentioned in his letter to Guglielmo, adding an ominous charge: they were to look into the legitimacy of the marriages of all the judges of Sardinia. The results of these investigations were to be forwarded to Rome. Innocent did not follow up on this initiative for two more years, so far as we know, probably because of his preoccupations with the mainland. But the order to investigate the marriages of the judges is an indication that Innocent was looking for powerful weapons to bring the judges under papal control.

In September 1202 the death of Markward of Anweiler delivered Innocent from his most formidable German opponent in Italy. The following December, responding to a letter from Judge Comita of Torres (or Logudoro), the pope began a prolonged offensive. The judge had sent a messenger informing Innocent that at some earlier time the Pisans had forced him to swear fidelity to the archbishop of Pisa. He had agreed to make war on the other judges and to expel Genoese merchants whenever the archbishop told him to do so. The judge was now clearly asking Innocent to relieve him of these obligations. Innocent wrote the judge and the archbishop that since "the judge holds his land, which belongs by right to St. Peter, in fidelity to the Apostolic See and to ourselves," an oath of this sort was improper and injurious to the Roman church. Innocent did soften the force of his letter somewhat. Instead of simply annulling the oath, he told the archbishop not to give any commands to the judge without papal approval—an odd, even illogical arrangement, perhaps aimed at placating the old archbishop.

About the same time the pope somehow arranged to place a trusted cleric from his own household as archbishop of Torres. Biagio was still in the curia in February 1203, signing papal documents as the archbishop-elect of Torres. Soon thereafter he was in Sardinia, and it is clear that Innocent had from that time on a reliable agent on the scene. On March 10 the pope wrote to the prelates of Sardinia concerning the murder there of the bishop of Ploaghe and two monastic officials. He criticized them bitterly for doing nothing, for being like mute dogs, and ordered them solemnly to excommunicate the murderers and to use ecclesiastical censures to force the judges of Sardinia to move against the guilty. At the same time he informed the archbishop of Pisa and his suffragans that he had placed the judge of Torres and his lands under apostolic protection, and they were to see that the protection was not violated. He mentioned specifically that they should restrain their "parochianos." Biagio had arrived in Torres and was doing his job.

Shortly thereafter, in the spring of 1203, came a series of letters to Sardinia. One to Archbishop Biagio conceded to Judge Comita of Torres that his dead brother and predecessor, Costantino, could have a Christian burial, even though he had died under the sentence of excommunication placed on him by the archbishop of Pisa (this concession justified by death-bed signs of repentance). Another letter went to Judge Comita. The judge had been acting as agent of the Pisans in enforcing payments from people in his territory, including clergy, and Innocent informed him that he should do so no longer.

A third letter reminded the judges of Torres, Cagliari, and Arborea that Sardinia belonged to the Roman church, "both in things spiritual and in things temporal," and that he wanted to restore peace there. He told them that he had charged Archbishop Biagio to act in his place and that they were to attend carefully to the archbishop's instructions and carry them out. The archbishop's charge had to do with the judgeships of Cagliari and Arborea and with the arrangements for the marriage of Elena, the young daughter of the recently deceased judge of Gallura.

A fourth letter required all the judges to swear fealty to the Roman church through Archbishop Biagio or suffer the consequences, probably ecclesiastical censure. Finally, a letter to everyone in Sardinia required them "to respond" to Biagio concerning the census owed to the Roman church.

In September 1203 the pope sent another set of letters to Sardinia. To Guglielmo di Massa, judge of Cagliari, he said that Archbishop Biagio had sent word that Guglielmo had removed his "relative" from the land of Gallura—presumably someone who sought the hand and land of Elena. Innocent commended Guglielmo for this contribution to peace and warned him to prevent Elena from marrying any "suspect person," especially Ittocorre, brother of Judge Comita of Torres, to whom she was related in a forbidden degree. Guglielmo was to follow Biagio's direction in this matter. He sent the same warning to Judge Comita. He also wrote to Guglielmo that Biagio had informed him of Guglielmo's refusal to swear fealty to the Roman church, on the grounds that he had already sworn fealty to the archbishop of Pisa. Innocent told Guglielmo that he clearly owed fealty to the Roman church. If that fealty was contravened by the oath to the archbishop of Pisa, then the latter oath was invalid; if it was not so contravened, then there was no problem about swearing fealty to Rome—which he was to do without further excuses. Innocent also granted Archbishop Biagio the right to take possessions from those refusing to pay a census owed to the church of Torres.

The following July (1204), another set of letters left Rome for Sardinia. Innocent wrote letters to Elena, heiress of Gallura (commending her for agreeing to follow papal direction), to her mother, to the archbishop of Cagliari, and to the bishops and freemen of Gallura, warning all of them to follow the counsels of Archbishop Biagio in the matter of Elena's marriage and telling the mother and the archbishop to send the bishop of Città to Rome to receive the pope's instructions. He wrote a similar letter to the judge of Cagliari, in which he also commended the judge for removing one of Elena's suitors, a Marquis G. Innocent stated in these letters that the deceased judge of Gallura had left Elena and her lands under apostolic protection, a claim that cannot be verified, but the deceased judge may have known that Innocent had carried out a similar charge well in the case of Constance and Frederick of Sicily. In several of the letters Innocent also expressed his intention to provide for Elena a husband who would not be "suspect" to the other judges.

Letters written at the same time show Innocent's efforts to support Biagio and to prevent clergy from being called before lay authorities. Biagio was clearly encountering opposition. The clergy of Sardinia had been refusing Biagio hospitality and expenses as he traveled about on papal business; they were ordered to extend to him these courtesies or he would, with papal approval, suspend them from their offices. Biagio was also authorized to take measures against the archpriest and canons of his church in Torres, even to the extent of moving them elsewhere and replacing them with canons regular. Furthermore, Biagio was told to respond to the archbishop of Pisa as papal legate only when the legate was in Sardinia, and then only at certain defined times. The following October, Innocent granted Biagio's petition that he not be bound to pay debts incurred by his predecessor if they were not incurred for the use of the church.

In another letter of July 1204 Innocent told the archbishop of Pisa to order the judge of Cagliari to swear fealty to the Roman church, something the judge was still declining to do on the grounds of his oath to the archbishop of Pisa. Innocent opened the letter, "Your fraternity is not ignorant of the fact that the island of Sardinia belongs to the right and property of the Apostolic See, and that its judges owe, and customarily take, an oath of fidelity to the Roman church." He proceeded sternly to a concluding warning that the archbishop might lose a privilege if he abused it. Innocent also instructed the judge of Torres and the clergy of Sardinia that clergy were not to go before lay judges.

The final letter in this series of July 1204 concerned the delicate matter of the marriage of the judge of Torres. It is clear that the fishing expedition Innocent had ordered into the marriages of the judges had brought to the surface a creature not easily landed. Innocent wrote:

You have informed us through your letter that the noble man [Comita] judge of Torres and his wife [Ispella] are related to each other in the fourth and fifth degree of consanguinity, and that they have shown each other marital affection for so long that they have a son, to whom the land is now sworn, and two daughters, one of whom is married. And since Ispella is the mother of the noble man Ugone di Bas, judge of Arborea, a scandal is to be feared if the marriage is now annulled. The couple, it is believed, will be displeased, since they have remained so joined since the time of . . . Pope Alexander. The judge, however, seeks this: either that he may with our permission remain with his wife, or, an annulment having been declared, he may rush into another marriage. The judge has said that he could then dismiss the concubines whom—since he has long abstained from relations with his wife—he is employing, following the depraved custom of the land. In the meantime, he claims that he cannot dismiss them.

Since, therefore, you are not in doubt concerning the law and since we are in doubt concerning the scandal, we leave the matter to your discretion so that, with our authority, you can do what seems most useful.

Comita's nonchalance seems to have completely neutralized as a political weapon papal jurisdiction over marriage.

In 1206 Innocent came as close as he ever was to come to gaining substantial control in Sardinia. In that year he tried to place his cousin Trasimondo as judge of Gallura by marrying him to Elena, the heiress of the judgeship. With the papal clerk Biagio in the archbishopric of Torres and Trasimondo in the judgeship of Gallura, papal influence would have been strong in the north of the island; and if Guglielmo, judge of Cagliari, were finally to be persuaded to take the oath of fealty to the pope, Innocent would have been very close to replacing Pisa as the dominant power in Sardinia. Just as the threat of German imperial domination might make Italian cities turn to papal control and protection, the threat of Genoese or Pisan domination might have the same effect on the Sardinian judges.

At the same time Innocent pursued even more aggressively his efforts to restrain the Pisans in Sardinia. In March 1206 he wrote not only to the archbishop of Pisa but also to the bishop of Florence, telling them to use ecclesiastical censures to compel the commune of Pisa to stop taking money and land in Sardinia under the guise of claiming what was owed to it, since it was in fact taking what belonged to the Roman church. He threatened the archbishop of Pisa in the strongest language to date, saying that he must absolve the judge of Cagliari from his oath lest he be deprived of his legatine commission over Sardinia—or suffer even stronger penalties— since "he who abuses his power deserves to lose his privilege."

Things did not go according to plan. Elena did not marry Trasimondo. She married instead Lamberto di Eldizio, a member of the powerful Visconti family of Pisa. Lamberto and his brother Ubaldo were related to Sardinian families as well and were the two principal agents of the Pisan push into Sardinia at the time. Lamberto took control of Gallura by marrying Elena circa 1206, and a decade later he invaded the judgeship of Cagliari and captured Benedetta, heiress of the judgeship, whom he later married. His brother Ubaldo used his position as podestà of Pisa to provide military support.

Lamberto's marriage to Elena was a serious reversal for Innocent; but in 1207 and 1208 there were surprising signs that Pisa had suddenly become tractable. A delegation of distinguished Pisans appeared before Innocent in Viterbo in August or September of 1207, offering to give satisfaction to the pope in the matters of both Sicily and Sardinia. The three messengers promised under pain of a substantial fine to try to persuade the podestà of

Pisa to compel Lamberto to acknowledge the authority of the pope and accept his commands in the matter of Gallura and the damages done to Trasimondo. They also promised to try to persuade the podestà and the city not to do anything injurious to the king of Sicily.

The Pisan delegation agreed to these terms partly because a new political situation had developed in the empire and partly because Innocent had probably threatened to deprive Pisa of its archbishopric. In the empire, the civil war between the imperial candidates Otto and Philip was ending, with Innocent switching his support to Philip. An impending peace treaty promised to leave Innocent in a very strong position, on good terms with both Otto and Philip, with Pisa left out. Pisa would not be able to stand up to a combined papacy and empire. This new advantage for the pope was dramatically displayed at a great gathering of officials of papal territories held in Viterbo at about the time when Innocent received the Pisan delegation.

As for the possibility that Innocent would deprive Pisa of its archbishopric, it was a threat he had used to good effect elsewhere, and the advanced age of the archbishop, who died in 1208, probably made the threat more plausible. In his letter to Pisa reporting the agreements with the Pisan delegation, Innocent alludes to the fact that the "matter of your archbishopric" was being dealt with in the papal curia. A year later, on 11 May 1208, Innocent wrote to the Pisans describing the agreement he had made with a new delegation. They had promised to give the pope satisfaction in the matters of Sardinia and Sicily. In return Innocent confirmed Lotario, the new archbishop, with all the traditional privileges of the archdiocese and gave him permission to absolve Lamberto Visconti from the bonds of excommunication.

With their new archbishop officially confirmed, the Pisans were more secure, and in the following month Emperor Philip was murdered, leaving Innocent's settlement with Otto and Philip in shambles. On 4 October 1209, after promising to respect the Papal State, Otto was crowned emperor. He then proceeded to violate his promises, taking whatever he could of the papal possessions and invading the kingdom of Sicily. Under these circumstances Innocent was much less of a danger to Pisa. His letters to Pisa and to the bishop of Florence on 22 December 1210 show that the Pisans had returned to their independent ways, but also that Innocent was too concerned about Otto's successes to press Pisa about Sardinia. Innocent paraphrased a letter from Pisa in which the Pisans argued that they prevented Guglielmo di Massa from responding in the papal court concerning disputes between him and other Pisan citizens because he was himself a Pisan citizen, with a home in Pisa. They assured the pope that they had no intention of injuring papal prerogatives, and that the pope's rights in Sardinia were not really involved in the case. They also requested the pope to restrain the bishop of Florence, whom Innocent had commissioned to look into the matter, and to prevent him from imposing a sentence of excommunication on Pisa. The Pisans had evidently written with elaborate diplomatic courtesy, but they were clearly conceding nothing. Innocent conceded nothing as well, again charging the bishop of Florence to look into the matter and report back to him, but he did not make an issue of Guglielmo's going before a Pisan court. He merely expressed his hope that the deeds of the Pisans would correspond to their words and warned them sternly that if they gave assistance to Emperor Otto in his efforts to control the kingdom of Sicily, they could certainly expect the sentence of excommunication. Otto and Sicily were now more pressing problems than Sardinia.

By September 1211 Pisa had broken completely with Innocent and was supporting Otto in Sicily. Pisa had long sought advantages in Sicily by supporting German princes, and in 1210 Otto had promised not only greater possessions in the kingdom of Sicily, but also advantages against Genoa in Corsica and Sardinia. Innocent wrote Comita, judge of Torres, and Ugone di Bas, judge of Arborea, that Pisa was sending a fleet to Sicily in support of Otto, that the Pisans had been excommunicated, and that the judges were to be prepared to defend themselves against the Pisans and were not to enter into agreements with the Pisans without papal approval.

The registers of Innocent's last three years are missing, but the few remaining pieces of evidence, together with the actions of his successor, tell us that things did not really change very much. Innocent managed to have Sardinia included in one of the versions of the Golden Bull of Eger, in which Frederick II promised to respect the possessions of the Roman church. A letter dated 26 November 1213 ordered the bishop and two other clergymen of Florence to protect papal rights and Guglielmo di Massa from encroachments by Pisans. After Guglielmo di Massa died in 1214 and was succeeded in Cagliari by his daughter Benedetta, Innocent achieved a victory of sorts when Benedetta and her husband Barisone swore fidelity to him, no doubt as an alternative to Pisan domination. But the Visconti brothers were soon in control of her lands and of Benedetta herself (widowed in 1217). Honorius III excommunicated the Visconti, but when Ubaldo Visconti died in 1231, still excommunicate, he still had lands in Sardinia to bequeath to his heirs.

Innocent's Sardinian policy was to be followed with remarkable fidelity by his successors throughout most of the thirteenth century. Like Innocent, Honorius III confirmed the archbishop of Pisa's legatine rights over Sardinia, but he sought to restrain the Pisans there, even trying to enlist the help of Milan to do so. In 1224 a curial official represented Honorius as papal legate for "all Sardinia and Corsica" and received a renewal of Benedetta's oath of fealty. Gregory IX vigorously pursued papal claims in Sardinia and had them acknowledged in oaths of fidelity from the judges of all four judgeships. But in the 1260s the archbishop of Pisa was still trying to assert his authority as primate and legate in Sardinia; he was still getting support in Cagliari; and the archbishop of Torres, just as in Innocent's day, was resisting with papal support. Finally, in 1297 Boniface VIII bestowed the island as a fief on James II, king of Aragon. Papal claims grew weaker in the fourteenth century and, so far as I know, disappeared in the fifteenth.

This review of papal actions in Sardinia leaves little doubt that Innocent hoped to incorporate Sardinia into the Papal State, even when he lost hope of controlling the duchy of Tuscany. His methods were essentially the same in Sardinia as in the Papal State on the mainland. He did not try to put Sardinia under the government of papal legates as was his policy in central Italy, because the legatine commission over Sardinia had too long been the prerogative, with papal approval, of the archbishop of Pisa—a problem that did not exist in central Italy. And he may have shown unusual forbearance with Pisa because of his continuing hopes for a successful crusade. But he installed Biagio, a trusted member of the curia, as archbishop of Torres to act as his agent; and he did all he could to strengthen Biagio's position, short of depriving the archbishop of Pisa of his rights in Sardinia, and he threatened to do that. When Innocent tried to place his cousin Trasimondo as judge of Gallura, he was following the same policy that was working well on the mainland. His brother Richard, besides being a mainstay in Rome itself, was granted the important Poli estates to the south; his cousin James was papal marshal further south and commanded papal troops in Sicily; and two other relatives were papal rectors of Campagna and the Tuscan patrimony. His principal agents in central Italy were relatives and trusted curial officials; he tried to use the same policy in Sardinia.

One method Innocent used in Sardinia, however, seems both exceptional and morally suspect: namely, his use of his jurisdiction over marriage as a political tool. As we have seen, he initially ordered an investigation into the marriages of all the judges. Then when he discovered an awkward situation surrounding a clearly invalid marriage in Torres, he backed off and left the matter to the discretion of Archbishop Biagio. In 1217 Benedetta of Cagliari mentioned that Innocent had legitimated her marriage to Barisone of Arborea, despite the fact that they were related in "the fourth and fifth degree of consanguinity." One wonders whether her oath of fealty to Innocent in 1215, an oath her father resisted for many years, was related to that dispensation. Innocent's handling of the marriage of Benedetta's sister Preziosa raises similar suspicions. In May 1206 he told Biagio to investigate whether Preziosa was related to Ugone di Bas within the forbidden degrees. Her father had told the pope that the marriage would be very beneficial. Innocent did not tell Biagio to forbid the marriage if they were so related; rather he was to report his findings so that Innocent could choose the most useful course. The next year (October 1207) Innocent bitterly denounced the archbishop of Cagliari for having permitted the marriage, which Innocent said he had forbidden. Innocent had little patience with insubordination of any sort, but probably he was especially annoyed in this instance because the archbishop's action weakened Innocent's bargaining position with Preziosa's father, who was refusing to swear fealty to the pope. It appears that the pope was willing to block marriages within the prohibited degrees if doing so would bring about matches more to his liking, but to permit them if it seemed politically useful to do so. Robert Tenbrock and Helene Tillmann have effectively defended Innocent against charges of this sort in other contexts, but his tactics concerning marriages in Sardinia seem less defensible.

The language Innocent used about Sardinia shows that juridically he thought of it just as he did the patrimony in central Italy. When speaking of territories claimed for the patrimony in the early years of his pontificate, he would commonly say that the territory in question belonged "ad ius et dominium . . . ," "ad demanium . . . ," "ad ius et proprietatem ecclesie Romane," or "ad ecclesie patrimonium," [These all refer to the lands of the church,] sometimes substituting St. Peter, the Apostolic See, or merely "the church" for "ecclesie Romane." As we have seen, this is precisely the kind of language Innocent used with reference to Sardinia.

It is also true that when Innocent was trying to be conciliatory, when he suspected that such clear, proprietary language would antagonize a power he did not want to antagonize, he sometimes avoided the language without abandoning the claim. When he granted Sicily and related territories to Queen Constance in November of 1198, instead of the proprietary language described above, he used the language of feudal custom: "nobis et successoribus nostris et ecclesie Romane fidelitatem et hominium exhibere"; "accedes ligium hominium prestitura." At the very same time he used stronger, proprietary terms for Sicily when writing to others.

Similarly, the language Innocent used at first when addressing Pisa and the Tuscan League seemed to be more circumspect than that which he used for cities he claimed in Umbria, the March, and the Exarchate of Ravenna. His letter to the archbishop of Pisa in March of 1198, discussed below, was full of concern for the honor and well-being of the Pisans, without a word about his claim that Pisa and all of Tuscany belonged to the patrimony. In October of 1198, he wrote to the rulers of Tuscany (and of the duchy of

Spoleto), saying only that "vos nobis et ecclesie Romane gratum semper devotionis et fidei debeatis obsequium."

When Innocent wrote to the Pisans in February 1199, reporting to them that the rectors of the Tuscan League had come to Rome, that they and he had come to an agreeable version of the terms of the Tuscan League, and that the Pisans were now to join or be subject to interdict, he still did not invoke the proprietary language commonly used elsewhere. Rather, he told them that they must join the league for their own good and for the good of the fatherland ("totius patrie").

So we need not be surprised that Innocent made little of his claim to Sardinia in the early years. In March of 1198 he wrote to the archbishop of Pisa, reviewing and confirming the archbishop's rights in Sardinia as they had been granted and confirmed by popes for over a century. He was doing all this, he said, "so that the Pisan church together with the entire people of that city may persevere together in fidelity and devotion to the Holy Roman Church and be daily strengthened therein." There was no word about papal dominion over Sardinia. But from late 1200, when he was no longer courting Pisa, he regularly applied the stronger proprietary language to Sardinia.

Just as Innocent's methods in Sardinia were similar to his methods in central Italy, so also were his motives. His claims to Sardinia were based on ancient documents and on the precedents of his twelfth-century predecessors. In pursuing those claims, he was in part like any officeholder who feels obligated to preserve the prerogatives of his office. Like most conscientious popes, he felt a strong obligation to defend the "jus Ecclesiae Rômanae." In this regard, he was unusual only in his energy, determination, and skill—and good fortune. He was very probably moved also by the high-minded ideals attributed to his "Rekuperationspolitik" by Michele Maccarrone. He no doubt believed that Sardinia, like central Italy, would be better ruled under papal authority than otherwise. His cherished goal of "libertas ecclesiae"—clerical freedom from lay control—would certainly have been better served in Sardinia under his control than under the quarreling judges, Pisans, and Genoese. The need for better government was evidenced for him by the murder in Sardinia of a bishop and two monastic officials circa 1200, by the resistance met by Biagio in trying to reform the Sardinian church, and by the pressure evidently felt even by conscientious prelates to accommodate improper demands from Sardinian dynasts.

Another motive for his policy in Sardinia, as well as on the mainland, was surely financial. His ideas of papal responsibility were expensive as well as expansive. Everyone in the Middle Ages expected rulers to finance their governments, at least in part, from their own estates and from the territories they controlled, and Innocent was no exception. How much income he derived from Sardinia is unknown. In 1224 Benedetta promised an annual census of 20 lbs. of silver for Cagliari, a very modest sum. But in the early fourteenth century the king of Aragon acknowledged that he owed an annual census of 2,000 silver marks for Corsica and Sardinia, a sum twice what was owed by the king of England for his kingdom. It does seem likely that Innocent's efforts in Sardinia resulted in greater revenues for thirteenth-century popes.

One motive operating on the mainland, but much less so in Sardinia, was the perennial desire of the popes to preserve their independence from lay control, especially from the control of Roman emperors. Emperors in Italy were always more dangerous to the papacy than Pisans in Sardinia. But his aggressive policy toward Sardinia also shows that his overall "Rekuperationspolitik" cannot be explained merely as a defense of papal independence in central Italy.

Innocent's effort to incorporate Sardinia into the Papal State was not entirely successful, but neither was it entirely unsuccessful. He inherited a papal claim to Sardinia and pursued it with energy and ingenuity. He kept alive the claim to Sardinia rather than let it fade, as did the papal claim to the duchy of Tuscany, and his successors gave their approval to his policy toward Sardinia by pursuing it for over a century. Perhaps he and they can be faulted for not seeing the ultimate futility of their efforts. But we cannot expect thirteenth-century curial statesmen to have foreseen that the papacy would never be able to hold its own against a major secular power, like Pisa in the twelfth and thirteenth centuries and Aragon thereafter, any more than we can expect them to have foreseen that the secular power finally to end the Papal State, leaving only Vatican City to the pope, would be the kingdom of Sardinia.

FRIEDRICH KEMPF

Innocent III's Claim to Power

FEW POPES have identified themselves with their office, have contemplated their power so thoroughly, and so insistently placed themselves before their contemporaries as did Innocent III. He called himself the successor, but no longer as the vicar of Peter (as it had been until about 1150) but the vicar of Jesus Christ. In fact he employed this terminology so constantly that the new title won official acceptance. The concept of vicar of Christ became central to his thought. It burdened him with a difficult responsibility, as he stated in a sermon, nevertheless putting him in an all-powerful position "between God and man, under God and over man, less than God, but greater than man, judge over all and judged by no one (save the Lord)." For the pope, as we read constantly in his letters, took the place of Him Who is truly the King of Kings, the Lord of Lords, priest forever according to the Order of Melchisedech. Such a global claim to the vicariate of the priest-king Christ could naturally obtain only in limited circumstances. Innocent was aware that the rights pertaining to him referred directly to the church, while he could exercise power in secular affairs only insofar as temporal authorities were willing to permit.

Actually, he was able to secure lasting results only in the ecclesiastical sphere. He thereby strengthened and extended in ideological and practical terms the jurisdiction based on the papal primacy that had emerged in the twelfth century. To this end, he made greater use than his predecessors of canonistic teachings on papal primacy. In the last three decades, the canon-

Friedrich Kempf, S. J., "Innocenz III," in Martin Greschat, ed., *Das Papsttum I: Von den Anfängen bis zu den Päpsten in Avignon* (Stuttgart: Verlag W. Kohlhammer, 1985), 196–207. Excerpted from 197–201. Translated by the editor. I wish to thank Kenneth Pennington for his help with the translation.

ists had based papal power in a more decisive way and also in accord with Roman imperial law on monarchical principles. For both Innocent and the canonists the role of the pope as monarch rested on the plenitude of power that inhered in him alone. This distinguished the pope—Innocent makes the point repeatedly—in an essential way from the jurisdiction of the bishops and other members of the hierarchy. For they are summoned only to a share in the cure of souls, while the vicar of Christ has been entrusted with the care of the whole Church, and for this reason he has been granted a power that knows no limits in the area of positive canon law. It reaches all believers, prelates as well as their subordinates; it gives the pope the right to intervene in legal disputes directly, without recognizing the rights of lower courts and, in fact, without being bound by the positive law, for as the highest lawgiver he can dispense with the law under certain conditions. In agreement with the canonists, Innocent pointed out expressly that the jurisdiction of the entire hierarchy in the final analysis flowed from the plenitude of power, for the pope summons all officeholders to a share in the care of souls. The bishops could therefore say of themselves in relation to the pope, as he once wrote: Of his fullness we have all received. This bold formulation must assuredly be taken with a grain of salt. But Innocent doubtless held firmly to the point that the bishops were successors of the apostles and could therefore have considered that his claim to summon them was based on power that stemmed from Christ. In relation to metropolitans, primates, and patriarchs he nevertheless did not feel limited by these boundaries. For him, their jurisdiction was purely human, even if it was based on venerable traditions of established law. How strong a position he took on the dependence of these officeholders on the Holy See is evident from his letters to the Latin patriarchs of Constantinople. There he once went so far in an allegorical explanation of Rev. 6, 7 ["when he broke open the fourth seal, I heard the voice of the fourth living creature cry out, 'come forward' "] as to see the Holy See symbolized under the Divine Throne and, for the four living creatures, the four patriarchs surrounding the Divine Throne, "to serve as helpers of the Master." How far these exegetical escapades impressed contemporaries is impossible to say; they were certainly the basic elements that achieved lasting recognition that Innocent set forth clearly on behalf of the jurisdictional primacy of the papacy and pursued energetically in practice, and only were freed from their one-sidedness by the Second Vatican Council.

The claim of lordship that Innocent raised as vicar of Christ extended over the internal ecclesiastical sphere and throughout the Christian world. This fact is as well established as its meaning is controversial. It gets to the question: Was Innocent of the opinion that the power not only of ecclesiastical officeholders but also of secular rulers flowed from the plenitude of power of the vicar of Christ, with the consequence that secular rulership also comes from the papacy, or did he want to grant secular rulers an autonomous power directly from God?

He had often made it clear in his letters and sermons that he claimed to stand over people and nations. That means, for example: "While princes have only individual provinces, kings only individual kingdoms, Peter surpasses them in fullness as well as in breadth, for he is the vicar of the One to Whom the earth and its fullness belong, the world and its inhabitants." And in other places he embraced an allegorical meaning, in which the Apostle Peter not only would be the leader of the Universal Church but also would be entrusted with the world. Certainly, here Innocent based his position on his powers as High Priest, but a power according to the Order of Melchisedech. What is at stake here is a unity of order. For the people of God, whose head on earth is the Vicar of Christ is called in Sacred Scripture—as Innocent occasionally points out in specific terms—to a royal priesthood. Although the dual function of the people of God would be understood as referring to two different powers, namely priesthood and kingship, these two powers were drawn from one another, and in this case Innocent's view approaches in an unqualified manner the notion of the superiority of the priesthood. As the moon receives its light from the sun, so the royal power obtains its brightness from the authority of the High Priesthood, and this brightness increases or diminishes to the degree that monarchy reflects the High Priesthood or distances itself from its sight. What Innocent brings out here and in other places as an elaboration of traditional ideas had been formulated in a very general and unclear way. It contains too much rhetoric, as we recognize when he puts forward his relationship to secular powers in concrete terms.

He had taken a position on this question only when he had to justify particular political initiatives. His utterances reveal noticeably different positions. On the one hand, the pope claimed particular rights even in secular affairs; on the other, he recognized autonomous rights of kingship. For example, following an appeal from John I of England, Innocent desired to hand down a judgment about the war which Philip Augustus of France had launched against John. Philip rejected it on the ground that this matter concerned a dispute over a fief and feudal law was no concern of the pope. He defended his intervention in the decretal, "Novit," with a claim to be able, indeed to be required, to judge in matters of sin. He conceded, however, that in questions of feudal law not he but the French king would be competent to judge. With that he lost the opportunity to bring his involvement to a successful conclusion. For the fact as to whether or not there was a sin involved in this case depended primarily on a question of feudal law. In the conflict over the German throne, he bound himself by a self-imposed limit. Challenged by the protest of the supporters of Philip of Swabia against his decision in favor of Otto IV, he claimed in the decretal "Venerabilem" an authoritative voice in a disputed election for the German imperial throne, but recognized that the election of the German king was the right of the German princes, and he had to watch helplessly as the Hohenstaufen princes set aside his decision in favor of Otto on the basis of their electoral right and led their candidate to victory.

It is more difficult to interpret a third pronouncement, namely, the decretal "Per venerabilem." It takes up the question whether the pope has the right to legitimize illegitimate children in the secular sphere. Innocent decided thus: he would not have the right if the petitioner (in this case, the count of Montpellier) was subject to a secular Lord, but he would be able to if the petitioner (in this instance, the king of France) recognized no higher secular power. For the pope exercises secular jurisdiction on an occasional basis under certain circumstances even outside the States of the church. Indeed, as found in the Old and New Testaments, he exercises this jurisdiction on the strength of his High Priesthood according to the Order of Melchisedech. One may turn to the Apostolic See in all difficult, not otherwise solvable cases.

This decretal has become a problem for both medieval and modern interpreters on account of its unclear formulation of ideas. In whatever way it might be explained, Innocent can only have thought about such exceptional cases that secular rulers would or could not resolve, thus placing the Holy See in a subsidiary role, to be asked for by those involved (at least by one of the parties). Although the decretal may also have an important place in the thought of Innocent III, its practical significance was slight. Yet he assumed the willingness of the secular princes to make concessions. The claim of the pope to lead the world as vicar of Christ and the far-reaching recognition of the claims to autonomy of secular rulers—how do they go together? Were the political ideas of Innocent III in the final analysis hierocratic or dualistic? The research of the last decades has debated this question in a lively fashion. Although the discussion is still not concluded, it has been recognized that the hierocratism-dualism confrontation misstates the problem. It might be much more worthwhile to pose a genuine polarity, emphasizing the tension between two poles in order to unify the tension between two positions that scholars have taken with equal seriousness. The vicariate of Christ, insofar as Innocent gave it meaning in the secular sphere, was supported ideologically by the papal primacy and in practical terms by a series of concrete rights that had come into the hands of the papacy since the Gregorian reform and were taken up by Innocent and broadened as far as possible. These rights were chronologically limited and of doubtful worth as the autonomy of secular powers increased. Innocent knew this and handled it appropriately. He took advantage of all possible legal arguments that were granted him for leading the Christian world. He took it seriously if a ruler resisted his claim, and sought in cases of conflict a solution that was just to both sides. To this elasticity we must credit his deep insight into the limits of his spiritual-political claims to lead, with the result that—in spite of many setbacks—he reached a position of political power that exceeded that of his predecessors and that his successors would not surpass, because they lost sight of political realities and made the mistake of pursuing a rigid hierocratism.

HELENE TILLMANN

The Man

IN AUGUST 1202, Innocent stopped for a while in Subiaco. We have a happy find by Karl Hampe to thank for a description of this sojourn. It is a letter which a higher official of the curia, but not a cardinal, wrote from Subiaco to an absent colleague. The report makes a witty but genuinely perceptive complaint about the hardships there, to which the curia was exposed under the hot sun of Subiaco. Above the sea, enclosed by rugged, gloomy mountains, lay the place where the tents for the pope, the officials of the curia, and the baggage were pitched. On the south side, the cook had set up his smoky tent. The wrangling of the kitchen help over tallow and grease continually resounded. On the east, the apothecary held his flasks of urine up to the heavens in the morning, while all day long he disturbed his surroundings by the unpleasantly monotonous pounding of his mortar. On the north, the crowd of buyers and sellers streamed to market in the early morning. Their wrangling and crying put an end to sleep. The members of the curia were tired, and they remained tired all day. Often the pope, whose shabby tent was pitched on the west side, saw his fellow worker sleeping over his work. In spite of the cool breeze from the sea, the heat was hard to bear. From sunrise on, the gnats, whose hum itself was a torture, harassed them; from early morning the song of the cicadas disturbed their sleep. Night brought the chirping of the crickets to the despair of sensitive nerves. No less did the groans and wailing of those lying all round oppress them. On the other hand, the view of the sea was magnificent. The chaplains frequently refreshed themselves in its cool water so that they seemed to live like fish. The letter-writer described the sea as, for

From Helene Tillmann, *Papst Innocenz III* (Bonn: Ludwig Rohrscheid Gmbh., 1954), 233–42; 255–57. By permission of the publisher. Translated by the editor.

the most part, a tantalizing torture; he was afraid of the neck-breaking descent and the exhausting re-ascent, which blotted out of his memory the pleasures that the sea held out.

Innocent experienced hardships in the provisional camp under the hot sun of Subiaco that were hardly less than those of the letter-writer. We know that he had to forego mass and preaching in Monte Cassino on account of the increasing sultriness brought to the point of intolerability by the crowd of people. The summer months were always extremely critical for his generally poor health. For that reason, he spent them outside of Rome when no special demands made his presence in the city necessary. In Subiaco, Innocent was able to escape many hardships behind the protective walls of the monastery. But he wanted to share them openly with his retinue and perhaps he did not wish to be a burden to the monastery. In his modest simplicity, defying the hardships of the place and of the season, he was content with a shabby tent or a simple hut; he did not desire any special regard from his companions, but took the buzzing, crying, and groaning with apparent patience. The members of the curia could flee to him if the torture of the heat became unbearable. In the words of the letter-writer, they forced him, like themselves, to rest from work and, sitting intimately at his feet in stimulating conversation, they forgot the summer torture.

Thus, Innocent does not stand before us as a man unapproachable in his sense of the dignity of his office and in his consciousness of the oppressive burden of his responsibilities. The letter-writer, with a smile of intimacy yet in the respectful language of the curia, speaks also of Innocent as the third Solomon, our most reverend father, the successor of the prince of the apostles and the representative of Jesus Christ, the spring of all living waters, to whom have been allotted the treasures of all wisdom and eloquence. He also discovers important trifles about the pope; the third Solomon likes to live on islands in the sea and, therefore, he is not afraid of the dangerous descent and the exhausting ascent as the writer is. He dips his "holy hands" into the water and uses it as a refreshing gargle. When the writer tells us that he consulted the physician for a sick friend, he does not neglect to add that the third Solomon also esteems the doctor. Visitors to the curia, like the letter-writer, confirm the fact of Innocent's affable, humanly simple nature and his amiability. A monk from the monastery of St. Andrew, near Boulogne, relates with still happy memory the story of his audience with the pope. He approached Innocent when he was just awaking from his afternoon nap and still free of business. Just as the monk was kneeling down, Innocent called him, greeted him with a kiss, and, after finishing his business, told about his visit to the monastery of St. Andrew, whose hospitality he had enjoyed when he had made a pilgrimage to the tomb of St. Thomas of Canterbury while he was a student in Paris. During the Christmas season, Innocent twice sent game to the monk Thomas Marleberg of Evesham. It was not the first time that the pope did small favors for strangers who spent some time at the curia. His pleasant nature was revealed by his attendance at the tournament held in his honor by the men of Ceccano while he was on a trip to the southern borders of the papal state and by the way he enjoyed the sport of the young men in Viterbo, as it is reported. In the vivid description of Gerald of Wales, the famous writer who visited the curia, Innocent appears in the same kind and humanly simple way. Once, on an outing to Fonte Vergine, Innocent talked with him for a long time both seriously and in a humorous vein. He laughed heartily about the rough way in which Gerald indicted for slander a monk who thought Gerald had stolen his horse. Gerald even wants us to believe that Innocent joined him and the cardinals in making fun of the poor Latin and lack of theological education of Hubert Walter, the archbishop of Canterbury, who opposed him in a lawsuit. Undoubtedly, the gentleman from Wales is lying here, as he was in his dispute with the archbishop; those remarks he later retracted as mostly gossip. Innocent could not forget the special dignity and consideration due an outstanding member of the episcopate. Social frivolity certainly did not mean that one could let oneself go completely. He possessed a definite sense of what was fitting and proper. When, after the death of Pope Celestine III, some of the cardinals fled the Lateran to find greater safety in the Septizonium for the preparations for the new election, he was one of the cardinals who remained until the end in the Lateran in order to participate in the funeral of the pope. Feelings of personal intimacy were not important in influencing him to do this, for he was never, by any means, close to the deceased. We learn that now and then Innocent had the cross carried before him as he took a walk; he did not, therefore, try to escape the obligations to which he was bound as holder of his high office, even while he was relaxing. Gerald might be right in his assumption that it was hard for Innocent to hide his smile at Gerald's witty but malicious pranks. Innocent liked to have the company of this intelligent fellow, but did not take him too seriously because of his boundless vanity and his imperturbable cockiness, as well as the almost childish manner in which he displayed both. Gerald himself noticed once how Innocent, shaking his head at Gerald's speech, cast a smile at Cardinal Hugolino, who was seated at his side.

Gerald is not the only one who recorded the happy trait of wit and humor in the character of the pope. A visitor to the curia observed how Innocent turned in the middle of official business to tell a joke in Italian. Once when a proctor complained that his opponents had stolen his lawyers, Innocent answered with a smile that no one ever lacked legal advisers at the Roman curia. O what a happy event! he supposedly exclaimed when he heard the news that Archbishop John of Trier, whose vacillation did not permit him to attend the court of the Hohenstaufen or to stay away, had fallen from his horse. Even if it is only an anecdote, it confirms, as does another told by Salimbene, the view of the pope's humor held by contemporaries and by posterity. The Franciscan reports the amusing conversation of the pope with a witty fellow, whom Innocent answered in the same poor Latin in which he had been addressed, and he adds that the pope was a man who sometimes permitted himself joy among his sorrows. Now and then, Innocent's sense of humor was expressed in the more biting form of irony. He wanted to give the Bishop of Fiesole a chance to find out if he could, as he boasted, bribe the pope to forgive him. "Look here, Adam was created like one of us . . ." he stated ironically when the Bishop of Penne forgot, on his promotion, that he was bound to follow a simple life especially since he was a Cistercian. At the same time he reminded him of the words of Genesis, "I am sorry for having created man." Innocent did not consider it irony, but a kind of joke, when in his chambers he once addressed Gerald of Wales—who was working at the curia for recognition of his election to the bishopric of St. David's and also for metropolitan status for the diocese—as elect of St. David's and at another time as archbishop.

The Welsh author, to whom we owe so many exciting details of Innocent's private life, also furnishes particulars about the pope's interests. Once when poems were recited in honor of the pope and in his presence, Gerald received the most applause for his poem. It is not a false generalization to assume that the recitation of poetry or readings from scripture were a part of the social program at the papal court. Innocent was well acquainted with classical literature and had some notion of the grandeur of Greek culture. For him, Athens was the city from which much learning streamed out to almost every corner of the world, the city with a brilliant name and of complete beauty, the city which first taught the art of philosophy and which brought forth poets, the mother of all the arts, the city of learning. He had at least some knowledge of Greek.

It is significant that Gerald, who was extraordinarily well read and looked down arrogantly on others because of his own educational background and learning, acknowledged the breadth of the pope's reading and praised him as a lover of literature, and not merely of theology. We can also believe the contemporary biographer of the pope when he stresses the pope's education in secular matters. Gerald often had occasion to talk with Innocent. On one visit to the curia, he presented him with six of his writings. As the author proudly relates, Innocent had them lying beside his bed for nearly a month. The pope pointed out the fine points of style and content to the cardinals who visited him and finally lent them out to them one by one. He did not want to give up one work, the *Gemma Ecclesiastica*, however. Certainly Gerald exaggerated—because of his vanity as an author—but in fact the exciting works, namely the topography and conquest of Ireland along with the *Gemma,* must have interested the brilliant mind of the pope. It is a proof of the pontiff's noble impartiality that he enjoyed a book such as the *Gemma Ecclesiastica* or allowed himself to receive it with a smile. A lesser mind would have taken offense at the writing. The author expressed doubts about coercing the clergy to be celibate, repeated, in the midst of attacks on the worldly possessions of the church, the legend that the devil had exclaimed triumphantly on the day of the Donation of Constantine: "I have injected a poison into the church," and hinted at the immoderate financial burden of prelates because of their expenses at the curia and for the cardinals, their relatives, and legates.

The close connections of the pope with the Universities of Paris and Bologna testify to his lively interest in learning. His historical knowledge and his high critical ability appear to us as remarkable for his time. He had probably acquired this knowledge in part while studying in the papal archives. He was able to train his critical faculties and his then rare sense of historical development and use them for the comparison of source materials, an opportunity which the curia offered in a unique manner.

Innocent III had as keen an appreciation of the plastic arts as he did of literature and poetry. He had added a peristyle to the church of SS. Sergius and Bacchus, reconstructed by him during his years as a cardinal. He also undertook extensive alterations in the Lateran and Vatican palaces. The hospital of the Holy Spirit was rebuilt by him and, in the name of his brother, Richard of Segni, the huge tower later called the *Torre dei Conti* was erected. The hospital and the tower were praised by later generations as masterpieces. When an earthquake destroyed the tower in the time of Petrarch, the poet lamented the collapse of this unique building. Innocent had the mosaics in the ceiling of the apse of St. Peter's renovated and had his portrait put in—this reminds us of the popes of the Renaissance. He donated valuable products of the goldsmith's art, illustrated books, and embroidery to churches within and outside of Rome, or he contributed to their restoration and structural embellishment. In the judgment of experts, he united Roman majesty and aesthetic sensitivity to the best effect in the execution of his papal bulls. The "E" in the *Ego* of the papal signature and the small cross done by the pope himself are outstanding because of their beautiful clear lines. The same fine perception of forms and sureness and firmness of line already distinguished the signature of the cardinal-deacon of SS. Sergius and Bacchus.

This picture of the rich and varied personality of Innocent III is complete with the discovery that he was an able singer and wrote songs well and that his ear was sensitive to dissonant voices and harsh sounds. . . .

History has denied Innocent III its highest distinction, the title of great. Decisions of this kind are irrevocable. Would we appeal if it were possible? Must not the fact that Innocent III led the spiritual and temporal power of the medieval papacy to its highest point and that he, unlike his successor, had put substance in his claims ensure him of the claim to commanding greatness?

He performed in a commanding manner when he strengthened the papacy in the new papal states and in its feudal vassal-state of Sicily in the face of historical events. That his successors in great part weakly surrendered this strength, which like all strength was a relative thing, did not diminish the accomplishment of Innocent III. His efforts for church freedom and his work of reform, as well as the protection and promotion he gave the pathbreaking Catholic poverty movement, are witnesses for his spiritual greatness. If the Catholic Church had nothing else to thank Innocent for than this protection and the issuance of a doctrine which still binds the church today, i.e., to receive the sacrament of the Eucharist at least once a year, the great significance of his pontificate for the development of Christian life in the church would be assured. Innocent's rule has become distinguished for the further spread of canon law. It marked a turning point in the history of Germany, England, Italy, and France. The preparation of two crusades was an important, if in the final analysis, fruitless, accomplishment. And the man on whose shoulders the burden of work, worry, and the accountability lay, who was surrounded by the events and decisions of his pontificate, was a man in poor health, who more than once in the eighteen years of his pontificate had been extremely ill. The establishment and preservation of papal rule in Rome and the states of the church, the work of strengthening the Patrimony, and the papal regency in Sicily put an endlessly exhausting and grinding round with a thousand problems and a thousand often malicious impediments in the way. The ordinary problems of administration and jurisdiction would have been almost enough of a strain, given the conscientious attention with which Innocent discharged them. In less important matters, too, no real decision could be made by the chancery without his knowledge. He drew up his own letters, insofar as they were not purely formal, either completely or for the most part.

The faculty for sharply critical thought and for strong and determined action as well as a high degree of feeling for his limitations attest to Innocent's statesmanlike and human talents. He set clear goals for himself and held them fixedly before his eyes, but he was to a great degree flexible in the selection of ways and the preparation of means. Fundamentally conservative, he did not slam the door on fruitful new things, and he himself also pioneered new paths. He united the knowledge of duty, need, and the idealistic goal to a calm sense of the true, the possible, and the attainable.

Posterity, which refused Innocent the title of great, might take it into account that, he, with all the foresight with which he worked for the future, was still not always able to rise above his time and its immediate circumstances. The not unmerited failures of his policy in the Fourth Crusade and on the question of the union of the churches or the ambiguity of his position with respect to the crusade against heresy could possibly be an objection to his acceptance as a commanding historical and personal great.

Ideas of such kind, however, can hardly explain why Innocent does not live on in history as a great. The personality of a pope should not be evaluated only by the measure of his greatness as a statesman; it must also and before all be measured according to the obligations of his office and his worthiness as a vicar of Christ. In part, Innocent was suited to these. With a holy fervor, he had worked for the reform of the clergy and the Church; the purification of the church was his ardent desire and the object of fixed concern of his pontificate. He had a deep sense of his obligations as guardian of the faith and the moral law. His priestly life was irreproachable; his piety was genuine and deep. But he did not always act from the highest religious interpretation of his office; still, he did not often sacrifice the values of law and morality, for which he had often acted with a high moral sense, to his political goals.

With a fine sense of value, perhaps, has history withheld the title of great from Innocent, who could not resolve the ambiguity between his role as vicar of Christ and statesman and politician, in spite of his commanding significance in world history. At the same time it singled out Leo I and Gregory I, popes, who are also numbered among the saints of the Catholic Church.

GLOSSARY

ALBIGENSIAN   See CATHARI

ANATHEMA   A solemn ban issued by the church and accompanied by excommunication.

BULL   A papal letter sealed with a leaden seal, or *bulla*. These letters are usually of greater importance than the general run of correspondence.

CANON   Literally, a rule. See CANON LAW. Canon may also refer to a group of clergy, often those attached to a Cathedral, who follow a rule of life. This group acts as the electoral body for the selection of the bishop. Canons may also be used as a shortened form for canon laws.

CANON LAW   The law of the church.

CATHARI   A group of Provençal heretics who espoused a form of dualistic religion. Although Christ figured in their teachings, it is doubtful whether they could actually be called Christians. The heresy had its origins in the East and came to southern France from Bulgaria. Its relationship to the Manichaean heresy is not clear. See MANICHAEAN.

CELIBACY   The unmarried state. Celibacy of the clergy was advocated very early in the history of the church, especially in the West, but gained full acceptance only gradually.

CHAPTER   A meeting of monks or canons or other clergy. The term usually refers to the meeting at which a new abbot or bishop was elected.

CONCLAVE   The meeting at which the cardinals choose a new pope.

COUNCIL   A meeting of the bishops and prelates of the church to decide questions of faith and morals. A general or ecumenical council was usually summoned by the pope and presided over by his representatives. The

Lateran Council, summoned by Innocent III in 1215, was a general council. See SYNOD.

CURIA   The Roman, or papal, curia is composed of the heads—usually cardinals—of the various administrative offices of the church.

DECRETAL   A decretal is a papal letter answering a question of Canon Law. Decretals is the name given to the collections of these letters.

ENCYCLICAL   A papal letter addressed to many bishops, princes, and lay people.

EXCOMMUNICATION   An ecclesiastical censure "cutting off" the person punished from communion with the faithful. There are various kinds or degrees of excommunication.

GLOSS   A marginal note or explanation. Glosses were the usual way in which commentators on canon law offered explanations of difficult points. Hence, the name Glossator, referring to a commentator on canon law.

HOMILETIC   Pertaining to a homily, or sermon.

INTERDICT   An ecclesiastical censure which forbids the holding of any church services in a particular area. A form of compulsion used by the church to enlist popular opinion against the persons censured.

MANICHAEAN   A heresy compounded of Persian dualism (Zoroastrianism) and Christianity which flourished in the fourth century A.D. St. Augustine of Hippo espoused the heresy during his youth, but later opposed it vigorously. The Manichaeans were especially strong in North Africa and the East.

PATRIMONY   This term usually refers in the text to the Patrimony of St. Peter, i.e., the papal states.

PRIMACY   The claim of the pope to be supreme bishop, based in part on New Testament references and in part on the historical development of the church.

SIMONY   The buying and selling of ecclesiastical office.

SUFFRAGAN   A bishop who is subordinate to an Archiepiscopal See.

SYNOD   A local council, composed of the bishops from a certain area.

USURY   In medieval usage, all forms of interest on loans for consumption were usurious. Both church and state tried to enforce strong penalties for violations.

SUGGESTIONS FOR ADDITIONAL READING

The writings of Innocent himself remain for the most part untranslated from the original Latin. They have been collected by J. P. Migne in the closing volumes of his Patrologia Latina (Paris: Migne, 1844–64). His papal register is being edited as *Die Register Innocenz' III* By O. Hageneder and A. Haidacher (Graz: Böhlau, 1964–). Two volumes have been published to date. A critical edition of his *De Miseria Humane Conditionis* (Lucani: In aedibus Thesauri Mundi, 1955) has been edited by Michele Maccarrone for the series Thesaurus Mundi. An English translation is available, *De Miseria Condicionis Humanae* (Athens: University of Georgia Press, Ga., 1978). An important critical study of Innocent's letters is Friedrich Kempf, *Die Register Innocenz III* (Rome: Pontificia Università gregoriana, 1945). However, *Selected Letters of Pope Innocent III concerning England (1198–1216)* (Edinburgh: T. Nelson, 1953), has been edited and translated into English by C. R. Cheney and W. H. Semple. These letters will permit students without facility in Latin an opportunity to study some of Innocent's actions and policies first hand.

Fortunately, there are many fine works in English dealing with the medieval church and various aspects of its development. There is an excellent recent history of the medieval papacy in this period, *The Papal Monarchy: The Western Church from 1050 to 1250* (New York: Oxford University Press, 1991), by Colin Morris. A still-useful volume is Geoffrey Barraclough, *The Medieval Papacy* (New York: Harcourt, 1968). Walter Ullmann's study, *Growth of Papal Government in the Middle Ages* (London: Methuen, 1955), is a good introduction to ecclesiastical administration. His work might be supplemented by R. L. Poole's *Lectures on the History of the Papal Chancery down to the Time of Innocent III* (Cambridge: Cambridge University Press, England, 1915) and W. E. Lunt's *Financial Relations of the Papacy with England to 1327* (Cambridge, Mass.: Mediaeval Academy, 1939) and his *Papal Revenues in the Middle Ages* (2 vols., New York: Columbia University

Press, 1934). Stephan Kuttner, *Gratian and the Schools of Law, 1140–1234* (London: Variorum, 1983) brings together important essays on the development of canon law by an international authority.

There are many important studies of the church in other languages. The *Handbuch der Kirchengeschichte,* edited by the late Hubert Jedin, has been translated into English as *History of the Church* (10 vols., New York: Crossroad, 1981–82). Augustin Fliche and V. Martin edited and contributed to the *Histoire de l'Eglise depuis les Origines à nos Jours* (Paris: Bloud & Gay, 1934–). However, the quality of scholarship in this series is somewhat irregular. Fliche himself published a fine manual, *La Chrétienté médiévale* (Paris: Boccard, 1929). His major work, however, remains *La réforme grégorienne* (3 vols., Louvain: Spicilegium sacrum lovaniense, 1927–37), a truly significant background work to any study of Innocent III. The papacy is the central focus of Ferdinand Gregorovious, *Geschichte der Stadt Rom im Mittelalter* (8 vols., Stuttgart: Cotta'sche Verlag, 1859–72; English trans. London: G. Bell, 1903–12), which remains, from a literary point of view, one of the great monuments of German historiography. For an up-to-date view of papal Rome in the thirteenth century, Robert Brentano's *Rome before Avignon* (New York: Basic Books, 1974) is invaluable. Innocent III received considerable attention in Daniel Waley's, *The Papal State in the Thirteenth Century* (London: St. Martin's Press, 1961). C. J. Hefele's *Conciliengeschichte* (9 vols., Freiburg: Herder, 1869–90) is much more than a history of the councils: it is a major study of the doctrinal development of the church. There is a French translation by Henri Leclerq (Hildesheim: Olms Verlag, 1973) and a partial English translation by W. R. Clark (5 vols., Edinburgh: Clark, 1871–96). However, the Leclerq edition is to be preferred. For the Fourth Lateran Council, see Raymonde Foreville, *Latran I, II, III, et Latran IV* (Paris: Editions l'Orante, 1965). Johannes Haller's *Das Papsttum* (5 vols., Basel: B. Schwabe, 1951–53) provides a viewpoint on many issues sharply contrasting to that of Hefele or Fliche. For a listing of more specialized works in English or other languages, the student should consult *The International Medieval Bibliography* (Leeds: School of History, Leeds University, 1967–) as well as the bibliographical supplements to the *Revue d'histoire ecclésiastique* (Louvain: Bureaux de la Revue, 1900–). Gray Boyce's *Literature of Medieval History, 1930–1975* (Millwood: Kraus, 1980) is also useful.

The best study of Innocent III in English is Helene Tillmann, *Pope Innocent III* (Amsterdam: North Holland, 1980), which has been translated from the German (Bonn: L. Rohrscheid, 1954). S. R. Packard's *Europe and the Church under Innocent III* (New York: Holt, 1927) is out of date. The biography of Innocent by Leonard Elliott-Binns, first published in 1931 (Hamden, Conn.: Archon, 1968), suffers from the same difficulty. Joseph

Clayton's *Innocent III and His Times* (Milwaukee: Bruce, 1941) is rather uncritical; it belongs to the genre of apologetics rather than scholarly history. Charles Smith's *Innocent III, Church Defender* (Baton Rouge: Louisiana State University Press, 1951) is valuable insofar as it focuses attention on an aspect of Innocent's career that has received scant notice in earlier English works. There are now numerous articles in English dealing not merely with Innocent but also with his period.

Some of the more interesting selections in this book have been taken from authors whose work is previously untranslated. The student would be well advised to continue reading on Innocent by consulting the complete works from which the selections have been taken. For example, Achille Luchaire's *Innocent III* (6 vols., Paris: Hachette, 1905–8) is still an important place to begin seeking for a fuller understanding of this pope. There are also many studies dealing with limited aspects of Innocent's reign or with special problems of the period. Works like Joseph Gill's *Byzantium and the Papacy, 1198–1400* (New Brunswick: Rutgers University Press, 1979), and David Abulafia's *Frederick II: A Medieval Emperor* (London: Allen Lane, 1988), while not limited to the period of Innocent III, provide insights into important aspects of his policy. For his involvement in the crusading movement, readers should consult Donald Queller's *The Fourth Crusade: The Conquest of Constantinople, 1201–1204* (Philadelphia: University of Pennsylvania Press, 1977), in addition to James M. Powell's *Anatomy of a Crusade, 1213–1221* (Philadelphia: University of Pennsylvania Press, 1986), from which a selection has been taken for this volume. The major study of Innocent III's relations with the Empire is Friedrick Kempf's *Papsttum und Kaisertum bei Innocenz III* (Rome: Università pontificia gregoriana, 1954), which may be supplemented by Manfred Laufs's interesting but controversial study, *Politik und Recht bei Innocenz III* (Cologne: Böhlau, 1980). On ecclesiology, see Kenneth Pennington, *Pope and Bishops: The Papal Monarchy in the Twelfth and Thirteenth Centuries* (Philadelphia: University of Pennsylvania Press, 1984) and Wilhelm Imkamp, *Das Kirchenbild Innocenz' III (1198–1216)* (Stuttgart: Hiersemann, 1983). On Innocent III's relations with England, Christopher Cheney's *Innocent III and England* (Stuttgart: Hiersemann, 1976) is invaluable. Recently, Kenneth Pennington has collected a series of his articles, many dealing with Innocent III, in *Popes, Canonists and Texts, 1150–1250* (London: Variorum, 1993). Christopher Eggers's article, "Papst Innocenz III. als Theologe: Beiträge zur Kenntnis seines Denkens im Rahmen der Frühscholastik," appeared in *Archivum Historiae Pontificiae* 30 (1992): 56–123.

This list of readings scarcely does justice to the study of Innocent III and his pontificate, but it will, I hope, prove helpful to students interested in pursuing the topic further.

CONTRIBUTORS

Brenda Bolton teaches medieval history at Westfield College, University of London. She is the author of *The Medieval Reformation* and various essays on Innocent III.

The late Christopher Cheney (1906–87) was professor of medieval history at the University of Cambridge. His major works include *Pope Innocent III and England* and his Ford Lectures, *From Becket to Langton*.

Alexander (1861–1943) and Robert (1859–1934) Carlyle were educated at Glasgow and the University of Cambridge. *Mediaeval Political Theory in the West* is an essential basis for study in the field.

Augustin Fliche (1884–1951) was professor of medieval history at the Universities of Montpellier and Paris (Sorbonne). His major work was *La reforme gregorienne*. With Victor Martin, he edited the multi-volume *Histoire de l'église depuis les origines à nos jours*.

Johannes Haller (1865–1947) was professor of history at the University of Tübingen. He was the author of *Das Paspsttum: Idee und Wirklichkeit*.

Albert Hauck (1845–1918) studied at the Universities of Erlangen and Berlin. His *Kirchengeschichte Deutschlands* remains a basic work in the field of German church history.

Friedrich Hurter (1787–1865) authored his biography of Innocent III in 1834, ten years prior to his conversion to Catholicism. In 1852, he became court historian in Vienna.

Wilhelm Imkamp earned his doctorate in theology at the Università Pontificia Gregoriana in Rome. He is the author of *Das Kirchenbild Innocenz' III* and of numerous essays on the history of medieval and modern theology.

Friedrich Kempf (1908–) is a leading international authority on the medieval papacy. He is professor emeritus of the Università Pontificia Gregoriana and author of *Die Register Innocenz III* and *Papsttum und Kaisertum bei Innocenz III* in addition to many other works in the field.

Elizabeth T. Kennan received her doctorate at the University of Washington and taught at The Catholic University of America prior to becoming President of Mt. Holyoke College. She translated (with John Anderson) St. Bernard of Clairvaux's *Five Books On Consideration.*

Achille Luchaire (1846–1908) was one of the leading medieval historians in France, having taught at the University of Bourdeaux before moving to Paris, where he succeeded Fustel de Coulange in the Chair of Medieval History.

Michele Maccarrone (1910–93) taught at the Pontifical Lateran University in Rome. His published works include *Chiesa e stato nella dottrina di Papa Innocenzo III* and *Studi su Innocenzo III.*

Charles H. McIlwain (1871–1968) taught at Harvard University, where he established an international reputation for his work in medieval legal and political thought. His *Constitutionalism Ancient and Modern* is a classic in the field.

John C. Moore (1933–) is professor of history at Hofstra University and author of *Love in Twelfth Century France.* He has written a number of articles on Pope Innocent III.

Kenneth Pennington (1941–) is professor of medieval history at Syracuse University. He is the author of *Pope and Bishops: The Papal Monarchy in the Twelfth and Thirteenth Centuries* and an edition of Johannes Teutonicus's *Apparatus ad Compilationem Tertiam.*

James M. Powell (1930–) is professor of history at Syracuse University. He is the author of *Anatomy of a Crusade,* which was awarded the John Gilmary Shea Prize in 1987. He recently published *Albertanus of Brescia: The Pursuit of Happiness in the Thirteenth Century.*

Brian Tierney (1922–) studied with Walter Ullman at the University of Cambridge. He taught at The Catholic University of America and at Cornell University. He is the author of *The Foundations of Conciliar Theory* and *The Origins of Papal Infallibility.*

Helene Tillmann (1896–) received her doctorate at Bonn. In addition to her biography of Innocent III (English trans., 1980), she has authored articles on the medieval papacy and the college of cardinals in the twelfth and early thirteenth centuries.

INDEX

ABOUT THE EDITOR

James M. Powell is professor of medieval history at Syracuse University. He is the author of *Anatomy of a Crusade* (1986), which was awarded the John Gilmary Shea Prize of the American Catholic Historical Association. He has edited a number of works, including *Medieval Studies: An Introduction* (2d edition, 1992) and *Muslims under Latin Rule, 1100–1300* (1990). His most recent book is *Albertanus of Brescia: The Pursuit of Happiness in the Early Thirteenth Century* (1992).

ABOUT THE BOOK

Innocent III: Vicar of Christ or Lord of the World? was composed in Garamond #3 by BookMasters, Inc. of Ashland, Ohio. It was printed on 60 lb. Phoenix Opaque and bound by Baker Johnson of Dexter, Michigan. The design of the book and cover is by Kachergis Book Design of Pittsboro, North Carolina.